THE "PERFECT TEACHER"—AND THE YOUNG GIRLS
HE SELECTED FOR HIS PERSONAL ATTE

SECRET

LESSONS

THE TRUE-CRIME SHOCKER BY

DON W. WEBER AND CHARLES BOSWORTH, JR.,

BESTSELLING AUTHORS OF <u>SILENT WITNESS</u> AND <u>PRECIOUS VICTIMS</u>

ONYX ☆ 451-JE480 ☆ (CANADA $6.99) ☆ U.S. $5.99

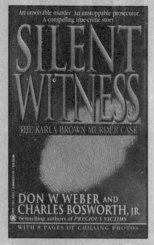

WHAT WENT ON
IN "THE PRIVATE ROOM"?

In his sixth-grade public school classroom, Richard Van Hook was all that a child or a child's parent could want in a teacher—innovative, entertaining, warm, supportive, leading his eager students along the pathway of learning.

But Richard Van Hook had another room in which he conducted a much more private schooling. His "office" in the school library. Only select students were allowed there. His favorite students. All of them little girls. And all of them afraid to tell anyone about what he did to them there. Afraid that the teacher was always right, and it was wrong to resist. And even more afraid that no one would believe what they themselves could barely believe even when it was happening to them.

Then one by one a skilled social worker, a state police detective, and a dedicated prosecutor freed them of their fears enough to tell the unspeakable truth about what Richard Van Hook did to little girls behind closed doors, as a courtroom froze in shock, a community was split in two by controversy, and a school exploded in scandal. . . .

Secret Lessons

ALSO BY DON W. WEBER
AND CHARLES BOSWORTH, JR.

Precious Victims
Silent Witness

SECRET LESSONS

Don W. Weber
and
Charles Bosworth, Jr.

AN ONYX BOOK

ONYX
Published by the Penguin Group
Penguin Books USA Inc., 375 Hudson Street,
New York, New York 10014, U.S.A.
Penguin Books Ltd, 27 Wrights Lane,
London W8 5TZ, England
Penguin Books Australia Ltd, Ringwood,
Victoria, Australia
Penguin Books Canada Ltd, 10 Alcorn Avenue,
Toronto, Ontario, Canada M4V 3B2
Penguin Books (N.Z.) Ltd, 182–190 Wairau Road,
Auckland 10, New Zealand

Penguin Books Ltd, Registered Offices:
Harmondsworth, Middlesex, England

First published by Onyx, an imprint of Dutton Signet,
a division of Penguin Books USA Inc.

First Printing, April, 1994
10 9 8 7 6 5 4 3 2 1

Ⓡ REGISTERED TRADEMARK-MARCA REGISTRADA

Printed in the United States of America

To my father, Norman J. Weber, former mayor of Collinsville, who taught me that courage and integrity are more important than votes.

—D.W.

To my parents, Charles and Martha Bosworth, who taught me how to dream about the future, and to my children, Christopher and Kyle, who give me such hope for the future.

—C.B.

FOREWORD

This is a true account of the investigation and prosecution of a teacher accused of molesting a startling number of his young female students. It is a painful story for all involved, on both sides of the issue. This book was not written to reopen old wounds or exact revenge. It was written because the lessons still need to be learned so that this kind of tragedy can be avoided for children, and adults, in the future. The lessons are too important to be ignored, and there is strong evidence they have been. The abused, and the abusers, must be helped.

The authors wish to express their sincere gratitude to Pam Klein, the former director of the Rape and Sexual Abuse Care Center at Edwardsville, Illinois, and Master Sergeant Dennis Kuba of the Illinois State Police, for the myriad hours spent recounting their efforts. We also want to thank Pam Klein for her permission to use portions of her writings on this case as reference material for this book.

And thanks must be offered to all the other sources who shared their memories with us, including Randy Massey, Captain Larry Trent (retired) and Sergeant Jere Juenger of the State Police, Ed Gurney, Pat Shahini, and other sources who asked not to be identified.

A special debt is owed to the victims who courageously relived very painful memories to offer insight into the abuse they suffered, and the damage they still carry today. Their words must be heard.

A large number of pseudonyms have been used to protect the victims, and some others, from embarrassment or harassment because of the sensitive nature of the issues discussed. All of the girls, their families, and friends are portrayed under names chosen randomly and arbitrarily by the authors.

But the other events, the investigation, and the trial are portrayed as factually and accurately as possible, using contemporary notes, records, police reports, and court transcripts at every possible point. Conversations are reported from notes, records, and the memories of all of those involved whenever possible, or are carefully reconstructed from documents, notes and the memories of some of those who participated.

We wish to thank our editor, Michaela Hamilton, and her staff, for their guidance, support, and encouragement. As always, they made writing this book—and we are sure reading it—a much better experience.

And we owe special thanks to our agents, Arthur Pine and Richard Pine, for their continuing counsel, encouragement, and efforts on our behalf.

PROLOGUE

This must be how it feels to drown, Katherine thought. She slid down into the chair at the kitchen table, awash in painful memories. She struggled to get a breath, and felt her heart pounding. How had they found her, these two strangers who stood there looking at her so intently? She had kept the secret so carefully—the awful secret. It had been so hard for a 12-year-old girl to hold inside. But she had, even when it was tearing her apart. She had told no one, not even her best friends. And especially not her parents.

But now this man and woman she had never seen before were standing in her own kitchen. Something in their eyes said that they knew the secret. Oh God, how could they know? Fear was dragging Katherine down, as if she were sinking to depths from which she would never return. She still couldn't breathe. She twisted the dish towel in her hands, thankful for anything real to hold onto. Was there no way out?

Did they know about . . . him? How could they? She couldn't even believe it herself. It had started so innocently, and then had become something else—something she didn't understand. She was so scared, so ashamed. But she hadn't known how to stop him. She had tried to stay away from him, but even that didn't work. He had found her, no matter where she hid. How could she tell him no? It was all so confusing.

She could feel the tears welling up from deep inside; she could feel the awful fear sucking out her breath. This must be how it feels to drown.

The panic in Katherine's heart that night was prophetic. Her secret was burden enough, but she was about to find herself plunged into a nightmare she never could have imagined. She was about to find herself betrayed again—this time by her hometown, her school, her friends, and everyone she had been taught to respect. Katherine's secret left her ashamed. When her secret came out, it would be her community that shamed itself.

CHAPTER 1

The bleak January afternoon outside her office window confirmed Pamala Klein's decision to spend this Friday plowing through paperwork, cloistered away from the activity in the rest of the rooms outside her door. She came dressed for her agenda: old jeans topped by a faded blue sweatshirt, set off by run-down running shoes. Her short, curly dark blond hair hung limply along her face, the least of her worries while she sorted through stacks of reports and files for the Rape and Sexual Abuse Care Center.

She had been the director at the center for four years, nurturing it from its start as a barely funded afterthought of a program hidden away in a four-room tract house on the campus of Southern Illinois University at Edwardsville. She had recruited talented and dedicated volunteers and professionals, and they had worked hard to make the center a place where women and children could turn for help when the most secret parts of their bodies and souls had been violated.

It had been a long, hard struggle, and the results were about to be tested in ways no one could have predicted. Pam Klein thought she had just about seen everything, especially involving child abuse. But there would be one more telephone call to take.

Pam looked up from her desk to check the time, and was glad it was four o'clock. The day had been different than she had planned. She had spent much of her time sprawled on the floor talking and playing with some children who were coming to the center for counseling. One little boy who had remained mute during the three weeks she had worked with him finally had broken through and, in halting words, had shared with Pam the details of the abuse he had endured. He even drew Pam a crude picture of the man who molested him. That kind of progress with a troubled child was the reward Pam worked for; it was a gratifying way to end a long week.

As Pam stared at the clock, she already was looking forward to a relaxed evening in front of the fire with her husband and kids in their comfortable home in nearby Collinsville. Those nights were too infrequent, and this one was well deserved. She was beginning to imagine the warmth pushing away the winter chill when her secretary buzzed with a call. Probably her 16-year-old daughter, Leslie, checking to see what time to expect dinner.

But the voice on the other end was a surprise.

"Pam, this is Mike O'Malley from the state's attorney's office. I'm down at the Caseyville Police Department. They have a couple of little girls here who are making allegations of sexual abuse against a male sixth-grade teacher. Would it be possible for you to come down and talk with the girls and their parents?"

Pam was pleased that the young prosecutor from St. Clair County was concerned enough about the girls to call the center for assistance at such an early point. Too many people in the police and court system, especially men, were slow to understand the need for that. When one understood, Pam liked to say, "He gets it." About the others—well, she had learned long ago that you couldn't teach a crow to sing.

"Sure, Mike, no problem. I'm just finishing up here and was about to leave for home. I can run by on my way. Thanks for calling."

She turned up her coat collar against the wind and headed toward her car in the gravel lot outside. She really didn't mind the last-minute change of plans. Caseyville was a village right next to Collinsville; in fact, the Caseyville police station was just a couple of miles down Route 157 past the turn to Pam's house. It's not far out of the way, and it shouldn't take that long, she thought as her car reluctantly chugged to life. A 20-minute drive in the wintry dusk, enough counseling to ease the girls' fear and trauma, and an appointment for them with counselors at the center.

Home by 5:30, Pam thought.

Mike O'Malley and Caseyville Police Chief Mike Buckner met her at the door to the police station, shook her shivering hand, and ushered her into a small office.

"Pam, thanks for coming," O'Malley said in relief. "Let me see if I can fill you in before I introduce you to the girls and their parents."

O'Malley offered a quick explanation that an 11-year-old girl named Michelle had gone to her stepfather, Officer Ron Tamburello, several nights earlier with a startling story. She was reluctant to tell him because she and several other little girls had sworn an oath of secrecy, and she took the pact quite seriously. She was so distraught, however, that she finally broke down and told her parents how she had discovered two of her friends crying in the rest room at the Caseyville Elementary School. They were upset about an incident with a male teacher; they told Michelle and several other girls how the teacher had gotten too friendly with them. Now, O'Malley said, Michelle was feeling like a traitor; he asked Pam to say something that could patch up things between the girls. Michelle had done the right thing by telling her folks, but she was afraid her friends wouldn't understand.

The prosecutor added that Officer Tamburello had been concerned enough to talk to the other girls, and what he heard worried him. Since then more girls had come forward with similar complaints against the teacher. The girls and their parents were waiting for Pam in the City Council chambers down the hall.

"Well, I'll be glad to do what I can to help," Pam offered.

She was not prepared for what she saw when O'Malley opened the door to the chambers.

Sitting around the semicircular table were nine girls, all

of them between 10 and 13 years old. Some of their parents sat nearby or stood behind them. Most of the fathers were lined up against the wall, standing there sternly with their arms folded across their chests and anger flashing in their faces.

The silence in the room was oppressive.

How do I work this crowd? Pam Klein wondered.

Looking at the girls' faces, she could see their tension and fear. Some fidgeted nervously; others sat motionless. She read in their eyes the realization that their secret was out, and powers beyond their understanding had taken control of this grave situation. It was escalating beyond their reach and understanding, and they were terrified.

Pam was confident in her ability to calm frightened children and help them cut through the grownup stuff to the real issues that concerned them. But she knew, standing there in the midst of this group of more than 20 people, that this would not be a routine counseling session. This situation would require strong professional intervention—and she was standing there in a sweatshirt and tennies.

Mike O'Malley introduced her, and Pam opened by explaining that her first priority was the welfare of the children; she was there to help the girls and the parents understand the emotional side of the situation, and to offer advice and counseling. She described how the Rape and Sexual Abuse Care Center worked, adding that she and the staff were dedicated to helping children deal with such problems with the least amount of trauma.

One father in the back of the room interrupted to demand impatiently from behind his folded arms, "What happens next?"

O'Malley stepped in, explaining that the Caseyville police would be assisted by the detectives from the Illinois State Police—special agents in the Division of Criminal Investigation—who would help the local police in this delicate case. They would investigate the girls' complaints, and the state's attorney's office would review the police reports to decide if charges would be filed.

"When is a police officer going to talk to my child?" one woman asked anxiously.

"When can we expect to hear that this guy's been arrested?" an angry father asked.

As O'Malley explained the process that would follow, Pam was sure he was shooting well over the heads of this group. She didn't know how serious the allegations were against this teacher or even who he was. It didn't matter. But she did know that these people really needed different information now. The girls needed calm, warm reassurance that they had done nothing wrong and, in fact, were right to tell the authorities what had happened. The parents needed a professional to tell them that their daughters would be all right, and that someone would be there for all of them through the confusing, uncertain events that lie ahead.

Not one of the girls had said a word. They obviously weren't understanding much of what O'Malley said. They were terrified and no one was getting close to dealing with that. Pam stepped out front and spoke to the parents.

"I would like your permission to speak privately with the girls. I can assure you that I am very aware of your frustration, and I know you all must be extremely concerned about your daughters." She gestured at the row of girls. "I think they must be having a lot of their own feelings right now, and I'm sure they must have their own questions. So, if I could just have a few minutes alone with them, maybe they might like to talk about their concerns and begin to feel a little less anxious about what's going on tonight."

To Pam's relief, the parents nodded, collected their coats and handbags, and headed toward the door. Pam knew they were just as lost in this jumble as their kids; they were willing to trust her enough now to take over and lead them through the confusion.

It was time for Pam to turn this night over to the girls. She smiled and dropped cross-legged onto the floor, motioning for the girls to join her. "I think we might be more comfortable down here. You all look pretty uncomfortable in those chairs."

The tension in the girls' faces melted as they rushed to join her on the floor. She was the first adult to operate on their level. They fanned out in front of Pam, leaning forward eagerly to hear what she had to say.

She scanned the group. Nine sweet, little-girl faces. So young, and so serious. Blondes to brunettes; skinny to chubby. All turned toward her expectantly.

"I'm pretty sure none of you is really clear about what my job is, so maybe I should start with a little explanation of what I do. I work with children who have been abused. I help explain what's happened to them and I try to give them some information they need. I don't believe in keeping secrets from children. So, I will always be as honest with you as I can. Do you have any questions?"

She was as unprepared for the response as she had been for the sight when she walked into the room. She immediately was barraged from all sides as chattering voices poured out their concerns and fears. What came through most plainly, however, was their dread of the idea of testifying in court against Mr. Van Hook.

There was the name. Pam Klein hadn't heard the name before that instant. Richard Van Hook, the girls said. Pam didn't recognize the name, even though her children attended the same school district as these girls.

But Pam realized the girls had made a big step. They already had projected themselves past an investigation and an arrest to the time when they would have to face this teacher from the witness stand. For them to have moved so far ahead was very unusual, Pam knew. What did that say about what had happened?

Pam asked for their names. Lori. Elizabeth. Sally. Ellen. Tammy. Bobbie. Paula. Bethany. Carrie.

Then the allegations began to pour out. The girls almost tripped over one another, each trying to get her turn but wanting to hear what her friends had to say.

"Mr. Van Hook French-kissed me."

"Once he put his hand up my dress."

"Yeah, one time he walked up behind me and unzipped my jumpsuit."

"He touched my butt," one little voice offered.

The tears were starting as each girl listened to her friends, and the realization sunk in that they all had been hurt by this man in some way. Some of the girls were holding hands. The sweetness in the children touched Pam again.

"He tried to kiss me, too."

"He tried to put his hand in my pants."

"He did that to you, too? I don't believe this!"

"He always scared me. One time he threw a chair across the room."

"He's a real perv," another tiny voice added.

Their eyes were boring into Pam Klein's, as if these girls wanted to crawl under Pam's skin to make sure she knew. Someone had to know.

One of the littlest girls looked at Pam intensely. "He tried to play with my boobs—and I don't even have any!" Her eyes searched Pam's face as if to ask, "Can you figure this out for me? I don't get it." It was such a relief finally to be able to talk about this to someone.

Pam felt the urge to smile at the innocence, but then their pain pushed in. These frightened kids were ashamed and confused by behavior that was beyond their comprehension. She wanted to take them all in her arms and tell them it would be all right. But she knew more hurdles lay ahead, and it was time to prepare them for that.

"I will always be here for you through this. I will help you when it comes time to take the witness stand; I know how scary that seems. I'll be with you when the police talk to you. I promise you I will never lie to you. Whatever happens, you'll know, and I'll tell you the truth. You're the ones who have been hurt, and I'll do everything I can to help you."

The nine solemn faces looked at her in absolute silence, hanging on every word she said. And tears rolled softly down their cheeks.

Pam swallowed hard, then began to wrap up this first session. She asked each girl to write her name, age, address, and phone number on a piece of paper. In addition to getting necessary information for Pam, that would let each one know she was a special individual, not just part of a group. Pam passed out business cards so they could reach her, too.

Then she asked one more question.

"By the way, if you had to pick one girl you would call the teacher's pet, who would it be? Who was Mr. Van Hook's favorite?"

The girls looked back and forth at each other, searching for the answer.

"Oh, that's easy," Elizabeth said flatly. "Katherine Howes. She and I were in class together last year. She would be the one, his favorite. He liked her best; he spent a lot of time with her. She's 12. Her dad's a Baptist minister."

Bingo, Pam thought. There was the one missing from the group that night. Among these eager girls one should have held back, refusing to open up. One should have been more upset than the others. Her absence meant the worst case hadn't been found yet. Maybe that case would be the teacher's pet.

As Pam started to open the door to let in the waiting parents, she offered the girls one more bit of advice.

"Now, leave all of your 'scares' with me tonight. I'll take care of them for you."

That brought quick smiles. Several of the girls hugged Pam as they left the room. Chief Buckner told the families to go home for the night. The police would contact them later.

Pam joined Buckner and Mike O'Malley in the chief's tiny, cluttered office. Stacks of police journals and other papers were piled about, and the room that surely had been designed as a janitor's closet smelled of dust. The air was so thick with cigarette smoke that Pam coughed and fanned her hand back and forth in front of her face.

"Would you please put out those disgusting weeds?" she asked with her characteristic bluntness. "Chief, is it okay if I leave the door open to get some air in here?"

Buckner didn't know Klein very well, and he cleared his throat before he answered. "Well, uh, we wanted to keep this private."

Pam chuckled. "What's to keep private? Everyone except the dispatcher is already in here."

A familiar voice boomed from the side.

"Well, you can always tell when Klein has arrived."

Pam smiled back at one of the best cops she had ever met, Special Agent Jimmy Bivens from the State Police Division of Criminal Investigation—the DCI as everyone called it.

"I guess someone thought I should be here to keep you on your toes, Bivens," Pam shot back. She knew she couldn't let him get too far ahead of her in the give-and-take chatter that marked her work with the cops she knew.

Bivens lived in Caseyville, and Chief Buckner had called him for help. He was an old pro who had handled every kind of case there was over the past 21 years as a road trooper and detective. He was tall and lean and hard-nosed and tough, and he had one of the foulest mouths Pam Klein ever heard on a cop. But he had a soft center when kids had been hurt, and his gentle interviewing technique left every sex-abuse victim with dignity and hope.

"Pam, I can't handle this case," Bivens mumbled as he shook his head. His hound-dog face was beet-red, a sure signal that he was mad as hell. "This is my town; I live here. I'm too close to it to stay objective. The chief wants DCI to handle this, so he called me. But I need to turn this over to someone else."

Pam nodded. "How about Dennis Kuba?"

It was almost 6:30 when the telephone rang at Dennis Kuba's house in Edwardsville, ten miles north of Caseyville and across the line into Madison County. He had just arrived home after getting a fish dinner with his wife, Joanie, and his two-year-old son, Kory, and was about to ease into a relaxing Friday evening with the family. Joanie put her hand over the receiver and rolled her eyes knowingly.

"It's Bivens."

"What's he want?" Dennis frowned. "I'm not the duty agent this weekend."

Bivens's voice was ominous. "Kuba, I'm down at the Caseyville police station and we've got a roomful of irate people claiming a schoolteacher molested their daughters. We want you to handle some interviews to help Mike O'Malley with the case."

"Wait a minute. Is Klein there?"

Bivens laughed. "How did you know?"

"It's not funny. She has me up to my eyebrows in sexually abused kids."

"I know. She's a genuine pain in the ass. But you'd better come down and hear this one out. I think this is going to be a rough one."

"All right," Kuba sighed as his wife shook her head. So much for their quiet evening together.

Dennis Kuba—a husky, athletic blond with a handsome, friendly face—had been a DCI agent for eight years. He and Pam Klein had worked together on more rape and sexual abuse cases than they cared to remember, and they had developed a special professional relationship based on mutual respect for each other's abilities and dedication. With that had come a friendship forged in the heat of their duties; they loved to slam each other, but they knew they could count on each other, even in the most difficult situation.

None of that meant, however, that Kuba wanted to get a call on a Friday night on one of Klein's cases. Why couldn't this wait until Monday? On second thought, Kuba realized something must be up. Bivens had said Mike O'Malley, the prosecutor, already was there. Klein was there. And the Caseyville police already had called in DCI. Something important had to be going on. He put on a suit and headed south.

Kuba's curiosity was piqued by the time he hurried out of the cold and into the Caseyville police station. He walked into Buckner's smoke-filled office and immediately shot Pam Klein his familiar "thanks a lot" look. She was on the phone to her office, but caught the look and its message. She grinned in response, thinking of all the times he had dragged her out of a warm house to help him on a case.

Kuba was briefed on the somewhat vague details from Buckner and Bivens, and sized the case up as a teacher who had patted some girls on the rear and rubbed against their chests. It would mean a lot of interviews and hassles over relatively minor incidents that may not even justify criminal charges—certainly not on the felony level. Kuba shook his head; he wished he was back home in front of the fire with Joanie and Kory.

Pam Klein hung up the phone and turned to the agent.

"Hi, Kuba." She smiled as she took another sip of coffee.

The agent was in no mood for small talk. "Okay, Klein, what do you think?"

"I asked them who the teacher's pet was, and they said Katherine Howes. You know what that means."

Kuba nodded sadly; he felt his stomach tighten. He knew all too well.

Klein stayed on the attack; she knew she would have to push Kuba to get him to move at her pace. "We have to interview her tonight, Dennis. This is going to be all over town tomorrow. We can't wait."

Kuba pulled his trench coat back on. "Yeah, I know."

As they shivered in his car and prepared for the short drive to the address provided by Chief Buckner, Klein offered her assessment of the case: some fondling, kissing, and relatively minor molestation. Klein was concerned because it involved a significant number of girls, but no evidence so far justified a felony charge—nothing like vaginal penetration, even by a finger. The evidence did indicate to her, however, that this Van Hook was a serious pedophile. That much was certain from the long list of girls.

Klein also told Kuba about the girls' demeanor during the session with her. They showed all of the signs Kuba and Klein recognized as proof children were telling the absolute truth. They were sincere and candid, and so innocent in the special way these two had seen so many times. Their stories came naturally, with no long pauses while they searched for the most incriminating answers or allegations. There was none of the body language that indicated they were lying or hiding something—no averted eyes or jiggling feet.

But the next interview could be the most important of the night. They needed information from someone who hadn't been at the police station. Someone who couldn't be accused of succumbing to peer pressure and group psychology. Someone who didn't know the police were about to drop by.

Kuba turned into the driveway about eight o'clock, and the headlights swept across the front of the Howeses' mobile home. In the frigid night air they threaded their way around the little bicycles and other toys in the yard. Klein saw Kuba slip his badge and ID case out of his breast pocket as he knocked on the door.

The Reverend Jim Howes was a big man and he filled the doorway. He was six feet tall and easily 220 pounds. He wore dark blue polyester slacks, and a light blue dress shirt open at the collar to reveal the top of his T-shirt. He smiled a warm greeting from behind his eyeglasses.

"Reverend Howes, I'm Special Agent Dennis Kuba of the Illinois State Police, and this is Pam Klein from the Rape and Sexual Abuse Care Center in Edwardsville. May we speak with you a minute?"

Reverend Howes was puzzled. "Well . . . sure. Come on in, please."

Klein was met first by the tantalizing smell of fried chicken—her favorite and a nagging reminder that she hadn't eaten since breakfast. She scanned the inside of the trailer for clues about this family. Several little boys were scampering around. Dinner was over, and the dishes were done and put away in the kitchen that she could see from the living room. The place was neat and tidy, and felt like the home of good people about to settle in for a cozy night.

Jim Howes led his guests to the couch as his wife walked into the room. Sheila Howes was a big woman, too, wearing a flowered blouse over black slacks.

"What's this about?" Reverend Howes asked as he and his wife settled into chairs.

Dennis Kuba slid forward to the edge of the couch, propped his elbows on his knees, and pressed his fingertips together. It was a sight Pam Klein had seen often: he was about to get serious. He always leaned forward like that when he wanted to convey his concern and sincerity. He knew it was important to spend a lot of time with these parents, explaining what was happening. He was very aware of how he would feel if two people came to his house with this kind of news involving his son. This minister and his wife could be facing a crushing reality, and Kuba didn't want to make that any harder than it would be.

"Mr. and Mrs. Howes, we've just come from the Caseyville police station. There were several parents there with their children, who have made complaints against Richard Van Hook. They said he has made sexual advances toward them. We'd like to speak to Katherine about it."

The look in the Howeses' eyes was unmistakable, and Sheila Howes's hand flashed to her mouth in horror. Hearing this allegation against a respected teacher obviously was a shock, but it grew to frightening dimensions when followed by the implication from these two investigators that their daughter was somehow involved.

"No, not Richard Van Hook," Sheila protested. "There must be some mistake. He's a fine man; he's done a lot for our family. He's been very good to Katherine. He knows things have been hard for us financially, and his wife arranged for us to save some money on the kids' medical exams for school with the doctor she works for. And Mr. Van Hook and Katherine have had a very good relationship. He's even called her and asked her to baby-sit for him."

Jim Howes was nodding emphatically. "He's been

wonderful to Katherine and to us. He's a very caring man. I can't believe something like that about him. There's got to be some mistake."

The warning bell went off for Klein and Kuba as they exchanged glances. An extra close relationship between Mr. Van Hook and young Katherine could be quite ominous. She may well be another victim of the petting and fondling they already had heard so much about tonight. Did Katherine make ten little victims?

Klein decided it was time for her to ease into the picture and try to prepare these shocked parents for what could be a disturbing and painful explosion in their happy home.

"Mr. and Mrs. Howes, did Katherine baby-sit for Mr. Van Hook?"

"No," Sheila answered. "There always was some reason why she couldn't go." The look on her face changed suddenly, as if her own answer enlightened—and frightened—her.

Klein glanced at Kuba again. Another red flag: Katherine was avoiding Van Hook. Klein pushed ahead. "Have you noticed any changes in Katherine's behavior or her moods lately?"

Sheila nodded. "Well, yes. For the last year or so, she's been a lot moodier and she's been spending a lot of time alone in her room with the door locked. She's been so short-tempered most of the time that her brothers—we have four boys younger than Katherine—have been calling her 'Crabby Kate.' I just thought it was hormonal—you know, normal puberty for a girl."

The ugly possibilities for explaining the changes in their daughter's personality were dawning on the Howeses now, and they exchanged stricken looks.

Pam softened her voice. "I know this is hard, but we need to speak to Katherine. Could we see her alone for a few minutes? It would be better if you and the other kids could leave us alone in the room with her."

Jim Howes's face was sad and his voice was pained; he was scared. "Sure. She's in her room. I'll call her."

Moments after the big man disappeared down the hall, his daughter walked uncertainly into the room. Klein and Kuba were struck immediately by how young and innocent the 12-year-old looked—still so much a child with a sweet, pretty face. She had on jeans and a white T-shirt, with only white socks on her feet. She was slim and angular, without the rounding of pubescence. She had shoulder-length blond hair; her skin was fair and her ice blue eyes glittered in contrast.

Reverend Howes stepped out of the hallway behind her and introduced their guests. As he mentioned the State Police and the Rape-Crisis Center, the color drained from Katherine's face. The look in her eyes changed from a curious girl to a trapped animal.

Jim Howes turned and cupped her face gently in his big hands.

"Just tell the truth, Katherine," he said softly and lovingly. "The truth never hurts."

Then he and his wife walked slowly down the hall, herding their boys in front of them.

Dennis Kuba motioned toward the kitchen table. "Sit down, Katherine; we just want to talk to you for a minute."

Katherine picked up a dish towel as she walked by the sink, and then slid uneasily into a chair. Pam sat next to her at the round table; Dennis sat on the other side. The pattern the investigator and the counselor had established in so many interviews was kicking in automatically.

As Kuba began to speak, Katherine looked intensely at this handsome man who had blond hair and blue eyes just like hers. She was searching his face for some clue about this unexpected and uncomfortable visit.

Dennis began slowly and his soft voice was soothing.

"Katherine, we've been talking to some other girls from Caseyville School, and they've been telling us some things about Mr. Van Hook."

Katherine's eyes widened and she leaned back abruptly in her chair. She started twisting the dish towel nervously.

Dennis pushed ahead: "They said some things have

happened to them, and they gave us some names of other kids to talk to. They told us we should talk to you. They knew you were close to Mr. Van Hook; they knew he was a friend of yours and your family's."

The look in Katherine's eyes was turning to terror. Pam almost could see the girl's mind searching for some way out. There was something in there; the question was whether Katherine would find a way to let it out, or stonewall these two unknown adults.

Pam put her hand gently on Katherine's arm, and the child turned to look into her face. "You're not in any trouble, Katherine. You haven't done anything wrong," Pam said softly, hoping Katherine would trust her.

Dennis leaned forward a bit. "Katherine, the other kids referred to you as 'teacher's pet.' "

Katherine's head dropped suddenly, and she began to cry. She was wringing the dish towel harder as her crying intensified.

Kuba and Klein looked at each other again; they knew something significant had just happened. Pam put her arms around Katherine's shoulders and hugged her. She could feel the girl's heart pounding.

"Kate, I know you're really scared. We're here for you. I want you to trust us. Now, you cry if you need to; it's okay. But there's something you need to tell us, right?"

Katherine nodded slowly.

Pam kept her voice low and soothing. "Okay. We'll be here until you're ready to tell us. Just take a deep breath and relax."

Dennis Kuba watched patiently. At such moments he was acutely aware of the importance of having Pam Klein along on this kind of case. This was so much better than putting Katherine between two male cops, no matter how sensitive and understanding they were. Katherine could lean into Pam Klein's arms and know she would understand.

Dennis had to move slowly; this could not be rushed. He had to pursue Katherine and the truth without terrifying her or putting words in her mouth. He started with easy questions.

"What grade were you in when you first met Mr. Van Hook?"

Katherine shrugged and whispered, "I don't know—fourth or fifth."

"What did you like about him?"

Katherine shrugged again but did not answer.

She's a very confused child, Kuba thought. And he was certain something had happened. She probably had been fondled, just like the rest of these little girls. But how do you get a 12-year-old girl to talk about sex? The question always tugged at his mind while he was conducting an interview like this. Even most adults won't talk about sex. How do you make a 12-year-old who never saw you before feel comfortable enough to open up? Dennis did the only thing he knew might work; he kept talking to her.

"Katherine, it's okay to like Mr. Van Hook. We're not here to try to change your mind about him. But adults have rules and laws about their behavior. Some of these rules are to protect kids. Has there ever been a time when you didn't feel good about Mr. Van Hook?"

She nodded again and softly said, "Yes."

"When?"

"When he gave me good grades, but something else happened."

"Where did this happen?"

"In his little office in the library. He made me a librarian."

Dennis knew something else was lurking just within reach. He moved closer to her and asked bluntly, "Kate, did Mr. Van Hook ever kiss you?"

As Katherine stared at the towel in her hands, Pam recognized the change in Dennis's tone. He still was being gentle, but he had become more authoritative. The message was clear: he was a friend, but he also was a cop and he was going to ask these questions until he got the truth.

Finally, Katherine nodded slowly and whispered, "Yes."

Dennis felt his heart breaking as he sensed what was next: surely Van Hook had fondled her, too.

"Kate, will you look at me? He did more than kiss you, didn't he? It's okay to tell me. If he did, we need to know."

Her eyes scanned his face again, and tears streamed down her cheeks. She buried her face in the towel and cried harder, gasping for air between sobs.

Pam Klein looked at her colleague. He was leaning forward, his elbows on his knees; his eyes were focused on his folded hands. Pam knew it was his unspoken signal for her to move in.

She hugged Katherine again. Her well-being was the most important issue here, and Pam wanted to be sure the interview did not worsen the emotional injuries this little girl already had suffered.

"Kate, we have all the time in the world. I honestly know how difficult this is for you, and you don't have to tell us anything until you're ready. We understand how scared and embarrassed you are. But you've kept this secret long enough. You might feel better if you get this all out in the open."

Katherine took a deep breath, and then looked up into Pam's face. "I don't know how to start."

"Well, how did he kiss you?"

She hesitated, and then said, "He put his tongue in my mouth."

"Did he touch you?"

"Yes." She took a breath. "He put his hand in my pants."

"Front or back?"

"Both."

"What else?"

"He took my clothes off."

Pam glanced at Dennis and he read the look. They both knew they had reached the threshold that, so far tonight, had not been crossed. Pam Klein held her breath for the next question. "What did he do with his hand?"

"He . . . he put his finger in me."

"He put his finger in your vagina?" Pam asked slowly. Katherine hesitated a moment before nodding.

"Do you know what the vagina is?"

"Yes, I know."

"Did he do more than that?"

Katherine didn't answer. Klein and Kuba looked at each other again. He shook his head slightly in disgust.

Katherine said in a whisper, "He put his thing in me."

"He put his penis in your vagina?" Klein repeated.

Katherine nodded slowly.

"Did he do more than that?"

"Yes. Sometimes he put his mouth on me there."

Katherine buried her face in the towel and cried uncontrollably. Finally she had relieved herself of the awful burden of carrying around the secret.

The entire situation had changed for Klein and Kuba. What had been a troubling case of a teacher clumsily pawing his students had become a sickening case of a man in a position of trust manipulating a girl into intercourse and oral sex before she even understood what was happening. A case that minutes earlier meant some misdemeanor charges at most had just been catapulted to a Class X felony—the most serious offense in Illinois. If Richard Van Hook had committed these crimes, he could be facing 20 years in prison.

Kuba pulled a spiral tablet from his pocket and explained that he would need to make some notes. Now that she had given them the basics, Kuba explained, she would need to tell him in more detail what happened. It took another hour to get the full story; Katherine cried off and on during the rest of the interview.

Richard Van Hook had been her sixth-grade teacher for the 1980–1981 school year at Caseyville Elementary School; she had been 11 years old. He was the head librarian, and he chose her as a library worker. She often spent the lunch hour in the library grading papers with him. As the year progressed, he became increasingly friendly. He began with a kiss on the cheek, but eventually started rubbing her breasts and buttocks. She was confused and frightened, but didn't know what to do. After all, he was her teacher. What could she say or do?

One day shortly after Christmas vacation, Van Hook took her into a little office he had off the library; he had a sign on the door that read, "Bear's Cave, Enter at Your Own Risk." He locked the door, undressed her, and then undressed himself. He rolled a sleeping bag across the floor, and put on a prophylactic he got from a box that looked like a book on one of the shelves. Then he had intercourse with her. She told Kuba that Van Hook took her into the room about twice a week for the rest of the year. Sometimes he had intercourse with her. Other times he rubbed himself against her legs until "sticky stuff" came out, or he put his mouth on her. When the sex was done, he cleaned himself up with tissues, and gave her some to use. She thought it usually lasted 20 to 30 minutes. Before the sex acts he sometimes showed her pornographic magazines. Katherine said she thought the first act of intercourse was the second day after the end of Christmas break, and it happened again on her twelfth birthday on February 3, 1981.

During this time Van Hook began to give her answers to tests and homework, and she got higher grades than she deserved. On her birthday he gave her a folder with a five-dollar bill inside. On other occasions he gave her three pairs of earrings, a little brass elephant, and a key ring with the word "Love" on it. He told her he knew her father wasn't working, and offered to give her money if she needed it. He told her not to say anything about what was happening because he might go to jail.

She had last heard from Van Hook four days ago, on January 11, when he called her at home and asked if she knew Lori Parker, another student. He said Lori was spreading rumors about him, and he asked Katherine to call her and tell her to cool it.

That last tidbit shocked Kuba. It was a brazen step for a man who had molested a little girl to call her and ask her to run interference with someone who could be another victim. This guy must be something, Kuba thought.

At the investigators' request, Katherine gave them more names of girls they should interview—including some she had no way of knowing had been at the police station earlier that night.

Then she looked up and asked, "Will Mr. Van Hook be in trouble?" Her voice showed real concern for the man she had begun to realize had been tricking and using her. She still was confused enough about this former teacher to wonder if she had caused him problems.

As Pam Klein listened to the whole story, the knot in her stomach corroborated her intellectual assessment that she was hearing the truth. Katherine's demeanor was a textbook example of how kids act—and her words were exactly what they say—when they tell the truth about sexual abuse. She had described a classic child molester and how he would manipulate the victim and her family. And why would Katherine lie? What could she possibly gain by concocting such a story?

The details proved her account just as surely as her demeanor. How else would this 12-year-old know about prophylactics—"rubbers" as she called them? Dennis Kuba had tested her on that point.

"How did he use the rubbers?"

"He put them on his thing."

"Why did he do that?"

"He said it was so I wouldn't get pregnant." She looked innocently at Pam Klein and added, "I didn't think I was old enough to get pregnant. He wanted me to help him put it on, but I didn't want to touch it."

Katherine's story had come haltingly, in a weak voice, amid constant wringing of the towel and tears that sometimes gave way to almost uncontrollable sobbing. She often hid her eyes, looking at her hands rather than risking the embarrassment she felt when she faced these adults. Toward the end she had begun to relax a bit; Pam read that as relief that the secret was finally out.

Kuba was convinced that no little girl surprised in her own house by two veteran investigators could improvise with such lies and convince them she was telling the truth. Attention, trust, affection, gifts, fondling, and then sex. He had heard the story before. He had no doubt that he had just heard a factual account of what had happened—and damn

Richard Van Hook for it. Kuba already was thinking ahead to the next phases of the investigation, from more interviews to search warrants to criminal charges to the final confrontation, face to face, with Van Hook.

As the interview ended, Pam again heard muffled voices and other sounds behind the door at the end of the hall. She winced as she thought about what was next. She looked tenderly at Katherine and spoke the words the girl had begun to realize were coming.

"Kate, you have to tell your parents."

She began to cry hard again and shook her head. "I can't tell them about this."

"You have to, Kate. Dennis and I will stay with you while you tell them. We can explain why you didn't tell them before. You know, most girls don't tell their parents."

Katherine's eyes widened. "Really? Is that true?"

"Yes, it is," Pam said softly. "Most of the girls we've talked to feel the same way you do. They carry this around alone, and they try to protect their parents from the pain of knowing what has happened to them."

Katherine seemed stunned. "I always felt alone. I never thought other girls have gone through this. I thought maybe there was something wrong with me, and that was why Mr. Van Hook did those things."

Dennis Kuba could be still no longer, and his voice came out firm and strong, almost angry. "That's not true, Kate. There is absolutely nothing wrong with you. You have to believe that. What Mr. Van Hook did was totally his responsibility and his alone; you are not to blame in any way."

Then he softened and wrapped his hand around hers. "This won't be easy, but I think it's time to bring your folks in and tell them what's going on."

Katherine sighed and nodded. Pam kept her arm around the girl's shoulders while guiding her slowly from the kitchen table to the couch in the living room. Dennis walked down the hall and asked Jim and Sheila Howes to join them again. The parents' faces showed no fear until they walked in and looked at their daughter. They hurried over to the couch and sat on each side of the little blonde. Katherine looked pleadingly at Pam, and she decided to start the conversation.

"Katherine has something to tell you, and it really is difficult. She hasn't told you before because she really loves you. When kids don't tell their parents something like this, it's because they love them—not because they don't love them."

The Howeses' eyes were beginning to show their concern and fear. Pam could tell Katherine still couldn't find the words; Pam swallowed hard and kept going.

"Mr. Van Hook engaged Katherine in some sexual activity . . ."

Katherine began to cry again, and Sheila Howes gasped as she wrapped her arms around her daughter. Jim Howes leaned in and threw his arms around his daughter and his wife, and all three of them cried.

Pam Klein felt tears well in her eyes and a knot swell in her throat. She never had seen three people absorbed wholly into one being at such a moment, and it was a heartbreaking sight. Dennis Kuba, leaning forward on his knees again, stared at his folded hands.

Within a few minutes, Katherine started to recount for her parents the story she had revealed over the past hour. When she finished, Jim Howes's faltering voice said, "Katherine, no matter what, we love you and we always will love you. Absolutely nothing will change that."

Then he turned to Kuba and his voice hardened. "I want this man in jail tonight. I want him prosecuted."

Dennis nodded, "I understand." A father himself, he knew that what Jim Howes really wanted was "this man" dead.

After a few more minutes, Dennis explained briefly that there would be an investigation into the girls' allegations, and then the state's attorney's office would decide on charges. But it wasn't the time for a detailed explanation of the criminal justice system for these emotionally devastated people. Dennis added only that they must not discuss the situation with anyone else, and that he would be in touch with them again.

And then Kuba and Klein slipped out of the house and closed the door softly behind them. This family needed to be alone.

CHAPTER 2

Katherine had suspected nothing when she walked into her kitchen that night and found two strangers standing there. But when she heard the words "State Police, and Rape-Crisis Center," fear rose in her throat. Every part of her body began to shake and tremble, and then she felt sick to her stomach. She knew why they were there. It had to be about him. Her first thought was that she would tell them nothing about her awful secret. But then her father took her face in his hands and told her to tell the truth. He had always been right before, so that's what she did.

The experience had been terrifying, almost as if she were drowning. She felt so helpless against all these forces she didn't understand, against all these adults. It had been such a crushing secret to carry alone for so long. How, she wondered, had these two strangers found out? How had they found her and come to her home on this cold Friday night?

All of this pain had begun so innocently; sometimes she couldn't believe how it had turned out. She first met Mr. Van Hook when she was 11 years old and in the fifth grade. She was a library aide, and he was the head librarian in addition to being a teacher. He seemed really nice, not like the teacher she was having so many problems with that year. She was glad when she was assigned to Mr. Van Hook's class for sixth grade. She began spending a lot of time in the library helping him, especially during lunch hours. She put the books and index cards away, or stamped the books when they were checked out. She liked being an assistant librarian. But mostly she goofed off; Mr. Van Hook was so nice, he didn't even mind that. Some time later, one of the girls began to talk about

Mr. Van Hook pinching her bottom and making passes at her. Everyone thought this girl was a little strange, anyway, and they didn't know whether to believe her or not. They were surprised when they heard she had told the principal. Mr. Van Hook had talked to the other girls in the library about it, saying that the girl was trying to get him into trouble. He said he never touched her and was shocked that she would make such accusations about him. He seemed to be looking for sympathy from the other girls.

They were confused about it all and decided to be careful around him. They tried to stay in groups of twos or threes when they went into the library with him. But he still seemed okay; he always was in a good mood, telling jokes and kidding around with the girls. He got mad if the boys goofed off, but he liked having fun with the girls. He gave them birthday swats with a big dictionary, and taught them how to carve wooden plaques.

Mr. Van Hook always ate lunch in the library; he never ate in the teachers' lounge with the other teachers. He put down some of the other teachers a lot, and seemed to have just one real friend among his colleagues—Mrs. DeConcini. He always seemed to prefer being with the kids than with the teachers.

He always was bragging about what a good swimmer, diver, and coach he was. The girls knew he coached diving teams; he once climbed up on a desk and showed everyone the best diving form. All he talked about was diving, and his family; he talked a lot about his wife and son and daughter.

The boys seemed scared of him, and even Katherine once saw a flash of temper. When he got angry because she hadn't done her homework, he kicked a chair across the classroom. It was obvious when he didn't like someone; he constantly griped at them, almost mercilessly. The other kids felt sorry for anyone on his bad side.

Just before Christmas 1980, Mr. Van Hook started getting friendlier with Katherine. He patted her on the back a lot, and then he surprised her by kissing her on the forehead one day. She didn't know what to think about that, but she guessed it was okay. The next time, he kissed her on the cheek, and that really bothered her. She started trying to keep some distance from him. She wasn't sure why; she just knew what happened made her uncomfortable. Other teachers didn't do things like that.

Then he began making comments—but only when they were alone. Katherine looked older than she was; she had a body more like a 17-year-old than a 12-year-old. When she got eyeglasses, he said that really made her look older and more sophisticated. She stopped wearing the glasses around him. He said she always wore just the right amount of makeup; it made her look older, too. One time he told her he couldn't look at her in class because he would lose his train of thought. She made him feel like a teenager again.

Mr. Van Hook got moodier when his father died. Once during the lunch period, he was sitting at his desk with his head down, and Katherine saw him digging his fingernails into his arms. He acted strange for quite a while, and Katherine tried to stay away from him. But before long he became friendly with her again. He was like three different people, Katherine thought. Mr. Van Hook in class; Mr. Van Hook with other students; and Mr. Van Hook alone with Katherine. She decided she didn't trust any of those characters.

One day after the Christmas vacation, he sent her a note asking her to meet him in the library at lunch. He said he wanted to talk to her. He took her into the little storeroom off the library that he used for his office. He locked the door, and began to say the kinds of things that bothered her. He told her how pretty and sweet she was, and how grown-up her makeup made her look. He told her again how she made him feel like a teenager. It sounded different coming from him. She didn't get along well with boys, but it sounded different coming from Mr. Van Hook.

And then he unbuttoned her blouse and began to rub her breasts. She was shocked and terrified, too frozen to say or do anything but stand there. After a few minutes, he stopped and they left the room. She didn't know what to think.

But the next day he took her back to the room at lunch, and this time he undressed her completely. She still didn't know what to do. She knew it wasn't right, but he was her teacher. She was really confused now. How could she resist him? How do you tell a teacher no?

Then he had sex with her. It was awful, and she couldn't wait until it was over. She told him it hurt; he said he was sorry and slowed down a little. It was all so strange. How he put the rubber on his thing; he wanted her to touch it, but she pulled her hand away. He asked if she had begun menstruating—if she'd had her first period. He said it was good that she had not, because she couldn't get pregnant. But he said he would wear a rubber anyway. He said he had brought the sleeping bag from home; he had told his wife he was lending it to a student.

When the sex was over, she was so confused she didn't know what to do. She went to the rest room and cried.

Just before New Year's Eve, Mr. Van Hook made Katherine and Elizabeth McBride give him a new year kiss. Katherine wondered if he was doing the same things with Elizabeth that he was doing with her. Katherine wanted to ask Elizabeth, but she just couldn't.

The rest of the year, Katherine and Mr. Van Hook were embattled in a bizarre and sickening power struggle. She would look for ways to avoid him at school, but he usually would find her and take her into the little room at lunch. If she hid in the rest room, he would send in another girl to tell her that Mr. Van Hook wanted to see her. Once she slipped out of the bathroom window when she knew he was outside the door, waiting. She could never stay away from him and the little room for more than three or four days in a row.

She began to look for ways to avoid going to school. She claimed to be sick, until her mother quit accepting that. Then Katherine stuck her finger down her throat to make herself throw up. Her mother once called Mr. Van Hook and told him something was wrong with Katherine—she was acting strange and trying to avoid school. Mr. Van Hook came up to her that day and stunned her by asking if she wanted him to leave her alone. He stayed away from her then, but started up again the next day.

After a while he was taking her into the room two or three days a week. He didn't always perform intercourse with her; that only happened four or five times. But he undressed her and did other things; she didn't like any of it, but she didn't know what to do.

Sometimes she surprised herself when she thought about what was happening; she tried to tell herself it wasn't so awful. Mr. Van Hook made her feel needed, made her feel that someone really cared. It was a special feeling. And he gave her little gifts. He would tell her that he loved her, and that he had dreamed of going to a motel with her. He said his wife complained that he was not sexually attracted to her; he even mentioned that his wife had to have "female" surgery for cancer.

Knowing he shared so much with her made Katherine feel special. But she knew this was not right. She just didn't know what to do about it. She couldn't tell her parents. She used to be able to talk to them about everything. But she couldn't talk to them about this. She wanted to—oh, so many times. But she didn't know how. Instead she would retreat to the solitude of her room and cry. She once told her mother that she was scared and didn't know why. She stopped short of letting it all out; surely her mother would think she was lying about this teacher, this fine man who had been such a friend to the Howes family. Katherine didn't want her mother to get mad at her.

Her mother had joined the class for the trip to the Magic House and the Museum of Transport in St. Louis; that was the day Mr. Van Hook gave her the little brass elephant statue. He told her not to tell, and then he gave her a quick little kiss. Surely her mother wouldn't believe that had happened while she was along.

Katherine's grades were improving while all of this was going on. If she did poorly, he gave her a better grade than she deserved. Some of the other kids noticed it, and called her the teacher's pet. She thought the stu-

dent teacher suspected something. She once walked into
Mr. Van Hook's little room while Katherine was putting
her shoes back on; Katherine lied that she had a rock in
her shoe.

Eventually, Katherine decided that Mr. Van Hook really
didn't care about her. He knew she didn't want him to do
these things, but he did them anyway. He was such a jerk;
she wondered how she could have liked him before. She
was thrilled when the school year ended and she could
leave Caseyville for Webster Junior High School in
Collinsville. He frightened her again, however, by calling
over the summer and asking if she wanted to baby-sit for
him. She worried that, even though she refused to go,
somehow it would start all over again. But that passed
and, while she was in junior high, she went back to visit
Mr. Van Hook one day. He said he missed her, and then
he kissed her.

Telling all of that to Pam Klein and Dennis Kuba was
a horrible experience. Katherine felt so dirty, so guilty.
She couldn't even look at these people who said they
were trying to help her. She wasn't sure what to believe,
until they told her what happened was not her fault and
she had no reason to feel ashamed or guilty. She was the
victim, they said, and Mr. Van Hook was the criminal.
That made her feel better.

Telling her mom and dad was torture, too. She didn't
want to hurt them. She was afraid they would be disappointed in her, and angry because of what she had let Mr.
Van Hook do. It was a relief when they hugged her so
tightly and told her nothing could damage their love for
her. Katherine even heard her mother—her gentle, loving
mother—say she wanted to kill Mr. Van Hook. Finally, all
the secrecy was over.

Now she wondered where all this would lead.

CHAPTER 3

The night air seemed even colder as Pam Klein and Dennis Kuba left the mobile home and walked through the bitter wind to the car. They slammed the doors behind them quickly as they slid onto the creaking seats. Then the two of them just sat there in the dark; neither spoke a word as the vapor from their breath fogged the windshield.

Kuba finally started the car, but Pam hardly noticed. She was thinking that she never had been so chilled in her life, and that she couldn't remember any experience harder than watching that family's comfortable life and safe cocoon collapse on them in a matter of minutes. She felt like a doctor who had cut someone wide open and then walked out of the operating room without sewing up the wound. Her only comfort was the knowledge that these parents would help their daughter heal. She had seen enough to know that. She had seen the other kind of parent, too. She had watched a mother slap her sexually abused daughter in the face and scream, "How could you do this to me?"

Pam still was struggling with the tears in her eyes when the lightning bolt from the interview with Katherine struck. Oh, my God, how many more are there? How many more lives has Richard Van Hook ruined?

Kuba had found it incredibly difficult to walk out of that house, knowing what had just been done to the lives there. He knew they would spend a horrible, sleepless night, regretting the past and fearing the future. He was glad Jim and Sheila Howes were gentle, loving parents with a strong faith in God. But Kuba understood the emotional damage of what had happened, and he knew about the tough times that could lie ahead for everyone. How many more were out there if the investigators had found this kind of abuse and betrayal behind the first door they knocked on? This was something frighteningly unique in Dennis's experience; he never had heard of a teacher having sex with an 11-year-old student right in the school building before.

There went the weekend. He couldn't walk away from this; it was too serious to wait until Monday.

"Damn," he finally mumbled as he backed the car out of the driveway.

Caseyville Police Chief Mike Buckner and DCI Agent Jimmy Bivens still were at the station when Klein and Kuba returned after 9:30. Weary and numb, the pair headed directly for the coffeepot before beginning to tell the waiting cops about the nuclear explosion at the Howes trailer. Buckner and Bivens were stunned at how far things had gone, but what they had heard earlier convinced them there would be more victims.

Klein and Kuba agreed that there had to be even more out there if Van Hook had inflicted that kind of abuse on Katherine. And there weren't two people in the area with better credentials to handle this than Klein and Kuba. They had no doubt in their minds that this was their case; Bivens and Buckner seemed to be taking that for granted, too.

Klein gritted her teeth as she looked at Dennis. "I won't rest until we make a case against him, Kuba."

He was nodding. He not only agreed with her, he also was thinking how obsessive and unrelenting she would become about this. He had seen this before with her, and she could be a real pain. But he knew she cared and she would push ahead. He was glad to have the resources of the crisis center behind them; they would need everyone and everything the center could offer.

"These are felony offenses," he said to everyone in the room. "This isn't just fondling anymore. This guy crossed the line a long time ago."

Chief Buckner offered an astute suggestion. "Why

don't you call the superintendent of schools in Collinsville, John Renfro, and fill him in?"

Kuba nodded again. "Good idea. This investigation would be a lot easier to handle if Van Hook wasn't in the classroom on Monday when these kids go back to school."

Kuba called prosecutor Mike O'Malley to fill him in and urge that search warrants be issued for Van Hook's little office and the library as soon as possible. It would be up to the state's attorney's office to prepare the forms to submit to a judge, along with an affidavit from Kuba explaining what evidence the police believed could be found. And, Kuba added, felony charges against Van Hook should be considered immediately.

O'Malley also agreed that Superintendent Renfro needed to be consulted—that night if possible.

Klein noted that Renfro lived near her in Collinsville. She made a quick call to him to set up a visit within the hour. She already had called one of her staff members and asked her to set up a medical examination for Katherine the first thing the next morning at Cardinal Glennon Children's Hospital in St. Louis. That was one of the steps necessary in every sexual assault case, and Pam wanted to be sure it was handled right. She didn't want Katherine traumatized by it; she would be accompanied every step of the way by experts from the crisis center.

By a little after ten o'clock, Klein and Kuba were knocking on the door at Renfro's house. The short, stocky man with close-cropped brown hair and prominent eyeglasses greeted them with a friendly hello and invited them in with an offer of coffee; they declined. They walked into a beautiful, very formal living room that Pam noticed, despite all of the things on her mind, was decorated with a collection of the loveliest sea shells she ever had seen.

Kuba moved directly to an account of the interviews at the police station and the Howeses', detailing the charges by several girls whose demeanor indicated they were being truthful. Kuba added that he expected criminal charges to be filed very soon.

Renfro looked distressed, but he was making an effort to remain calm as he listened; the investigators wondered why Renfro did not seem more surprised.

Kuba continued. "We're very concerned about there being more victims in the school, and we would appreciate anything you could do about Van Hook on Monday. It could be a real obstacle to the investigation for him to remain in the classroom."

Renfro said softly that it could be a problem to remove a teacher from the classroom. He wanted to call the school board's attorney.

As he headed for the phone, Renfro asked if the girls had taken lie-detector tests. That was exactly the wrong thing to say to Kuba and Klein; they were outraged at the implication that the girls might be lying. Klein could feel her blood pressure rising and her face beginning to get hot. Kuba was furious, but he kept his professional composure and coolly explained that his agency did not give polygraphs to sexual assault victims. "We rely on the truth-finding of the investigation," he said with an air of finality.

Kuba glanced at Klein and could read the anger in her face. It had been an unexpected jolt for someone to question the girls' accounts of what had happened. Klein began putting her coat on and was ready to leave by the time Renfro returned to the room. He offered no response about Van Hook's presence on Monday. Kuba explained again that criminal charges would be issued soon, and that this had been a courtesy call to inform the school district that it could have a teacher who was dangerous to children, in case officials wanted to consider removing him from the classroom. Renfro politely thanked the investigators, and they left.

Back out in the cold, Klein and Kuba were steaming over Renfro's reaction, and the fact that he never inquired about the girls or their welfare. He didn't ask if they were handling this dreadful burden well, let alone suggest that the district might be willing to provide counseling for them. He never asked for a recommendation on how to handle Van Hook. He just wanted to know if there had been polygraph tests, and then he called the lawyer.

"We've got a crow," Klein mumbled. Kuba easily caught the reference to her oft-used phrase about teaching crows to sing—her way of saying one of the boys just didn't get it.

Unfortunately, Klein and Kuba failed to recognize the meeting as a sign of unbelievable events to come, things that would lead to more tragedy than anyone could imagine. The community of Collinsville would not welcome this investigation into a respected hometown boy. But it still had not dawned on Klein and Kuba that the girls' veracity would be doubted. As they got in the car, Kuba mumbled, "I'm glad this is your damned town."

On the drive between Caseyville and Collinsville, it also escaped the investigators' attention that they were crossing the boundary line between St. Clair County and its neighbor to the north, Madison County. The Collinsville School District straddled the line and had schools in both counties. That vague bit of geographical trivia would soon become perhaps the most compelling component of the investigation.

Kuba pulled his car alongside Klein's in the parking lot at the Caseyville police station to let her out. They agreed to meet back there at nine the next morning to decide how to proceed and, more likely than not, start interviewing the long list of names they were compiling.

As Klein crawled out of the car, Kuba called to her. She glanced back, and he grinned. "Thanks again. You owe me big this time."

"I know," she said, smiling weakly.

When he got home, Kuba called Chief Buckner again to describe Renfro's reaction, and to explain that the investigators would return early the next morning to resume their efforts.

Kuba's wife woke up as he slipped into bed, and he told her what had happened. He knew that Joanie, also a teacher, would be appalled; she was shocked by the episodes in the school library. As he lay awake in bed,

Dennis was concerned about supporting evidence. How could he corroborate this story from a 12-year-old girl? Would medical evidence be enough? What would happen Monday? If there was justice, that would be the day that Richard Van Hook went to jail.

The Klein house was dark when Pam arrived; everyone was in bed except her dogs, who greeted her with nudges and cold noses. She checked the microwave and found the dinner left by her husband. She ate without realizing what was on the plate. Then she crawled into bed, barely ahead of the exhaustion overwhelming her. Although her body ached for rest, she lay awake for a long time thinking about the tragedies scattered through the evening. Before she finally surrendered to sleep, she remembered thinking there were others in far more pain than she was then.

But she couldn't begin to imagine how much more pain was ahead, or the brutal tragedy that awaited farther down the road.

CHAPTER 4

Pam Klein wheeled her car into the parking lot at the Caseyville Police Department about nine o'clock Saturday morning, comforted to see Dennis Kuba's car in the next spot. She hopped out and hurried toward the building, hunching her shoulders against the piercing cold that refused to be warmed by a bright winter sun. At least it was light now, for the first time since she found herself plunged into this case. The light offered Pam at least symbolic support; this all could be brought out of the dark now.

She knew she would find Dennis already at work, another of the distinctions that made these two such an interesting team. Dennis was an early bird, hitting the ground running every morning amid a great surge of energy. Pam had to ease into the day, waiting for the coffee's caffeine to work its way into her gray matter and kick start her into consciousness.

But she had awakened this day with an unusual sense of urgency. She and Kuba needed to get a lot done in a short amount of time; the investigation was going to get very complicated, very quickly. Kuba needed to get the police work done, and Klein needed to focus the resources of the crisis center with an intensity and on a scale she never had before. She had 15 or 16 volunteers and one paid counselor, and she already had one family—the Howeses—who needed in-depth assistance. There surely would be more as this tree of poisoned fruit spread its roots. The center would be expected to provide a wide range of services for these girls and their families, taxing its resources in new and demanding ways.

Kuba was on the phone with the state's attorney's office when Pam walked into the police station and headed directly for the coffeepot and a caffeine fix. As she dropped into the chair at the next desk, Kuba motioned toward the box of glazed doughnuts he had brought in. Klein instead picked up the phone to check with Mary Free from the crisis center, and was pleased to hear that Mary already had set up a medical examination for Katherine at 10:30 at Cardinal Glennon Children's Hospital. Katherine wasn't thrilled about undergoing her first pelvic exam, but it helped that Mary had arranged to pick up Katherine and her parents, take them to the hospital, and stay with them during the exam.

Klein thanked Mary for her proficiency and hung up. After years without medical resources for abused kids, she was relieved to have Cardinal Glennon's trained teams of doctors, nurses, and social workers just 20 minutes away. They knew how to deal with the needs of traumatized children, provide medical assistance, and compile evidence needed by the police and courts.

Across coffee cups, Klein and Kuba began to plan their approach to the rest of the case. Obviously, the next step was to begin interviewing the nine girls whose appearance at the police station the night before had set off such an amazing chain of events. Investigator and counselor agreed that the police station probably was not the right place—not very private or conducive to frank discussions of embarrassing details with schoolchildren. Kuba suggested his office at DCI headquarters at Fairview Heights, five miles south of Collinsville. Pam and Dennis began calling the girls to set up the interviews.

Agent Jimmy Bivens, whose concern and curiosity brought him back this morning, also helped Klein arrange to use a room at nearby St. Stephen Catholic Church to talk to Katherine after her medical exam. Pam thought it might help for Katherine to talk about how she felt about the exam, and about herself in the middle of all this frightening activity.

This also was the first chance for Klein and Kuba to review the reports of the Caseyville police officers who already had conducted a preliminary investigation of the girls' complaints. This had started a week ago, on Saturday, January 9, when Officer Tamburello's stepdaughter, Michelle Sedlacek, came to him with a story she couldn't keep to herself any longer: Mr. Van Hook was a real pervert, the girl said. Michelle had seen Lori Parker run crying from the library and dash into the rest room at school that Thursday. Lori was reluctant to reveal what happened, but finally confided that Mr. Van Hook had grabbed her and "French-kissed" her. Lori complained that he always was "grabbing her butt" and acting real weird with her, and that he had done some things like that to Sally Morton, too. He told Lori not to tell anyone because he would be fired, or perhaps even sent to jail. Tamburello asked Michelle if the teacher ever did anything to her; she said no, because she refused to get close to him.

On Sunday, January 10, Michelle brought Lori to Tamburello's house, and he confronted her with the allegations against Van Hook. She told him even more: Van Hook would ask her if she wanted to be treated as a grown-up instead of one of his students, then he would rub her buttocks and kiss her. He had kissed her on three different occasions, and the fourth time, in the library that Thursday, he forced his tongue into her mouth. He told her the last time he felt that way about a woman was in high school.

Lori had then escaped to the rest room. She never told anyone what had happened. "My dad would kill him," she said.

As Pam Klein read the reports, a portrait of a classic pedophile began to emerge. Paula Birch, who was just ten years old, told Caseyville's juvenile officer on Monday, January 11, that she was standing alone in the hallway in front of the library the Tuesday before when Van Hook came up behind her, slipped his arms around her, and grabbed her right breast. He squeezed it three times as he giggled, "Tickle, tickle, tickle."

How juvenile and shameful, Klein thought in disgust.

He kept fondling Paula until she told him to stop. She

had laughed nervously, and he kidded, "I bet you laugh when you get kissed, don't you?" She said no.

Ten-year-old Sally Morton told Tamburello that she had been the recipient of about 15 kisses from Van Hook, from pecks on the cheek to longer kisses on the lips. He also had hugged her for about 15 seconds, until she pushed him away. Sometimes he gave her the little kisses in front of other girls. The longer kisses came only when they were alone, however, in his little room off the library. The Bear's Cave again, Klein thought.

The incident the previous Thursday began when Van Hook told Lori's and Sally's teacher that they were in trouble and he wanted to see them in the library. He took Sally into the little room first, held and caressed her hand, and said, "I don't know how to put this. How would you like to be treated? Like a kid from class, my daughter, or a grown-up? I wish you were ten years older." Then he hugged and kissed her, while putting his hand on her behind and squeezing it. She pushed him away, and he sent her out to tell Lori to come into the office. Twenty minutes later, Lori came out of the office crying, and the girls ran to the rest room. Lori told Sally, Michelle, Paula, and Ellen Spanos what had happened. When Sally and Lori went back to class, their teacher asked what was wrong; the girls said they had stomachaches.

The report from Lori Parker was almost identical. He had given her a few small kisses before that Thursday. Earlier that day, she had been standing on a stool while helping Van Hook in the library when he walked up, put his hands on her rear, and gave her a little kiss; she walked out. Later that day, Sally had come out of his office crying just before Lori went in. Van Hook took Lori's hand and said, "It's been a long time since anyone made me feel like this. Do you want me to treat you and tease you like Michelle and Bobbie Hunter and the others, or like my daughter, or do you want me to treat you like a teenager? I don't care if you get me fired or send me to jail. And I don't want you to think I'm a rapist or anything." Then he stood up, put his arms around Lori, and French-kissed her. She pulled away and ran out in tears.

Lori said Van Hook often made comments such as, "I wish you were ten years older or I was ten years younger."

On Monday, the eleventh, Van Hook hugged Lori and asked what she would do if she were in the back room with him. She laughed it off and kept walking. Just before school was dismissed that day, he asked if she could stay late with him and help with the files in the library. When she said she had to go home, he said Katherine Howes used to call her father and tell him she was staying late with Mr. Van Hook. He even offered Lori a dollar to stay late and help, and said he wouldn't harass her or do anything else she didn't want him to. But she refused and left.

Two other girls who were in the rest room with Lori also told identical versions of her tearful accusations. Bobbie Hunter added that Van Hook had started kissing all the girls who worked in the library. She had seen him kiss Sally on the mouth one day, and Paula had said he touched her breast.

Ellen Spanos said she had seen him touch Paula that way, and knew he had been kissing the girls from the library. On Friday, January 8, Van Hook was hugging Ellen when he slid his hand onto her behind. She escaped by telling him it was her turn to jump rope on the playground.

The next report added a whole new dimension to Van Hook's activities—he hadn't confined his roaming fingers to the school building. When a 19-year-old woman named Barbara Maxwell was approached by Officer Mark Goodloe for an interview about allegations against Van Hook, her first question was, "Is he still doing those things?" She said Van Hook had been her diving coach at the Oak Hill Racquet Club in Belleville from 1976 to 1978, while she was 13 to 15 and a student at Collinsville High School. Van Hook often touched her on the thighs, back, and buttocks while giving her diving instructions.

Klein and Kuba glanced at each other, wondering if

such moves couldn't be defended as reasonable during such lessons. But they read on. Barbara also said Van Hook had driven her home during the winter months and would pull up at the corner, a block away from her house, to let her out. Before long he began forcing himself on her—pinning her to the car door—and kissing her on the lips. She told her father about her coach's moves, and Dad put an end to the rides with Van Hook. After that, Van Hook had tried nothing else improper with her.

Klein and Kuba shook their heads. These preliminary reports not only showed Van Hook almost running amok for the last two weeks, but they traced his assaults back at least six years. In these pages alone were five victims at Caseyville School and a sixth from the diving team. And that didn't include Katherine. What would the rest of the interviews show? What other victims and sordid little stories were waiting?

All of those details were troubling enough. But buried at the end of the report from the Caseyville police was more shocking information that Klein and Kuba wished they had known when they talked to Superintendent Renfro the night before. Now they understood why he hadn't seemed appropriately surprised by the allegations against Van Hook. The reports said the Caseyville police had informed Renfro and the principal at Caseyville School, Gerald Ellis, on Monday about the girls' allegations. Renfro's response then had been to ask the police to document the allegations and let him know if any action against Van Hook was planned. That precipitated the meeting with the nine victims Friday night at the police station.

Klein and Kuba looked at each other in amazement. Renfro had known about the molestation charges for four days, but never let on to the investigators as they sat in his home in a courteous effort to warn him and the school district about the storm on the horizon. He had known about the allegations for four days, and he still didn't express a moment's concern for those girls.

It was Klein's turn to mutter incredulously to her partner. "Kuba, can you believe this?" He shook his head slowly.

It didn't take long Saturday afternoon for Klein and Kuba to find out how the rest of the case would shape up. They met Elizabeth McBride at Kuba's office at 1:30. Elizabeth was 13, and probably the most mature of the ten girls Klein had met the night before. She was taller and more physically developed than the others. She looked older, with her hair dyed blond and a touch of makeup on her face. She was in the seventh grade now, but had been in Van Hook's sixth-grade class the year before.

She was a bit hesitant to reveal much—cooperative but not too cooperative, Kuba thought. Her story was the essence of what Klein and Kuba had assumed they would hear from all the girls involved, before they had sat down with Katherine.

Van Hook had started bestowing kisses on Elizabeth's lips as a reward for good homework. When she injured herself slightly during gym class, Van Hook assisted her by placing his hand on her tummy, under her shirt, and then massaging her back. Once, when she wore her red jumpsuit uniform from gym to the library, Van Hook unzipped it and slipped his hand onto her buttocks. That frightened her and she ran out of the library. He hadn't pursued the physical contact beyond that, but he once took a Polaroid picture of her when she wore a dress to school; he kept the photo on his desk in his library office. Polaroids—the perverts always used Polaroids.

After she became the library captain—leader of the girls assisting Van Hook there—he gave her a pair of gold earrings in a design of two hearts. And, even though she no longer was his student, he recently had given her a pendant with the high-school mascot—the Kahok Indian. She had lost one of the earrings, but gave the other one and the pendant to Kuba as evidence.

Elizabeth also offered corroboration for Katherine Howes's story. During the last school year, Elizabeth had seen Katherine and Van Hook go into his office a couple of times a week and stay for what she thought was five or ten minutes each time. Elizabeth also had noticed a *Playboy* magazine on Van Hook's desk in his little office. After the Christmas vacation, Elizabeth noticed that Katherine had started getting more A's on her schoolwork from Van Hook. When she did poorly, Van Hook would become quite upset and berate her in front of the class.

Elizabeth related similar evidence of Van Hook's dalliances with other girls, too. She remembered seeing Susan Williams flee Van Hook's library office in tears and hide in the rest room. Susan wouldn't tell Elizabeth what had happened, so Elizabeth asked Van Hook. He said Susan had blamed him for trying to get her pregnant, and then he asked Elizabeth if she would testify in court that nothing had happened between him and Susan. Elizabeth was stunned, and responded that she couldn't testify about anything because the office door had been closed and she had no idea what had happened.

Elizabeth said Van Hook never took boys into the office and closed the door, nor did he show them the same attention he showed girls.

Elizabeth's story had been told in an unemotional voice. But Klein wondered what the little girl behind it really felt.

Lori Parker met with Kuba and Klein next, and left no doubt about her feelings. The interview was an emotional roller coaster for the tiny, delicate, and very introspective girl. She was bright and pensive, and gave each question deep thought. And she cried almost constantly as she confirmed her earlier statement to the Caseyville police. Pam wanted badly to hug Lori. She was a pretty child, with dark, wavy hair that hung to her shoulders and set off her pale skin.

The last little girl for that day, Tammy Ann Pauley, told a story that was becoming quite familiar already. She was a 12-year-old seventh grader, but was more mature in appearance and behavior than the others. She was slim and attractive with dark brown hair. Her father was a deputy sheriff, and Tammy answered the questions with police-like precision; she gave the facts without embellishment.

She had been a cocaptain in the library last year. After Christmas, Van Hook had started putting his arms around her and kissing her on the cheek. Then he moved to rubbing her shoulders and back, before beginning to pat her on the buttocks. She hadn't seen any activity with other girls. But Tammy did remember seeing a beanbag chair and some pillows in Van Hook's little office. That lent support to Katherine's claim about bedding in the Bear's Cave.

Dennis Kuba tried to relax and enjoy a Saturday night at home with his family—to make up for missing his regular Saturday breakfast at McDonald's with his son. But thoughts about the Van Hook case kept intruding. He and Klein now had accounts of abuse from seven of the nine girls from Friday night—either from personal interviews or statements to the other police officers. Plus, they had the worst-case scenario from that heart-wrenching interview with Katherine Howes. Eight little girls, all describing sexual molestation by a trusted teacher in terms so genuine and innocent and clear and concise that they could be telling nothing but the truth. Not one of the girls ever exhibited anything that remotely suggested they were lying, or even exaggerating. Dennis prided himself on knowing when he was being conned; these girls couldn't have faked the telltale signs of sexual abuse if they had a Ph.D. in psychology.

Just as important in his mind, the girls' stories had contained common threads—subtle bits and pieces the girls couldn't have been sophisticated enough to put together as part of a grand scheme to frame an innocent man. Van Hook made similar comments to many of them, made similar moves. These little details constructed for Kuba a crime profile that was well defined, and described Van Hook's careful and skillful manipulation of his prepubescent victims. He was falling face-first into the predictable patterns Dennis had been trained to expect from a child molester.

This investigation wasn't just seeking justice for past crimes anymore; there was a serious issue of community protection. How many more girls were about to slip within the grasp of Richard Van Hook's probing hands?

Dennis couldn't stop making mental lists of things to do. There were so many more interviews; every girl they had talked to so far had given them the names of several more girls—more suspected victims. Two more interviews were lined up for the next day, even though it was Sunday. Kuba knew that Monday had to bring the descent upon the Caseyville Elementary School by the DCI, including a careful search and interviews with teachers, administrators, and others at the building. Reports had to be filed—Dennis hated paperwork—and documents justifying the issuance of criminal charges had to be drafted. There was so much more to do, and it all needed to be done right away.

The Caseyville Police Department was quiet at noon Sunday when Klein and Kuba met to begin that day's activities. They took their time over coffee and enjoyed the calm, such a contrast to the atmosphere Friday night and Saturday. They decided to interview the last two of the original nine girls upstairs in, ironically, the village's library. It was closed on Sunday and using it would avoid the hectic procedure from the day before, as Klein and Kuba picked up the girls, drove them to his office in Fairview Heights, and then back to Caseyville. The trips had been exhausting and unnecessarily tense for everyone. Using the room upstairs would be much better

But the day would not be that simple. As Klein and Kuba picked up 12-year-old Bethany Crothers, her mother met them at the door with her arms folded defiantly across her chest. She would allow her daughter to talk to them, but first she wanted to inform the police of her feelings about this whole affair. Angrily, she told them she thought they all were crazy to make such allegations against one of the finest teachers she had ever met. Richard Van Hook would never do such things. She couldn't understand why her daughter had gotten involved in this, and there would be hell to pay when her father got home and found out what was going on.

The outrage Pam Klein had felt building for 36 hours nearly boiled over; she wanted to go for this woman's throat. How cruel could she be to her frightened daughter? How could she reject these girls' accusations without knowing the facts? And how could she support this teacher over her very own child? This was the most bizarre reaction Klein had seen yet.

Kuba was nearly as angry, but he kept a lid on the situation. "Mrs. Crothers," he said calmly, "I know these allegations have been a shock for a lot of people. But if you could just stay calm, we really would like to hear what you have to say."

Klein was glad Kuba had taken the diplomatic route again, and it seemed to work. Mrs. Crothers composed herself and took a much less hostile and combative tone. She explained that she had been on a lot of field trips with Van Hook, and she never had seen him act improperly toward any of the children. She just couldn't believe any of the things that were being said about him.

Kuba nodded politely. "I can assure you that we only want the truth, Mrs. Crothers. Your daughter can help us get it. If the allegations are untrue, we want to find that out, too,"

"Okay. I guess she can talk to you. But I can tell you now, her father won't be happy about her having anything to do with this."

Pam Klein turned to Bethany. "Do you want to talk to us?"

Bethany nodded, "Yeah, I do." She glanced sideways at her mother, and then back at Dennis as she headed toward the detective's car. She curled up in the backseat in a coat that didn't look very warm. Pam still found it difficult to push out her anger and maintain her professional composure on the ride to the police station. Kuba was glad to rescue the girl for a while, even if he would have to take her home later.

Bethany was tall and slender; her light brown hair was cropped close to her head. She was extremely agitated as she talked; her eyes darted rapidly back and forth. But she was so anxious to tell what she had experienced with Van Hook that she didn't even wait to be asked questions. Her story made it unanimous among the girls. She was in the seventh grade now, but had had Van Hook for sixth grade and had been a cocaptain of the library girls in fifth and sixth grades. She, too, had been subjected to the kisses on the forehead and cheek, but had managed to turn her head to avoid being kissed on the lips. Van Hook often hugged her and patted her rear; sometimes his hand would "slip" between her legs. When he helped her in math class, he would hold her hand or rub her leg.

She also described a yellow beanbag chair in Van Hook's office, and added that she had seen two striped pillows and, sometimes, a tumbling mat like they used in the gym. He kept soda pop and candy there, and occasionally offered her some. She had seen him take Elizabeth McBride or Katherine Howes into the office and lock the door. Bethany once listened at the door and could hear Van Hook telling Elizabeth how attractive she was. Bethany knew he had given Elizabeth a necklace, some earrings, and a Kahok pin, and had given several gifts to Katherine, too.

On the drive home, Bethany obviously was troubled. Pam was worried about dropping her off to face her mother without any support. Pam asked if Bethany wanted her or Dennis to talk to her mother. Bethany's face turned plaintive and she scooted forward on the car seat. "Oh no, please don't. That'll make things worse for me. I know my mom. She will have cooled down by now. I'll be okay—honest."

Pam and Dennis exchanged uncomfortable, unsure glances.

"Are you sure?" Pam asked.

"Yes, please," Bethany pleaded. "I'll be okay. I've been through things like this with my mom before. It'll be okay, really."

She offered a weak smile as she got out and hurried toward the house. Klein and Kuba watched, feeling helpless to affect what was awaiting Bethany behind that door. She waved when she got to the house, but the pair in the car weren't reassured. They drove away knowing they had left a victim without the love and support she needed so desperately. Klein wondered who had declared it open season on little girls.

Klein and Kuba needed a lift, and the last of the nine girls provided one in fine style. Ellen Spanos—an olive-skinned, dark-haired cutie with a slightly plump middle and an infectiously sweet face—had been interviewed by the Caseyville police already. But she still was tense when Klein and Kuba arrived at her family's mobile home. Her mother reassured her and sent her off to be interviewed. As Kuba started the car, he tried to comfort her a bit more and cracked, "Relax, Ellen, this won't be as bad as being eaten by a lion." Pam and Dennis laughed, but Ellen was stone-faced and intense. In the library for the interview, sitting at a children's reading table across from Kuba as he comically squeezed onto a little chair, Ellen finally seemed to soften.

When the investigators began to ask their questions, Ellen's resolute grimace turned to rubber. As she contemplated each question before answering, her little face contorted and twisted into hilarious shapes. Klein and Kuba wanted to laugh out loud with delight, but had to squelch even the slightest grin to avoid insulting Ellen. Pam had felt like hugging quite a number of girls that weekend to offer solace and support. But she felt like hugging Ellen out of sheer pleasure.

From her facial gymnastics Ellen was obviously searching her memory for every applicable detail in response to each question. She was not about to offer a wrong or incomplete answer. As Pam had noticed in all of the girls' interviews, Ellen seemed extremely conscious of the gravity of the situation.

She had just finished recounting how Van Hook kissed her and patted her rear when the stairs leading to the library resounded with an awful commotion. Klein and Kuba were surprised to see Bethany Crothers racing up the stairs, crying and screaming as she nearly crawled up the last step. Pam ran to meet her, unable to understand a word the hysterical girl was saying.

"Calm down, Bethany. What's the matter?"

"You've got to tear up my police report," she sputtered. "My mom and dad are so mad at me for talking to you, I think they're going to kill me."

Her eyes pleaded with Klein for help and understanding. Klein held Bethany by the shoulders. "My God, Bethany, let's talk about this, okay? Now, we can't just tear up your report. What do you think you said that your parents are going to be upset about?"

"I don't know," she wheezed through her tears. "It's the whole thing. My folks are just furious that I'm involved. I just don't know what to do."

"Okay, Bethany. Look, I promise you"—she glanced over and got a nod of approval from Dennis—"we won't seek any charges against Mr. Van Hook for anything he did to you. The only way we'll use what you said would be to back up what the other girls said. Okay?"

Bethany was quieter, but still crying. "Can I tell my mom that's for sure?"

"Yes, you can tell your mom. We promise. But, please, if you have any more problems, have your mom call me or Dennis. We'll be glad to talk to her."

Bethany clutched Pam's hand and looked into her face. There was a haunting look in her eyes as she studied Pam. Then, without another word, Bethany turned and quietly walked down the stairs. She never looked back.

Pam met Katherine Howes at St. Stephen Church about five o'clock for a counseling session Pam thought the girl might need after the examination at the hospital. As they struggled to find comfort zones around the protruding springs on an old couch, Pam could see the strain of the weekend in Kate's face. She was pale and suffering from a lack of sleep and a flood of tears. Her sunken eyes were ringed with dark circles. Her mouth was pinched tightly and her face was puffy.

As they settled in, Kate opened the conversation by angrily snapping, "Why did I have to go to the hospital and have that physical exam? I didn't like that at all."

Pam made sure her voice conveyed her empathy and concern as she explained that medical evidence would substantiate her statement to police. Weren't the people at the hospital kind? she asked. Kate turned away. "They were all right. It was just so embarrassing. They kept asking all kinds of questions I've already answered several times. They wanted to know everything."

Pam was glad Katherine still had some anger in her. Repeated sexual abuse sometimes took all the fight out of the victim, leaving behind a malaise that sapped the spirit. But Katherine's anger could provide the reservoir of strength and resolve for the new ordeals she could be facing. Pam warned Katherine that the difficulties of pursuing a case like this were just beginning; if she really wanted justice for Mr. Van Hook's crimes, more indignities probably awaited her at the hands of the system.

Katherine had sensed that, and she protested in a tone that conveyed her anguish and humiliation. "I've told you and Dennis what happened. Can't Dennis just put him in jail? Why do all those other people have to know everything that happened to me?"

The question wounded Pam because it came so directly from a child's innocence. And now Pam would be the adult who, one more time, had to tell a victim how things really were in the brutal world of the criminal justice system. She explained that the evidence and the girls' statements had to be reviewed by the police, the prosecutors, a grand jury, the defense attorneys, a judge, and finally, a jury, before the case ended.

Then she broke some more bad news. An assistant state's attorney in St. Clair County, Judy Cates, wanted Katherine in her office early Monday morning for an interview. That had struck Kuba and Klein as odd; prosecutors usually just relied on police reports to issue charges. But Klein knew this case would be more sensitive and difficult than most. Charging a popular schoolteacher with such disgusting acts was dangerous politically. Klein assumed the prosecutors' desire to talk to Katherine suggested the need for a carefully documented case. Klein would look back later and think that, in many ways, she had been as naive as Katherine.

But at the moment Klein thought she could explain it. "Kate, you know Mr. Van Hook is not going to admit what he did to you, don't you?"

"Yes," Katherine whispered softly. She looked at Pam. "I know he won't tell the truth. He always said he was afraid he would go to jail. You know, he kept telling me he would never do anything to hurt me, but all I've done is hurt from the very first time he started up with me."

This was the perfect opportunity for Pam to turn this conversation to the one thing that was more important than building a case against Van Hook—healing his victims.

"How are you feeling about Mr. Van Hook right now?"

Katherine's eyes turned away and she stared across the room. After a few seconds she said slowly, "I'm really mad at him now, but I'm mostly scared. Everything that has happened to me has me feeling so confused and weird. He said and did so many things that have me all mixed up inside."

Her gaze dropped to the floor and her voice got softer. "In some ways he treated me real special, so I feel guilty because I liked that part. But the other things made me feel so awful. I started getting angry over everything and fighting with my brothers. Mom and Dad used to ask me all the time if I needed to talk to them about something, but I would just get mad at them because I was so afraid to tell them. I even wondered what his wife would think if she found out. I figured she would be really mad at me."

Katherine's voice was growing even softer, as if she was talking to herself. "It's just all so crazy. I don't know why he did all those things to me. It wasn't right for a teacher to do that. He kept saying that he cared for me and wouldn't do anything to hurt me. I just keep remembering that over and over. When he was putting those rubbers on, he said they were so a sperm wouldn't get me pregnant. I didn't know exactly what that meant, but I knew what he was doing could make me have a baby. So I kept worrying about that part, too."

Pam let Katherine talk; it provided an important catharsis for her and valuable insight for Pam. But it still was painful to hear again how such abuse turned children's minds upside down and inside out. It shook their foundations and made everything uncertain. And ultimately, it simply caused the kids so much pain.

Katherine had started to cry, losing control of the tears she had struggled to hold back while she talked. "I can't believe this; I'm crying again," she said in frustration. "That's all I've done for the last two days." She took a breath. "Do you know that he called me this summer and asked if I would come over to his house and baby-sit for him? He told me he missed me and our 'special arrangement.' I made up an excuse why I couldn't go; I knew what he really wanted."

Katherine drilled Pam with direct eye contact. "How come you and Dennis talk to girls and get them to tell you these kinds of things that have happened to them, if you know they are going to have to go through all this other stuff?"

Another innocently brutal question. Pam swallowed hard again.

"Katherine, Dennis and I know there are certain kinds of men who do things to children that are against the law, and are very harmful to the children. If one of these men has done something with one girl, he probably has done the same thing with others. And he won't stop himself; he will continue to do those things to more and more little girls unless we stop him. It will take a lot of people working very hard to stop him. And the ones it will be the hardest on will be you girls. You'll have to get on the witness stand and tell the truth about what he did, because there will be a lot of people who will want to believe his lies."

Katherine looked at Pam intensely again. "He's a good liar, isn't he? He lied to me about a lot of things. I can't forgive him for that. He told me that if people found out what was happening, my dad would lose his job. I didn't want that to happen."

Van Hook was good, Pam thought. He was very good.

CHAPTER 5

By Monday, January 18, the rumor mill was churning full speed in Collinsville and Caseyville, grinding out misstated, exaggerated accounts of the girls' accusations. Pam Klein and Dennis Kuba had no idea what was happening and would not have believed the scope and intensity of the feelings generated by these allegations against Richard Van Hook. But the investigators were about to get a surprising taste of what would be a reaction beyond all reason.

Kuba arrived early at DCI headquarters in Fairview Heights to begin coordinating the blitz on Caseyville Elementary School that day and brief the two agents assigned to assist him with the interviews of administrators, teachers, custodians, and anyone else at the school who might have seen something. Kuba also called the principal at the school to explain that the agents would be arriving after lunch to begin the interviews and to search the Bear's Cave in the library. One of the department's crime-scene technicians—the inimitable Alva W. Busch—had been assigned to take photographs of Van Hook's lair and help look for the evidence that would support the accounts of the activities there from Katherine Howes and the others.

Kuba was excited; fewer than 72 hours after this case exploded into his life, the time was drawing near when Van Hook might be busted for his heinous behavior. That moment would make all the work worth-while.

As Kuba was huddling with some of the other agents to explain the events of the weekend, one of them asked if Kuba really believed the girls' stories. Kuba was taken aback; that was a strange question for a DCI agent after hearing the facts collected over the last three days. Then it dawned on Kuba: the other agent had been listening to the talk on the streets, and it wasn't behind the girls. The rumor mill was cranking in Van Hook's favor. Instead of building outrage because a teacher had violated the girls and his public trust, the rumors were generating doubts about the girls' stories. And Kuba knew that the inquiring agent's wife was a nurse who worked with Van Hook's wife at a doctor's office.

Although that question surprised Kuba, it confirmed one of the lessons he was learning about this type of investigation: everyone hates a child molester, until it's someone they know.

About eight miles south in Belleville, the county seat of St. Clair County, Pam Klein was escorting the Howes family into the office of Assistant State's Attorney Judy Cates. She was a slim, attractive woman with a stunning shock of long, red hair pulled back into a loose ponytail. After four years in the office, she had developed a reputation as an able and intelligent prosecutor, and had become the resident expert on sex cases.

Cates smiled reassuringly as she welcomed Katherine and her parents, and showed them to chairs. As anxious as the girl was about telling her story to another stranger, she was comforted somewhat to be facing a woman this time. But Klein was surprised by what she thought she heard in Cates' tone as she began the interview—an edge that Klein thought suggested Cates may have doubts about the allegations. She began to cross-examine Katherine, whose mind was drifting to the events of the weekend and the pain suffered by her parents. Katherine was brought crashing back to reality as Judy Cates bore in.

"Kate, why didn't you tell your parents when this all began?" the prosecutor was asking.

Katherine stuttered and groped for words. "I don't know . . . I didn't know what to do. I was scared and confused. I didn't want to hurt my parents . . ." She was shocked. She thought this prosecutor was supposed to be on her side, but it sounded like she didn't believe her.

Judy Cates asked how Katherine knew about "rubbers."

"Mr. Van Hook showed me; he told me what they were for. I never knew . . ."

"Do you use them with your boyfriend?"

Katherine was so stunned that she began to cry. "Why are you being so mean to me?"

"Kate, I'm trying to show you and your parents what it is going to be like when you have to testify in court and are cross-examined by a defense attorney."

Katherine sobbed, "I don't understand. I thought you were supposed to be my friend."

Pam Klein was startled by the direction the interview had taken and decided Katherine wasn't up to this. As she helped Katherine out of the chair, and ushered her and her parents into the hall, Pam looked back and snapped, "Good grief, Judy, I didn't prepare her for cross-examination. I thought this was just supposed to be an initial interview."

Judy Cates knew she had been tough on the girl. But the prosecutor had been following her habit in such cases—letting the victims and their parents see a glimpse of what lay ahead. The parents had to know that their children could be facing as much trauma from the judicial system as they already had endured from their abuser. Cates was concerned about whether the victim could hold up under such an onslaught. That kind of pressure was a cold, hard fact in the courts then, before laws were passed to protect victims from attacks on their sexual histories or to allow young victims to give a video-taped statement in lieu of testifying in open court.

And Cates thought Klein sometimes tended to focus more on punishing the offender than worrying about the impact of a trial on the victim. Klein certainly would have disputed that notion, but she still was as confused as Katherine about what had just happened. Klein wondered if the state's attorney's office was trying to convince the Howeses to back off the investigation. Was Cates looking for a reason to dump this one? Had State's Attorney John Baricevic—the boss and the one who had to face reelection—decided to short-circuit this investigation? Pam didn't know what was happening, and she could only hope a grand jury would be more receptive to the girls' stories.

Despite the impression left by the interview, Judy Cates actually believed Katherine. Cates was amazed that a teacher would be accused of such acts; she had never seen anything like this before. But she believed Katherine had been abused, even though she also believed this girl had a long way to go before her story would sound plausible in court.

There certainly had been no pressure on Cates from Baricevic or anyone else to kill the case. In fact, Cates was certain Baricevic was in favor of going to the grand jury for a decision on an indictment. He had been fair with the case, Cates thought, and she knew he always allowed her to prosecute any case she believed was valid.

But Katherine cried all the way home, wishing she had never told anyone what had happened. This was exactly what Mr. Van Hook had said would happen if she told on him; no one would take the word of a kid over a teacher. Pam had encouraged Katherine to be strong, but she was exhausted. This had just started, and all she wanted now was for it to be over.

Dennis Kuba felt his adrenaline pumping as he led the team of agents into the school building; it was a dramatic feeling to descend on that site with the full force of the State Police in a cause that was so just. But that feeling soon would fade into disappointment.

Kuba stopped first to talk to Principal Gerald Ellis. From behind his desk, the man in the heavy-rimmed eyeglasses remembered that he once had seen Van Hook give a girl a little smooch on the cheek, but never had observed anything remotely inappropriate. Van Hook's name had come up once before. A year earlier, student Susan Williams had told her parents that Van Hook had kissed and fondled her. Ellis checked with Van Hook; the teacher flatly denied it. Ellis learned later that Susan had admitted a strong attraction to Van Hook, and that she subsequently had required psychiatric treatment.

The episode registered with Kuba. Elizabeth McBride also had mentioned Susan Williams, recalling the time she ran crying from Van Hook's office. Van Hook had told Elizabeth that Susan was accusing him of trying to get her pregnant. All of that seemed to fit now, Kuba thought.

But Ellis's next statement really deflated Kuba. Ellis had been told about the investigation by Caseyville police a week ago, and he had told Van Hook that same day. The day after that—on Tuesday, January 12—Van Hook said he was sick and went home at noon. But Ellis noticed Van Hook's car parked in an unusual spot just before he left. Instead of parking in front, where he normally left his car, he was parked in the rear of the building—near the library.

Ellis's implication was clear; there would be nothing incriminating left in Van Hook's little office. While the cops cautiously were approaching the tender victims, Van Hook had been tipped off by school officials to the investigation and had dumped the evidence. That was damaging to the case, of course, and it was damning conduct by Van Hook.

As Ellis had warned, the search of the Bear's Cave yielded no evidence; no condoms in a box that looked like a book, no girlie magazines, no pillows or sleeping bag or gym mat. The room, barely six by eight feet, looked like nothing more than a simple storage closet— hardly the scene of depraved sexual molestation. The crime-scene "tech," Alva Busch, snapped some photos and noted that the doorknob locked with a key from outside, and unlocked from the inside with a twist of the handle. But he found no evidence to collect or analyze.

Then it was time to turn to the staff. Kuba was assisted by Agents Ron Snoke and Gary Lemming as they interviewed 13 teachers, 3 teacher's aides, 2 janitors, and a secretary. Every last one of them said they had never seen Richard Van Hook do anything improper. They had seen nothing suspicious in the library, never found the doors locked, and certainly never saw Van Hook kiss, fondle, or molest a student. Unanimously they insisted that Van Hook was a fine teacher and a wonderful man who obviously was the victim of some horrible miscarriage of justice. The staff members—even the ten women teachers who theoretically would have some sympathy for the girls—seemed to resent the agents' questions, and were incredulous at the implication that Van Hook was guilty of such a monstrous offense.

They were closing ranks behind Van Hook, all right.

Dennis Kuba was beginning to sense what the already traumatized girls were going to be facing. He didn't think the word "unpleasant" came close to describing what was ahead for them in their hometown.

When Klein told Kuba later about the session with Judy Cates, he was lost for words. He hadn't understood why Cates needed to interview Katherine at that point, anyway; his detailed reports usually were adequate when she was deciding on charges. If she had seemed too harsh with Katherine, Kuba wondered, had she just gone too far while trying to gauge the girl as a witness? But Cates still seemed cool to the case when he arrived at her office the next day, Tuesday the 19th, to describe the events at Caseyville School. He was optimistic she still would issue felony charges, but her tone dampened his hopes.

Cates was having trouble envisioning all this sexual activity in the room that had been described to her as a tiny, crowded storage closet. She looked across the desk and asked, "Dennis, do you really think they could have sex in that little room?"

Kuba felt the edge of sarcasm slice through as he responded, "Judy, do you think people really have sex in the back seat of a car?"

She shrugged; she saw a lot of difference between a back seat and a closet in a school. And she already had mapped out the course of action she described to Kuba. She was issuing three misdemeanor charges of contributing to the sexual delinquency of a minor on the three best cases. That would get Van Hook under arrest. Then the case would go before the grand jury the next month to let that panel decide whether to issue felony charges. The teacher's lawyer was Bill Gagen; Kuba was to call him and arrange the arrest.

Kuba was crestfallen. He had expected felony charges of taking indecent liberties with a child, or what used to be called statutory rape; that was the appropriate charge under the evidence. The misdemeanor charges carried a maximum sentence of a year in the county jail and a $1,000 fine—not even prison time. Surely Katherine Howes's story justified felony counts. But the prosecutors were not asking for Kuba's opinion. The decision already was made, and he assumed it had come down from the boss, State's Attorney John Baricevic.

When Cates handed him the misdemeanor charges, Kuba was even more disappointed. Not one referred to the incidents involving Katherine. One count was for touching Paula Birch's breast; the others were for fondling and kissing Lori Parker and Sally Morton. For some inexplicable reason the prosecutors had passed over the worst case and charged misdemeanors on the lesser offenses.

Kuba was starting to get uneasy. This was not going right at all. The case was sensitive politically, but he should be hearing some righteous indignation among prosecutors outraged by these unconscionable acts against so many girls. There should be talk of concern for the victims' welfare and the need to keep this man from hurting any more kids. There should be felony charges and pledges to win a prison sentence for this molester, despite all odds or public pressures.

Instead he was starting to wonder if prosecutors were planning the light treatment—probation, maybe with some counseling, and perhaps forcing the guy out of teaching. Kuba was starting to think that the only real desire in the prosecutor's office was for this case to go away, quietly.

Bill Gagen was a well known attorney in St. Clair County who practiced with his brother, Bob, a former county circuit judge. Kuba's call was expected, and Bill

Gagen said Van Hook would surrender at DCI headquarters early Wednesday afternoon—the next day. Kuba wouldn't even get to make an arrest; it all would be nice and neat.

Pamala Klein was unhappily surprised by the lowly misdemeanors filed against Van Hook, and the lack of charges on the allegations from Katherine. Klein had become suspicious about the way the prosecutor's office was going to handle the case, and these charges made her even more wary. She felt badly for Kuba as he broke the news to her. She didn't blame him, but she knew he would think she did. Her frustration was so overpowering it was hard to hide her feelings of disappointment and concern.

Klein and Kuba had another fear about the misdemeanor charges; they could send the wrong message to a community already plunging deeply into confusion and misinformation about the allegations against a popular teacher. The lesser charges would suggest lesser crimes or, even worse, that the case against Van Hook was weak and the girls' stories were dubious. The investigators were starting to wonder how this was going to play in the media once the news of Van Hook's arrest got out.

Klein had some bad news for Dennis, too. One of Bethany Crothers's classmates had called to report that Bethany had arrived at school that day with her face bruised. Had their worse fears come true? Klein could do nothing but call the abuse investigators from the Illinois Department of Children and Family Services, and hope their intervention would be enough to prevent further injury. Weeks later, Klein would receive a letter explaining that state investigators had found "credible evidence of child abuse," and the family was under observation. Bethany's fears and her mother's warnings had proved to be justified. Bethany said that, when her father returned home, he became enraged at her involvement in the investigation, and struck her. There had indeed been hell to pay.

Dennis said he would wait until the parents cooled down, and would drop by the Crothers home to discuss things. He and Pam wondered if there hadn't been something else they could have done. It was a bitter moment in an already frustrating case.

But they had to keep going. Kuba had lined up interviews with three more girls for that evening. Two of them were sisters, 11 and 9, the daughters of a city official in Caseyville who asked the police to interview his girls because he was concerned about the situation. The girls had not been around Van Hook much and knew nothing, Kuba and Klein learned.

But the third—a cute, chubby 12-year-old in the seventh grade named Sharon Bailey—had seen Katherine Howes and Elizabeth McBride go into Van Hook's little office alone with him several times, and he always closed the door behind them. Sharon had not been in Van Hook's office, but she had seen mistletoe hanging in the doorway. He had tried to get her to give him a "Christmas kiss," but she had slipped away clean. She had not seen him kiss anyone else, but had seen him hug some of the students. He had given Sharon a cutting board and a pair of earrings last year for serving as a librarian. She had a relatively good relationship with Van Hook until he sent the truant officer to her home when she missed school one day.

After the last of the girls left that night, Kuba showed Klein the report on Katherine Howes's examination at Cardinal Glennon Hospital on Saturday. The physical exam produced evidence of sexual activity that supported Katherine's story—absence of the hymen and a vaginal orifice large enough to accept a small penis.

The accompanying report written by the medical-social worker who interviewed Katherine showed that her account of how Van Hook abused her had remained consistent, more evidence of her truthfulness. The worker noted that, at the end of a long series of detailed questions about the sexual contact, "Katherine burst into tears in an angry rage after this set of questions." Pam winced: another painful moment for Katherine.

Klein was gratified to read the worker's conclusion

listed under "impression and assessment." It was good to
have another professional back up Klein's opinion.

"It is my feeling that this young girl is a very dedicated
and caring youth who was manipulated by her sixth-grade
teacher in playing on her sympathy and naivete. She has
been most dedicated in attempting to preserve the family
name and undoubtedly had this same integrity used
against her in this relationship with this sixth-grade
teacher."

Pam nodded; that is exactly how Van Hook had manipulated her to his purposes. That kind of "integrity" was
one of the traits such predators used to keep their victims
silent.

The worker's report also stated she was concerned
about psychological damage to the girl, and the possibility of widespread abuse by the same man. The worker already had contacted the abuse hot line for the Illinois
Department of Children and Family Services, and had referred the case to the hospital's special sexual-abuse
team. The agencies involved should provide assistance to
the other victims abused by the man, the social worker
added.

Pam nodded again. Dead right on all counts.

Dennis Kuba and Officer Ron Tamburello were waiting
at 1:15 Wednesday when Bill Gagen escorted Richard
Van Hook into the DCI offices on the third floor of the
Southern Illinois Bank Building in Fairview Heights.
Kuba's first look at the man he had heard so much about
was almost disappointing. Van Hook looked entirely ordinary, like any 34-year-old man walking along any street
in America. Pleasant-looking but not really handsome, he
was smaller than Kuba expected at five-foot-eight and a
trim 160 pounds. He had unremarkable blue eyes, and his
brown hair was combed across the top of his forehead.
He wore brown slacks and a brown sports coat over a
brown and white checked shirt. He looked much too innocent for the image Kuba had conjured up.

Kuba escorted the men into his office and, as they were
sitting down around the desk, asked if Van Hook wanted

to make a statement. The attorney responded curtly for him, saying there would be no statement or interview. As Kuba took the information for the standard arrest form, he realized Van Hook was extremely nervous. He was shaky and wouldn't look Kuba directly in the eyes. His voice was soft and low, but controlled, and his demeanor carried the message that he could not believe what was happening.

Kuba was frustrated to be sitting across a desk from this man, unable to confront him, to interview him the way he had taken on sex offenders before. Kuba let his thoughts wander to what might have happened under the best circumstances in this case. The police could have recorded a call by Katherine to an unsuspecting Van Hook, perhaps getting incriminating admissions. And Van Hook would have been an interesting subject to surprise at home after seizing the condoms and other evidence in his Bear's Cave. Kuba wanted desperately to have hauled Van Hook into headquarters for an interrogation, confronting him face to face about the charges from Katherine and all the others. Kuba wanted to look into Van Hook's eyes when he realized so many of his little victims finally had talked, despite all his pleading and warning and whining after he violated them. Kuba could imagine the look when Van Hook realized he couldn't lie his way out of this. The cop looked across the desk again, and felt absolutely sure he could have drawn a confession from this man.

Instead Kuba could do nothing but collect the barest biographical sketch. His name was Richard G. Van Hook; his nickname was Dick. He was born on March 27, 1947. He had been married since August 31, 1968, to the former Sandra Oliver, a 34-year-old nurse at a pediatrician's office. They had two children—a daughter, nine, and a son, seven. His father, Richard W. Van Hook, had died the previous April; his mother, Stella L. Van Hook, survived. He had a younger sister, Susan L. Meadows, who lived in nearby Glen Carbon. He had graduated from Collinsville High School in 1965, got a bachelor's degree from Eastern Illinois University in Charleston in 1969, and a master's from Southern Illinois University at Edwardsville in 1979.

The Van Hooks had lived at 214 Emilie Court in Collinsville for five years, and in the next little town to the north, Maryville, for six years before that. Kuba assigned no importance to this last bit of information, never dreaming how important it would become.

Kuba explained that Van Hook would have to be photographed and fingerprinted, and then excused himself to make the arrangements. He stepped into an office down the hall and asked Agent Jere Juenger to handle a mug shot for him; Juenger was probably the best photographer in the office. Juenger stepped into the room where mug shots were taken, and was stunned to see an old friend from Collinsville High School, Dick Van Hook, waiting. Juenger had not heard about the case, and had no idea why the respected teacher and prominent citizen would be there. As the men exchanged friendly greetings, Juenger wondered if there was some reasonable explanation. Did Van Hook need some kind of security clearance that required a photo and fingerprints? Van Hook was friendly and calm, but offered no explanation.

When the photography was done and Van Hook left the room, Juenger grabbed Kuba and asked, "What the hell is going on?" Kuba gave his colleague the brief version of the case, leaving Juenger stunned. How could these allegations have been made against Dick Van Hook, the popular and respected kid Juenger remembered from school? Juenger asked Kuba how good the case was, and got an uncharacteristically gruff response that it was rock-solid. Juenger had no way of knowing that Kuba and the others were starting to get very touchy about questions like that.

As shocked as Juenger was, he realized that the chance meeting had to be more troubling for Van Hook. How humiliating to have an old pal from high school turn out to be the cop who takes your mug shot on charges of being a child molester.

Juenger spent the rest of the day trying to deal with his own discomfort. How could this be Dick Van Hook, the kid Juenger had met at Webster Junior High School in

1959 when they were twelve years old? They went through junior and senior high schools together, and Dick had remained one of the nicest kids Juenger ever knew. Could Dick really be a child molester?

Pam Klein, Dennis Kuba, and other experts knew that the uncertainty nagging at Jere Juenger was common among people who knew only the public personas of secret sex offenders. They usually seemed so nice, so normal, so upstanding, that it was unthinkable that they could be pedophiles. People want child molesters to be drooling, wheezing, crazed cretins wrapped in battered overcoats and lurking in the bushes near the playground. There is comfort in hoping molesters are that easy to spot; children can be protected from such an obvious threat.

But that wasn't the reality Klein and Kuba had encountered. Sex offenders such as Van Hook almost always seemed like rock-solid citizens, offering few outward symptoms of their dangerous disorder. Their public face was so familiar and reassuring.

And that was what made them so insidious.

The life of Richard Van Hook was the perfect example. He was a nice kid from a regular, working-class family. The Van Hooks weren't part of the ruling class in Collinsville—just real people living the solid life promised to everyone who worked hard. His father, from whom he drew the name Richard, was a machinist. Mother Stella was a homemaker with two children—son Richard and daughter Susan, eight years younger.

Dick was a good kid; friends could remember no incidents that even hinted at hidden problems. He certainly never was in trouble with the police or school authorities. He was good-looking—not very tall, but trim and blond, with a crew-cut or similarly short style popular before the long hair of the late '60s and '70s became fashionable. He could have been a featured actor on any of the innocently naive television shows that pretended to chronicle family life in America's golden years.

At Collinsville High School from 1961 to 1965, Dick

Van Hook traveled in the best circles, a member of one of the most popular cliques among the kids at the top of a class of 500 or more. He was well liked and was invited to all the right social functions. He always wanted to be involved and at the center of things, and participated in a variety of activities. In addition to his outside accomplishments as a member of the swimming and diving teams at private clubs and as a lifeguard at local pools, he was on the track and cross-country running teams at school. He was a member of the science club as a sophomore and, as a senior, was on the student council. He seemed an ambitious kid, determined to be at the top of the heap whatever he did.

Van Hook didn't have a reputation as a ladies man and wasn't very old when he started dating Sandra Oliver. Other boys remembered her as a cute girl—not a knockout, but very attractive. She was a nice girl with a good head on her shoulders, and everyone was sure she would do something with her life. When Dick and Sandy got married later, they seemed like a perfect match.

He seemed on track again as he got his bachelor's degree in education in 1969, and spent the next ten years teaching while earning his master's in education. Growing up during the tumultuous Vietnam era, he was one of the fortunate who avoided military service with an educational deferment from the draft.

He spent his first two years teaching at Edwardsville Junior High School; district records said he was dismissed in 1971 for lack of tenure. He had received good evaluations there, although his principal wrote in 1970, "He seems at times to get his own need for attention interpolated into the learning activities." He was hired by the Collinsville School District in 1971 and began teaching at the high school.

Sandy had become a nurse, and they started a family in 1973. They attended the First United Methodist Church, where Sandy was on the board and Dick was the church librarian.

Until January 1982, Dick Van Hook seemed to be living the good life, perhaps even a charmed life.

* * *

While Agent Jere Juenger was lost in thoughts of old times, his old friend Richard Van Hook walked out of the DCI office and made the short drive to Circuit Court in Belleville for a brief arraignment before a judge. Van Hook posted $750 in cash—the 10 percent needed to satisfy the $7,500 bond—and walked out of the courthouse without being noticed.

The first newspaper story in what eventually would become a torrent of publicity about the Van Hook case appeared on Thursday, January 21, in the *Collinsville Herald*. A police source had tipped reporter Ed Gurney to Van Hook's arrest, and Gurney had put together a pretty comprehensive story. The biweekly paper's headline on the front page announced, "6th Grade Teacher Facing Allegations," and carried a photo of Richard Van Hook from the school yearbook. The straightforward and factual account reported the misdemeanor charges against a ten-year veteran of the district in his third year at Caseyville Elementary School. Gurney explained that the investigation had begun a week earlier and mushroomed under work by the Caseyville police, the DCI, and the Rape and Sex Abuse Care Center.

Superintendent John Renfro was quoted as saying Van Hook had been on sick leave since January 12, the day after the investigation began. Van Hook had not been asked to stay away from school, but Renfro said, "It helped the matter, certainly, because there were some very concerned parents." Renfro said the district had cooperated with the police, and the school board probably would discuss the situation at its next meeting the following Monday.

The board's president, Dick Cain, a lawyer, told the *Herald* the charges against Van Hook were "totally unexpected," and appropriate action would be taken once the truth was learned. "We'll make a complete investigation and until the results of the investigation are final, we don't expect him to go back into the classroom."

Now the word was really out, reaching far beyond the

halls of the school buildings; the community really was starting to buzz about a case that would test its true character.

The issuance of such lightweight charges didn't slow Klein and Kuba; a big push was put on between Thursday, January 21, and Friday, January 29. With help from Caseyville Officer Mark Goodloe and Mary Sudholt from the crisis center, they interviewed five more girls, three parents, and two student teachers. Two of the girls and a student teacher had seen nothing improper in Van Hook's conduct. But the other three had familiar stories. He had hugged the second student teacher, supposedly in an effort to make her blush; he once hugged her in front of Principal Jerry Ellis.

Another library helper, Carrie Vernon, was 12 the year before when Van Hook kissed her on the lips; she resigned from library duty the next day. When she returned to the post several months later, Van Hook apologized and never bothered her again.

An 11-year-old still in Van Hook's class said he often tickled her sides and tummy, hugged her tightly, and touched her buttocks. He commonly referred to her as his girlfriend, held her hand while they walked around the library, and teased her because she did not blush when he put his arms around her. She thought it was mostly just in fun.

But one of the parents reported what would turn out to be only a faint warning about what was ahead. Rita Bailey—whose daughter, Sharon, was one of the few girls who had managed to slip out of Van Hook's grasp without even a kiss—complained that the younger brother of a teacher at another grade school had approached Sharon and Tammy Pauley as they walked home from school. He sarcastically told them that he didn't believe the allegations against Van Hook.

And, on Monday, January 25, a male teacher at Webster Junior High School approached Sharon, Tammy Pauley, and Elizabeth McBride as they were standing in the cafeteria. He told them they were taking up too much space, and added, "Some girls should be painted red like fire hydrants so dogs can piss on them." Then he told Elizabeth McBride that he and Mr. Van Hook were good friends.

Elizabeth's mother, Donna McBride, also told Kuba about even more direct comments by the same teacher about the investigation. He had confronted Elizabeth again about the allegations against Van Hook, insisting that they were false and the girls were lying. Elizabeth had been so upset by the dual encounters that her mother called the principal at the junior high school to complain. The teacher later called Mrs. McBride to apologize.

One of the most enlightening interviews came on January 29, when Kuba and Klein interviewed Susan Williams's parents, Roberta and Donald Williams, in their mobile home. Their daughter was 12 when she complained to them before Thanksgiving of 1980 that Van Hook had been fondling her breasts and buttocks at school. The Williamses told Ellis, and the next day he reported that Van Hook had denied the allegations. His defense was that he may have patted or pushed Susan slightly from the rear, but it was kind of a "get moving" gesture. The Williamses said Ellis warned them that discussing the matter with anyone else could damage Van Hook's reputation, and leave the Williamses open to a slander suit.

They were angry and ashamed as they recounted how their trust in Ellis led them to accuse their daughter of lying about Van Hook. Their relationship with Susan deteriorated from that point, and she began making other, apparently wild accusations, including one about a sexual affair with a relative. A gynecologist found no evidence of sexual activity. Soon after that Susan was admitted to a hospital in St. Louis for psychiatric treatment. During the two months she was there, one of the doctors said she was going through a phase and eventually would overcome her chronic lying. In January 1981, Susan finally went back to school and, incredibly, was returned to Van Hook's class.

Then Klein and Kuba sat down with Susan, a plain-looking girl with dark hair, pale skin, and glasses. She said Van hook once pinched her buttocks and grabbed her breasts at least four times. Once, while he was sitting in a chair, he pulled Susan astraddle his lap and rubbed his erect penis on her buttocks.

And Susan added that she once had seen Van Hook try to remove Katherine Howes's blouse.

More almost incredibly bold actions by Van Hook told in consistent terms by another girl—this troubled girl— Klein and Kuba thought.

Reporter Ed Gurney was stunned by a blizzard of complaints about his story on Van Hook's arrest. Gurney had been a newspaperman for nine years, more than three of those at the *Collinsville Herald*, and he never had seen such a reaction to a down-the-middle account of an arrest. Van Hook's supporters were calling the *Herald* in unprecedented numbers complaining that the newspaper was ruining the life of an innocent man by reporting baseless allegations. Many of the callers insisted the only fair way to handle this situation was to refrain from reporting the case until it was resolved. The most outraged callers seemed to be people who went to church with Van Hook.

Gurney and editor Judy Taplin took the calls and were unable to mollify the protestors by explaining that the paper was simply reporting the details of a public event from the public record. Clearly, the callers thought these charges were unworthy of attention and should be ignored. Gurney and Taplin were amazed; the story on Thursday had been as accurate and unbiased as possible, and the journalists were at a loss to explain the numbers and intensity of angry calls. Although the school district was on Gurney's regular beat, he never had heard of Van Hook and had no idea whether he was innocent or guilty. That point really made no difference, anyway; this was a legitimate story and Gurney knew he had handled it properly. He was shocked that so many people were vociferously supporting the man when so little information was available about the allegations.

The school district "beat" always had been unusually

exciting in Collinsville, unlike covering most school districts for reporters. On Gurney's first day on the job in 1978, an acrimonious teachers' strike began, lasting two weeks. When it ended, the school board decided to make up the lost time by canceling Christmas vacation. Then the students walked out in protest. After a public meeting the school board reversed its decision and Christmas was saved. But about that time the high school's canonized basketball coach quit in anger over his contract. In a town where a winning basketball team was second only to breathing in importance, that was one of the most significant and debated events in decades.

But none of that had generated the kinds of calls the *Herald* was receiving over the Van Hook case. The protests had an unintended effect, creating the need for a follow-up story on the incredible support for Van Hook in the face of such charges.

The next edition of the *Collinsville Herald* sent Pam Klein into a rage. Across the top of the front page on Monday, January 25, was a headline that read, "Friends Rallying Around in Teacher's Trying Time."

She couldn't believe her eyes as she read Gurney's second story: "Many of Richard Van Hook's friends and coworkers have come to his support since it was announced last Thursday that the Caseyville School teacher had been arrested. His supporters have described him as an outstanding teacher, parent, and person. Many say they are shocked at the charges and believe he will be found innocent."

Klein wanted to scream; the story was just warming up.

"Some of Van Hook's friends have called the *Herald* to express the view that he is innocent. They believe publicity about the charges makes him appear guilty and that his life may be ruined, regardless of the outcome of court proceedings.

"Other members of the Caseyville School teaching staff appear to be solidly behind Van Hook.

" 'I think Dick is one of the best models for the kids I've ever seen,' said Donna Wetzel, a first grade teacher at Caseyville."

The story quoted Wetzel as commending Van Hook for his dedication in adjusting to the elementary level three years ago, after he was bumped down to Caseyville because of cutbacks at Webster Junior High School. Wetzel said Van Hook liked teaching elementary school, and was working on certification to teach grades below the sixth. "He's done really good things for the kids," she said. "He's gone beyond the call of duty many times."

The long story quoted several teachers calling Van Hook "a dedicated teacher and family man." The teacher whose brother had popped off to Sharon Bailey added, "There's no doubt in our minds that he's totally innocent." Van Hook's attorney added, "From everything I know of the guy, I think he's going to be found innocent of any charges.

Klein was almost as appalled as she was angry. How could so many people rush to this man's defense without knowing anything about the evidence? Worse, they weren't giving any thought to how their defense of indefensible acts would make the emotionally distraught victims feel. Hadn't these people stopped to think how they would feel if their daughters were involved?

To add to Pam's fury, a letter to the editor carried the headline, "Can man look innocent with article in the paper?" Pam's blood pressure headed toward the ionosphere as she read, "I thought in this country a person was innocent until proven guilty. Then how can a person still be considered innocent in the eyes of the public when his name and even his picture is plastered on the front page of the Thursday night paper for merely an accusation?"

"Merely an accusation? Damn it," she sputtered as she read on. "I was appalled at what I saw and read about a school teacher who was only accused of such a crime. It is ironic that the same thing happened on a television show last Wednesday night. An innocent man was accused of a crime he never did, and it ruined him and his family. I would hate to see this happen to this family or any other family that could be innocent. Today, families are split up fast enough. We do not need to push them into it. I am also a mother of a daughter, but I believe in 'innocent until proven guilty.' "

Pam Klein thought she would be ill. She never dreamed this case would draw out such ignorant, narrow-minded responses. Yes, Van Hook's friends should offer him support. But they should not be blind, and they certainly should not be attacking the girls.

Pam's husband, Gary, picked up the paper and read it quietly. Gary Klein was a city commissioner, and already had been taking some abuse around town about his wife's role in this investigation. He was used to his acquaintances having trouble dealing with Pam's career and the way she did her job. And Gary was supporting her in the ways he knew she needed while she was immersed in a case. He kept gas in the car and food on the table for the kids. But this story was even more than Gary could handle. He startled Pam by slamming the newspaper down on the kitchen table in disgust, a rare outburst for him.

The community's initial reaction was a shock, and a bitter pill for the girls and their families to swallow.

Katherine Howes had been under the worst assault. Some of the kids in the neighborhood had been teasing her about "going all the way" with Mr. Van Hook. She had been terribly upset, but was cheered a bit by a television set she received from her parents as a present for her thirteenth birthday on February 3. Klein and Kuba remembered that just a year earlier, Mr. Van Hook had celebrated Katherine's twelfth birthday with a session in the Bear's Cave.

No one outside of the schools in Collinsville could know what was happening within the teacher's ranks. First-grade teacher Pat Shahini watched as her colleagues struggled to keep from being completely consumed by panic. She taught at Summit Elementary School on the opposite side of the district from Caseyville School, but she wasn't insulated from the shock waves. Could this happen to me? the teachers all were wondering in almost paralyzing fear. Could disgruntled students make accusations against me, destroying my career and my life? The teachers all knew that kids sometimes twisted an event at school when they described it to their parents at home. Every teacher had tried to convince a parent that their child's version was somewhat exaggerated.

But Pat Shahini was even less prepared for the vehemence with which some of the teachers defended Van Hook. True, he was quite popular among most of his colleagues; he was personable, and some even found him charming. His reputation as a teacher was one of competence and dedication. While most of the staff expressed shock and disbelief at the charges, a few seemed extraordinarily angry. That occasionally came out in incredibly nasty comments about the girls. Pat seemed to be one of the few remaining neutral; she didn't know what had happened, so she would reserve judgment until all the facts were in.

One male teacher who had gone through the Collinsville schools shortly after Van Hook was genuinely disbelieving. Dick Van Hook was a friendly, competent teacher who treated his profession in a positive way. He got along well with everyone, and talked often about his wonderful family. He just wasn't the kind of guy who could molest the children he cared so much about. No one could convince this teacher that the Dick Van Hook he knew could do these things. And the word in the school district was that a movie about kids making similar allegations against a teacher had been on television just the week before this investigation began. Too coincidental, many people thought.

Pat Shahini had heard all of that, but she also had heard about Dick Van Hook's other reputation. He was known throughout the district as a flirt who loved making suggestive little remarks. Was it really so hard to believe that a man who would do those things might step over the line with the girls in class, too? And if the charges were true, these girls had been terribly traumatized. Sexual abuse by a teacher is incestuous for a little kid, Pat knew; it confused and wounded them deeply. If these girls were telling the truth, they needed help, care, counseling, and understanding. Pat kept wondering why no one was talking about that.

Pam Klein was disturbed by what was happening in her hometown. A group of vocal and angry supporters of Van Hook was taking control, influencing public opinion in a dangerous way. How could something like that happen in the town she knew and loved?

Collinsville was nothing if not Middle America. It sat on the edge of the bluffs in southwestern Illinois, overlooking the prehistoric bed of the Mississippi River. The mighty waters long ago shifted a few miles to the west, leaving a fertile bottomland below the bluffs. Collinsville had been settled in the early 1900s by miners who dug coal out of shafts directly under the town. After the mines closed, the workers' descendants stayed on and began a climb out of the poverty that accompanied the company store.

Collinsville was known for years as the home of Frank "Buster" Wortman, the gangster who controlled the downstate Illinois rackets in the thirties, forties, and fifties in conjunction with crime bosses in Chicago. For a while, Wortman was Al Capone's man in southern Illinois. Wortman lived on the edge of town in a squared off, fortress-like house surrounded by a moat; it was a well-known local landmark called "the castle" by most residents.

The city had grown to a population of almost 19,000 spreading along the bluffs, which offered a dynamic view of the skyline of St. Louis dominated by the glistening Gateway Arch, barely ten miles away. Collinsville was a link in a chain of small towns that had grown up on the east side of the metropolitan area. The city was smack in the middle, straddling the boundary line between the two large counties, Madison and St. Clair. They had a combined population of more than 500,000, and were a vital part of the regional identity.

Collinsville also had carved out a reputation as the home of the one of the winningest basketball teams in state history—the Kahoks. The mascot took its name from the nearby and world-renowned Cahokia Mounds, the artifact-rich earthen structures that were the center of a huge and impressive culture of Native Americans more than a thousand years ago.

Collinsville and the area around it were rich in diversity and tradition, but Klein feared that a sordid new chapter—one the town would not be proud of later—was about to be written.

CHAPTER 6

With the grand jury session in St. Clair County coming up on February 11, Dennis Kuba and Pam Klein dared to hope the tide was about to turn for the girls. The investigator and counselor looked at the impressive list of victims, and the credibility of their stories, all amassed in a very short time. Surely so much evidence would be more than enough to convince a panel of reasonable citizens that this teacher should be indicted on felony charges. Surely the grand jury would be outraged by this amazing pattern of abuse and molestation that went back years and could involve an untold number of victims. Surely the community and the school district would back off from their blind and wrong-headed support for Van Hook and open their hearts to his victims. Surely.

Katherine Howes had approached the grand-jury session with fear and loathing after learning that she and the three girls named in the misdemeanor charges would have to testify. Once again Katherine would have to tell her story, endure the prying questions, and suffer the humiliation. It probably would be even worse this time, because she would face a whole roomful of strangers—and many of them would be men. The event was daunting for a girl who had just turned 13.

Klein and Kuba had explained that a grand jury was made up of 23 ordinary citizens chosen randomly for the panel. A prosecutor would ask questions to draw out the evidence, and the jurors would listen to the girls' testimony. Then the jurors would decide if there was probable cause to believe a crime had been committed, and sufficient evidence to justify an indictment—the charge filed by the panel that would force Van Hook to trial.

Although none of the girls' support group could be in the room when they testified, Klein and Kuba assured them it would be okay. This was something they had to get through, and they would do fine. Despite those comforting words, Katherine became so nervous she quivered inside.

Kuba would be the first witness, and he was anxious to present the results of the investigation. He had summarized his reports and knew his material well. Some of the staff at Klein's crisis center had helped him prepare charts for the grand jurors that distilled the various aspects of the crimes against all of the girls into an easily understandable graphic. That alone, he thought, should build the proper perspective on what this case was all about. It was a list of the victims with X's across the graph to show each of the violations they had suffered, and establish a clear, constant pattern of misconduct by Van Hook.

The grand jury met in the County Board Room on the top floor of the St. Clair County Courthouse in Belleville—an imposing, brick and stone, five-story building only a few years old. A dramatic, central atrium—open the full height of the building and surrounded by glass banisters—served as its focal point. To the left and right, wings of offices and courtrooms veered off at 45-degree angles so the building formed a sprawling V-shape.

Kuba, Klein, and Mary Sudholt from the center picked up three of the girls that morning and drove them to the courthouse; Katherine Howes arrived with her parents. The group gathered in the lounge outside the boardroom, and Kuba chuckled as the little girls were swallowed whole by the huge, overstuffed chairs.

The girls were nervous, but they were glad they finally would get their chance to tell their stories to the grand jury. Katherine seemed the most intimidated; she wondered aloud if Judy Cates would be asking the questions. Klein and Kuba reassured the girls that the session would turn out well. It was a bit unusual for the victims to be called to testify; usually, Kuba's summary of the evidence was adequate. But this was an unusual case, and that a slightly more deliberate approach would be taken by the prosecutors seemed reasonable.

Assistant State's Attorney John Mohan always handled the grand jury. He was a pleasant young man, about medium height and trim, with brown hair and a mustache. For this session he was accompanied by Judy Cates.

Kuba sat on the witness stand to explain for the jurors how the investigation began and led to the meeting with nine girls at the Caseyville police station, and how a surprised Katherine Howes was interviewed that same night. He went through the allegations by Katherine and the other girls, and described the terrible story of Susan Williams and her committal to a psychiatric ward. He told the jurors he had seized as evidence Katherine's report cards that showed how her grades improved from B's, C's, and D's to A's and a few B's after Van Hook began having sex with her.

Kuba explained that he, Pam Klein, and the other officers had interviewed 16 girls, most of whom were 11 or 12 years old and in the fifth, sixth, and seventh grades; many of them did not even know each other and were unaware that Van Hook had taken similar liberties with other girls. Four of them had no improper contact with Van Hook and had seen nothing unusual; the other 12 all reported some kind of incident with sexual activities or overtones.

Then he passed around the chart with X's to show the scope of Van Hook's activities and the similarities in the girls' stories. Ten girls said he had embraced and kissed them—20 X's across those two categories. Two X's for "French-kissed." Nine more noted the girls who said he touched their buttocks; three X's appeared under "touched breast." Three more for "gave presents." Eight worked in the library. Five had been molested in the library office, three more in the other part of the library, and five more in other locations. Three had seen a girlie magazine. Two had been asked how they wanted to be treated.

One X stood out in the category marked "intercourse." All told, there were 64 X's that documented improper acts with 12 little girls—all located and interviewed in about two weeks.

Mohan, Cates, and the grand jurors asked a variety of questions, all of which struck Kuba as sincere and appropriate. When he left the stand, he felt good. He had presented the case with confidence and certainty that ample evidence existed against Van Hook. With details from so many girls, powerfully assembled on the chart, Kuba was sure the grand jury would indict Richard Van Hook on a good number of felony counts.

Katherine Howes looked nervously across the room of unfamiliar faces after she sat down on the witness stand. She was even more nervous than she had feared, and she was anxious to get this over with. The preliminary questions went by quickly, and soon she found herself explaining how Mr. Van Hook's increasingly intimate attention began just before Christmas and progressed quickly. She tried to ignore her embarrassment when she didn't know what attorney Mohan meant by the words "climax or orgasm." But she described how Van Hook had intercourse with her for a couple of minutes, and then some "sticky stuff" came out of him.

Did she resist or tell him to stop? "No, I was just scared. I didn't know what to do."

Why didn't she tell someone? There was that question again. Why couldn't grown-ups understand? You just couldn't tell these things to people. "Because I was scared. Because my dad is a minister and I was afraid it would ruin his reputation."

The questioning seemed to go on forever; the same questions she had been asked by so many different people. She began to cry just as Mohan finished, and she was sobbing in devastation by the time she reached Pam Klein's open arms outside the grand-jury room.

"They kept asking me those terrible questions," she cried. "It was so hard to answer them; I got so confused. Why didn't they understand? Didn't Dennis tell them what happened? Why did they have to ask me if Dennis already told them?"

Pam hugged Katherine again. "Kate, I know it was hard for you, but you did a great job and you told them the truth. And that means Van Hook will go to prison for what he did to you."

Dennis Kuba wondered if any 12-year-old girl could explain how something like this could happen. He had watched kids turn themselves inside out trying to explain it; they just didn't have the knowledge and the maturity to do it. They didn't understand it. How could a little girl explain it? How could she describe the feeling she got when a grown-up she trusted and cared for began to treat her so specially, giving so much attention and little gifts? He made her feel so great, saying she might even get to spend the rest of her life with him. And then, the special attention became something else, something more confusing. He was touching her, doing things she didn't understand, things that made her feel ashamed. Something was wrong, but how could she tell him to stop? And then the world explodes in her face, and she tries to explain to other adults. They look at her like she should have known that was "sex," the forbidden place. But she's only 12; how was she supposed to know? She thought it was wrong, but it made him feel so good. Was it wrong? Who was wrong?

Klein always was frustrated that people seemed unable to understand why kids didn't tell about sex abuse. Why did adults think that was illogical? Why should kids tell? They know they get in trouble when they tell about things they don't understand. They're afraid of the unknown. What will happen if I tell? They're confused and ashamed and embarrassed, and they're afraid no one will believe them. Adults do that to kids. The kids know something is wrong, but they're afraid telling will hurt their parents or the family's reputation; they will pay almost any price to "protect" their parents.

The situation becomes even more complicated when the abuser is an authority figure. Middle-class children are raised to obey such figures, not to challenge them, even when their conduct is confusing. After all, the adults know best; they must, since that's what they always tell the kids. Parents seldom really talk to their children to build real communication. They may chat, but they seldom talk about sex, about AIDS, about what to do when the almost mythical molester is a trusted adult close to the family. The message from parents is that sex is bad, so if something sexual has happened, children assume they've been bad. Why would they tell anyone about that? Once it has happened and they don't tell, how can they tell when it happens again? They know instinctively that their credibility has been compromised.

The list of reasons why kids don't tell is almost unending. The question Pam Klein always asked was, "Why don't adults understand that?"

The next witness before the grand jury was another tiny blonde with an animated face and a sweet disposition, Paula Birch. She explained how Van Hook had slipped up behind her and tickled her on the right breast as he oozed, "Gitchie, gitchie, goo." Then quiet little Lori Parker told the jurors how Van Hook gave her a "Christmas kiss," followed the same day with another kiss while he slid his hand onto her buttocks. She described Van Hook's maneuvers with her and Sally Morton in his little office. Sally—a stocky, almost tomboyish girl with yellow hair and blue eyes—told the same story when she followed Lori to the stand.

And then the girls were done. Klein and Kuba could see the relief on their faces. Despite the trauma of the experience, they felt they had done pretty well. The investigators took them out for ice cream to celebrate this milestone in what everyone felt was a courageous quest for justice by these little girls.

Kuba and Klein knew Richard Van Hook was to testify before the grand jury that afternoon. But what could he say to refute all of these very credible accounts of the abuse he inflicted on the children entrusted to his care?

Kuba knew it could be days, a week, even longer before they knew the results of the grand-jury review. He was a little surprised when he heard later that another teacher, Maria DeConcini, had testified as a character witness. Dennis had never heard of that before. But he was sure that Van Hook and all the character witnesses he could muster would be unable to overcome the simple truth from the girls.

The next day, on Friday, Kuba called Judy Cates to see if she had any word. She said the grand jury had taken no action yet, and Mohan had not suggested to her what the grand jury was doing. But Cates told Kuba to hold up on the interviews until further notice. Kuba really wasn't worried about the delay; he understood the bureaucracy.

The next week dragged by slowly. Parents called Pam Klein occasionally to ask if she had heard anything, and she explained patiently that the grand jury probably would not make a decision until its session next week, on Thursday, February 18.

When Thursday arrived, Kuba called Cates, expecting to get the good news. Instead, Cates informed him that the grand jury had returned a "no true bill." That meant the grand jury had decided against issuing felony charges. And worse yet, Cates explained, the panel had recommended that the misdemeanor charges be dismissed. Baricevic already had filed the motion, and the charges had been dropped by a judge. Cates didn't know what had happened, but she told Kuba that Lori Parker had smiled all the way through her testimony. That hadn't helped the girls' credibility with the jurors.

Dennis was too stunned to say anything for a moment.

Cates said quietly, "We're finished, Dennis. The investigation is over."

Kuba hung up the phone slowly. He hadn't even been able to offer Cates a reaction to the news. All he could think about was what it all meant.

Richard Van Hook was free and clear.

Kuba stared out his office window, his eyes barely focusing on the huge hardware store in the shopping center next door. What had happened? The case was all there. The girls' thorough and similar stories proved the charges so powerfully. Kuba and Klein had pulled it all together in an undeniable scenario of abuse and misconduct by this teacher. And the grand jury had rejected it.

Kuba stood slowly as he struggled to deal with this failure of the justice system. And then the real tragedy in this unbelievable twist struck him. What would he tell the girls? He rubbed his hand across his face. He wanted to scream. He had convinced these kids to trust him enough to tell him what had happened. He had promised the grand jury would give them justice. He had thought he could do some good, but he had let them down. Dennis felt personally responsible.

He began to pace in his office. Why hadn't the grand jury believed the girls? They had nothing to gain by lying about Van Hook; those little girls weren't liars. What had Van Hook told the grand jury? How could this group of average people believe Van Hook over the girls? What the hell could he have said?

Kuba's stomach rolled over and he fought another urge to scream. He walked down the hall and broke the news to some of the other agents; they were just as shocked.

As a cop, Kuba tried not to get involved emotionally in the cases he handled; that was one of the ways a cop kept his sanity. His job was to investigate and let the prosecutors take it from there. He accepted that, and moved to the next case. Kuba had been able to do that before, but this time it would be tougher—a lot tougher.

Kuba finally sat back down at his desk and picked up the phone. It was time to make the toughest call of his career; he had to call Pam Klein.

She had leaped at each phone call that day, expecting it to be Kuba with news of Van Hook's indictment. But when she heard the way he said, "Klein . . . ," she knew something was wrong.

"Klein, get ready for very bad news," he said softly.

What could he be talking about? she wondered. "What, Dennis?"

"The grand jury returned a 'no true bill,' " he almost whispered. "They dismissed the other charges. They didn't believe the girls; they believed Van Hook. We're finished, it's over. There's nothing else to do."

Klein was flabbergasted, and crushed. "Oh no, Kuba, you've got to be kidding. Oh, shit," she spat out.

She was so furious she couldn't speak for a minute. As her mind raced back over the investigation, she stopped on the reaction from the state's attorney's office. It had to have come down from the top, from State's Attorney John Baricevic.

"Dennis, something about the way they handled this case stunk from the beginning," she said as her voice rose. "There can be no good reason why they wouldn't indict Van Hook unless the prosecutor just didn't want to indict him. Everyone knows the prosecutor can get an indictment if he wants one. Instead they let him put on a pseudo-defense. They even let him call a character witness, for crying out loud! Something is rotten, I can feel it."

"Calm down, Klein," Kuba mumbled. "It's over. There's nothing else to do. We're finished."

"Have you told these poor girls yet?"

"No," Dennis said quietly. "I thought maybe you could call some of them, and I'll call some of them."

Klein could hear the despair in Kuba's voice. He was taking the news a lot harder than he was letting on; he always did.

"Okay, Dennis. I'll calm myself down, and then I'll call some and you call some."

She sucked in her breath for the first time since Dennis broke the news. She felt responsible, too. She had told the girls they had the right to seek justice, and that she would help them. They had trusted her, too. She ran through the list of the girls, visualizing each one and instantly recalling the little quirks and habits that made each of them so special.

"Oh, God, Dennis. I don't really want to believe this."

"Yeah, me neither," he mumbled.

Pam stepped out of her office to break the news to her staff members. They were astonished, and some shed tears. Klein was too angry to cry yet.

She called Sheila Howes first, and the woman was rocked to her soul by the news. Through an explosion of tears Sheila asked, "How could they possibly have doubted the girls' stories? It is inconceivable that the girls made all this up."

"I don't know what to say, Sheila. At this point I'm as confused as you are. I really don't know what to say."

"My God, Pam. If we thought the community has been unsupportive before, what in the world will these girls go through now?" Sheila was getting angry. "I'm going to demand some answers from John Baricevic. I'm sure all the parents will demand to know what happened. They'll be upset. I'll talk to some of the other mothers and see if we can set up a meeting with him. Would you be able to attend if we do?"

"Count on it," Pam snapped. "I think you have a perfect right to ask for an explanation. I'd like one myself."

Sheila Howes's voice quieted. "Katherine is going to be devastated by this, Pam."

"I know, Sheila. I'll be glad to talk to her and the other girls, although right now I can't think of a single thing that will be of any comfort to them."

Sheila Howes turned back to the criminal case. "We're not going to stop here. I'll go to the Illinois attorney general if I have to. I'll call Don Weber and see if he can do anything. We won't let this go. These girls have to get justice, and so do I."

"Do what you have to, Sheila, and I'll back you all the way."

It was the first time Pam Klein had thought about Don Weber, the state's attorney in Madison County, the adjacent county to the north. He was an aggressive prosecutor, probably the toughest Pam ever had met. When it came to sexual abuse cases, Don Weber definitely "got it." He was an advocate for sex-abuse victims, going after offenders with unswerving vigor.

But Weber was in Madison County; Katherine Howes, Caseyville, and the school were in St. Clair County. He had no jurisdiction in this case, Pam thought. But it might be worth talking to him about it sometime; it certainly couldn't hurt.

As Kuba and Klein called the rest of the girls' parents

with the news, at least two said they never would send their daughters back to that school or to any other public school in the Collinsville district. Several others threatened some kind of public protest against this miscarriage of justice.

Katherine Howes and the other girls were indeed devastated; Katherine thought she would faint when her mother told her the news. For her, whose wounds were the deepest, the grand jury's decision was the bitter realization of her worst fears, and the fulfillment of Mr. Van Hook's warnings. She had told the painful, humiliating truth to a roomful of adults, and they had rejected her, just as he had told her they would. They had refused to take the word of a kid over the word of a teacher, just as he had predicted. They had, in fact, refused to take the words of four kids—as well as Dennis Kuba's account of the other eight abuse victims. These adults had decided the kids were lying; they had called the girls liars, just as surely as if they had pointed to them on the witness stand and shouted it to their faces. Now it would be broadcast to the world. Everyone the girls knew—at school, at church, in their clubs, and on their sports teams—would see the girls branded as liars and sexual misfits who turned adolescent fantasies into hurtful allegations against an innocent teacher.

As the awful news sunk in, Katherine's shock and tears turned to anger. Pam Klein and Dennis Kuba had promised everything would be all right; they promised Mr. Van Hook would pay for what he did if the girls told the truth. But it was the kids who got hurt again. Her dad had been wrong, too, when he told her the truth never hurt. Where was this justice Pam and Dennis kept telling the girls about? How would they protect the girls now?

Why had she said anything? Why hadn't she kept her mouth shut? She probably would have gotten over it, anyway. She already was feeling a little better since she started junior high school and got away from Mr. Van Hook. The pain of being used that way still lingered, and it often pushed its way back into Katherine's thoughts just when she thought it was fading. But it probably would have gotten better if she had just left it alone.

She wished she had never said anything to Pam and Dennis; she was sorry she ever told them anything. She should have denied everything when they came to her house that first night. Now everything was a lot worse. Now everyone knew. The kids in the neighborhood were teasing her about "going all the way" with Mr. Van Hook. She felt as though everyone could see right through her skin; she couldn't hide anything anymore. She had no privacy, no thoughts that were her own. It was as if they had taken her soul.

Later Thursday afternoon, Sheila Howes called Pam Klein to announce that a meeting had been set up for that evening between the parents, State's Attorney Baricevic, Dennis Kuba, and his supervisor, Captain Terry Delaney. Klein couldn't believe the meeting had been scheduled so quickly; she already was committed to speak at a dinner meeting of the Collinsville Business and Professional Women that night. She promised to escape as soon as possible and get to the parents' meeting. The dinner and speech went well, and Pam even was able to relax and enjoy herself a little despite the horribly disappointing day. At the earliest moment, she excused herself and headed for Caseyville.

The meeting with Baricevic already was underway in an upstairs room at Delmonico's Restaurant when Klein arrived; she could hear the buzz as she approached from the hall. Inside, a group of about 50 people—mostly the families of girls involved in the case—sat clustered in front of a long table. Baricevic was fielding questions as he stood behind the table, and Kuba and Captain Delaney were sitting at Baricevic's side.

John Baricevic was a trim man of about 35, average height, with thinning reddish hair. His face was dominated by dark-rimmed, almost square glasses. He had a reputation as a blunt-spoken and direct man. He had been an assistant state's attorney for several years before being elected as the top prosecutor in 1980. He was a shrewd politician, and that was what concerned Pam Klein the most.

She stood in the back of the room and scanned the crowd; it confirmed what she had expected. There were a lot of men in cowboy boots and T-shirts that revealed bulging biceps. This was a working-class crowd, and these parents hadn't come to hear a politician dance around the questions about their little girls and the guy who molested them. The parents were getting angrier by the minute, Klein thought, as Baricevic tried to explain what had happened. She didn't like his comments, either; he wasn't giving the people any direct answers. He told the crowd the decision not to indict Van Hook was made by the grand jury, and state law prohibited him from discussing anything that occurred behind its closed doors. He could not speak for the jurors on that panel. Apparently they had not believed the testimony from the girls, but he did not know why. When asked if Van Hook could be charged if more evidence were developed, Baricevic explained that no further investigation was warranted— there would be no more evidence.

Klein had heard all she could stand. She even felt angry that Kuba was sitting there silently on the panel. She knew his boss was a friend of Baricevic's, but she still wanted Dennis to say something. He should defend the girls; he should tell their side. Where were his guts? Instead, she fumed, he sat there, just another blue suit taking orders.

Klein couldn't remain silent any longer. Her voice cut through the crowd murmurs from the back of the room. Even she could detect the anger and resentment in the tone.

"I have a question," she called out as she took a few steps toward the front table. "I would like this answered with a simple yes or no, please. Do you, or do you not, believe these children?"

Baricevic's eyes locked with Pam's, and she returned the stare defiantly as he responded that there had been some serious questions about their stories.

Klein shot back sharply, "Well, that answers our questions, doesn't it?"

She wheeled and stalked out of the room, mostly to make sure she didn't let her mouth get her into more serious trouble. She realized she was out of line, but she didn't care. Someone had to voice their anger and, having said her piece, it was wise for her to retreat. Diplomacy was not her long suit, and any further discussion with John Baricevic tonight could result in more blunt comments she knew she would regret later.

Kuba was mortified, and furious, at his partner. She had made a difficult situation worse and, he thought, made an ass of herself with such an immature exhibition. She was entitled to express her opinion, but the drama of a grand exit was not useful at this point. The case was dead, and there was nothing he could have done or said under the circumstances. He was just glad he had not been asked any questions that would have forced him to mouth the party line expected by his captain and the prosecutor.

Klein went directly to the bar downstairs and ordered a Bloody Mary. She needed it badly right then; she was so angry that she was shaking. She saw DCI Agent Jimmy Bivens sitting at a table, and joined him to report on the event upstairs. As the crowd from the meeting filtered in—apparently her departure had brought an abrupt end to the proceedings—she was joined by a few of the parents who shared her anger and doubts about the way the case had been handled. They were glad she had said what they were thinking.

Kuba walked by the table without stopping.

The publicity that had accompanied the arrest of Richard Van Hook was restrained compared to the news accounts of the grand jury's decision and Van Hook's reaction to his victory. The stories that appeared in the local papers were about to shake up the people involved and the community even more than the allegations had.

But more important, they were about to anger and

sicken another man in another county, and alter the course of events in ways no one could have predicted.

The first story appeared in the Friday edition of the *St. Louis Globe-Democrat* under the headline, "Caseyville Teacher Freed of Sex Charges." It announced that Van Hook had been "absolved" of charges of sexual misconduct, and quoted him as saying, "I've been through thirty-one days of hell and the last week of waiting." He added, "The nightmare continues as to why . . . and I don't think I'll ever know." He said he had lost 23 pounds during his ordeal, but wanted to get back to his classroom as soon as possible. He was sure the episode would change the way he and many other teachers acted toward their students. "I know I will be using verbal rewards and cutting out pats on the back for a long, long time to come," he said. He now feared that he would flinch anytime he started to reach out to help one of his diving students. But the experience had brought his family closer, and he was buoyed by the support from his students and colleagues at the school, as well as the more than a hundred telephone calls and 70 letters from well-wishers in his corner. He even received a letter signed by all the kids in his class. He and his wife had prepared their children for the worst, but had received not a single crank call.

The story quoted Dennis Kuba as saying the parents were shocked and angry, and that the DCI was shocked and disappointed by the grand jury's decision.

CHAPTER 7

The winter wind ripped through a dark parking lot as two figures hurried toward the telephone booth under the solitary streetlight. The young woman held her tiny daughter's hand, hurrying her into what little protection from the elements the booth offered. Their trip to the phone had been on impulse, and the woman had not even taken the time to dress herself or her child for the biting weather. The little girl wrapped her arms around her mother's legs, seeking any warmth she could find as she looked up and wondered why her mommy was crying. The woman couldn't hold back the tears as she dialed the telephone and held the newspaper story crumpled in her hand. The headline about the teacher freed from the sex charges was barely visible, but the woman already had memorized it.

"Don't cry, Mommy," the little girl urged softly.

"Those girls are telling the truth, Amy," the woman sniffed through the tears. "If anyone should know, it's me. I have to tell someone, but I'm afraid, too. Maybe they won't believe me, either."

She looked down at her innocent daughter, and knew again why she had to tell someone that the investigation had to continue. Those girls *were* telling the truth, and they had to stay strong and brave. They had to keep telling the truth until someone, somewhere believed them. The detectives had to keep looking for victims. This investigation had to go on. He could not be allowed to get away with it all again—and again and again. She had to call someone and tell them.

She pushed the coin into the slot with trembling fingers, but her hand stopped just above the dial. For what seemed an eternity she stood there, her heart pounding and her hand poised above the dial. She felt her daughter shivering against her legs. Fear rose in her throat, almost choking her.

Then slowly, gently, she hung up the phone. She felt her tears, so cold against her cheek.

"I'm so sorry," she whispered as she and the little girl turned back into the wind for home.

State's Attorney Don W. Weber was sifting through some files in his office in Madison County early Friday morning, February 19, when his secretary buzzed to tell him Pam Klein was on the phone. Weber really wasn't surprised; he had just read the story in the *Globe-Democrat*. It made him angry and suspicious of what had happened in the county to the south. He knew Klein and Kuba well; they wouldn't have gone to the grand jury without ample evidence to back them up. His experience with sex cases also had taught him how incredibly unlikely it was that four little girls with enough courage to face a grand jury would be lying. What he had found unbelievable was Van Hook's claim of a hundred calls and 70 letters of support. Weber especially had winced when he read about the letter from all of Van Hook's students; he wondered who put them up to it. Such concern and support was, at best, misdirected; at worst, it could lead to more verbal, and perhaps even physical, abuse of the girls who already were the victims.

Weber, a staunchly conservative Republican in a territory overwhelmingly controlled by Democrats, never had been too impressed with the prosecutors of the opposing party in St. Clair County. A "no true bill" in the Van Hook case did nothing to alter his opinion. Weber and the Democrats in Madison and St. Clair counties had little good to say about each other. Weber's candid comments and abrasive style left a lot of them—especially the losing defense attorneys—fuming after each encounter, and vowing to limit Weber's tenure to just one term. He had an impressive record of high-profile courtroom victories, dating back to 1976 when he began his career as an assistant prosecutor. The newspapers gave close coverage to each of his aggressive prosecutions, as well as all of his quotable comments.

Weber had worked with Klein often, and respected her instincts and dedication. The two were poles apart politically and philosophically on most issues. But prosecuting sex offenders was common ground, and they had developed a close friendship around that. Weber was from Collinsville, too, and even had served on the City Council with Pam's husband, Gary. Her brothers had helped Weber considerably two years earlier in his campaign to upset his former boss and claim the state's attorney's office—only the second Republican in that domain since the 1940s.

Weber knew Pam Klein well enough to assume she would be in a rage today. "Hey, Klein," he said in a voice trying to be upbeat but wary at the same time, "how ya doin'?"

"Okay," the voice on the other end said calmly. "How are you? You got any good cases going?"

Weber was surprised by the measured tone. Klein had never minced words before; that wasn't her style. "I'm fine. I thought you might be calling today. I read the *Globe* this morning."

"Yeah, I figured you would. That's what I'm calling about. Did you follow the investigation in St. Clair County?"

"A little bit, but I really hadn't paid that much attention to it."

"Well, Baricevic's office just washed this thing out, pure and simple. Everyone involved is pretty upset."

"I'll bet. Was Van Hook good for it, Pam?"

"You're damned right he was, Don. A lot of girls came forward and told us almost identical stories about what he had done to them. There was not a single indication that any of them were even exaggerating, let alone lying about it; some of them don't even know each other. There's no doubt that he was good for it." She hesitated a beat. "Do you think you could bring charges against him in Madison County?"

"He hasn't done anything in my county, Pam, and I have no jurisdiction over what he did in St. Clair County."

"Well, Kuba and I want to talk to you about it, anyway. Would you have a few minutes for us Monday afternoon?"

"Sure. Come on up about 1:30. I'll see you then."

Weber hung up the phone and leaned back in his chair. Klein had been a lot cooler than he had expected. She was controlling her anger extraordinarily well, for her. Weber realized she wasn't just working a case or trying to counsel victims anymore; she was on on a mission.

He knew that feeling; that was how he felt about being a prosecutor. He could make a lot more money in private practice—a hell of a lot more. But he had spent the past six years firmly in the grasp of the special feeling that came from extracting justice for someone who was wronged; someone who was injured, perhaps killed; someone who had been victimized; someone whose innocence had been lost to blind cruelty by the criminal on the street. He knew what Pam Klein and Dennis Kuba were feeling. It was what kept Don Weber going, too, when the bad guys seemed to be on top.

Over the weekend, Weber thought a lot about what Klein had said, and he began to develop more of a taste for pursuing the Van Hook case. He hated sex-abusers. A gang-rape trial had been one of the victories that had shaped his career early on; his anger at the disgusting abuse that the two teenage girls had suffered from those seven surly, sneering creeps had stayed with him ever since. He had helped send all of those guys to prison, and he would never forget the sense of justice for those women that swept through him when he watched the men's sneers fall from their faces as they were sentenced. That had whetted his appetite for a career in prosecution.

The Van Hook case was starting to appeal to that appetite. Not only was prosecution warranted for a grown man who victimized little girls, but this case presented a challenge. First of all, this was happening in Don Weber's hometown. His father had served as mayor, and his mother still taught first grade in the school district. Weber had graduated from Collinsville High School in 1967, and had served about 18 months on the City Council before being elected state's attorney in 1980.

Part of the Collinsville School District was in Madison County, too, including the old senior high school and both junior highs—Webster and North. But Caseyville Elementary School was across the line in St. Clair County. How could Weber get to Van Hook for crimes in another county? As Weber pondered, he remembered that a corporation could be sued in the jurisdiction where its office was located. The school board office was in the old post office in Collinsville, well inside Madison County. Did that give Weber jurisdiction over everything related to official school district activities? It was a stretch, but worth exploring.

He still was mulling over the possibilities Monday morning when he got a call from Sheila Howes. He had fielded many calls from infuriated parents; very often those people were beyond reason. This was different. Sheila Howes was an articulate woman who indeed was outraged and injured. But she had her feelings under control; she, too, was on a mission. She wanted to know if there was anything Weber could do, and mentioned that she was considering a call to the Illinois attorney general's office. Weber explained that the attorney general had no jurisdiction in such a case, and did not even have access to a grand jury. Weber told her of the meeting that afternoon, and he would let her know if anything came of it.

Klein and Kuba arrived at the door to the county office building in Edwardsville, the Madison County seat, at the same time, both of them hurrying against the winds of another frigid afternoon. The old building had housed a bank and had been bought by the county for extra office space. The state's attorney's office was on the third and fourth floors in relatively dreary old rooms along narrow hallways. About the only charm left in the building was the ornate elevator, still operated by a friendly woman.

Klein and Kuba had made their peace over the disagreement from the meeting last Thursday night. They had stated their opinions and cleared the air: Kuba thought Klein had acted like an ass and Klein thought Kuba had sat there like a gutless wonder. They agreed to disagree, and then dropped the matter entirely. There were much more important things that demanded their cooperation. Besides, their friendship and respect for each other certainly could withstand a challenge no bigger than that.

Weber welcomed his visitors into his office, a slightly worn room on the corner of the third floor, overlooking the adjacent courthouse across the street. The room was befitting the personality of its occupant, with an eclectic collection of photos—Robert E. Lee, George Armstrong Custer, the Pink Panther, Weber with President Ronald Reagan. Weber's desk boasted a jelly-bean jar bearing an etching of the White House. The desk was neat and clean, unlike his filing system, which was a collection of irregular piles on the floor behind the desk. It worked for him, and he always knew right where everything was.

After some chitchat Klein and Kuba turned to the Van Hook case. Kuba slid forward in his chair and propped his elbows on his knees as he began to explain the evidence collected during the investigation. His voice was restrained and seemed to get lower and lower as he described how the investigation had proceeded from girl to girl.

Weber was as surprised as Kuba and Klein had been to hear how serious the incidents were with Katherine Howes. Her mother had not offered any specifics when she called, and the newspaper stories were necessarily vague on graphic details. As he listened to Kuba's account, Weber began to feel angry: a girl still too young to understand what was happening had been maneuvered into sex with her teacher right in the school building after a campaign of calculated manipulation by a man she trusted to guide and protect her. The allegations from the other girls certainly were disturbing, too, but not serious enough to push Weber out on a limb by second-guessing the prosecutors and grand jury in St. Clair County. The Howes case was different. If Van Hook was capable of that, other, similar victims surely existed; he had to be stopped.

Then Kuba and Klein drew Weber further into the case by recounting Van Hook's moves on Barbara Maxwell near her home in Collinsville, and mentioning that Van Hook had taught at North Junior High School and the senior high school—all of which were in Madison County, Weber's turf. The spot where Van Hook had stopped his car to pin Barbara Maxwell against the door and kiss her was near the house where Weber had grown up. But that assault happened between 1976 and 1978, too long ago to fall within the three-year statute of limitations. The time limit for prosecution had expired.

All three people sitting in Weber's office knew that pedophiles were repeat offenders; Klein and Kuba were convinced Van Hook had been at it for years, probably practicing his secret hobby at the schools in Madison County, too. But three years had passed since Van Hook moved to the school in St. Clair County.

"Look," Weber said earnestly, "find me a case that occurred in Madison County, within the statute of limitations, and I'll take a real hard look at it. If it's good enough, I'll prosecute it."

Kuba and Klein looked at each other, both of them recoiling at the thought of more interviews. They had not contacted a lot of names on the list provided by the other girls; perhaps one of those would unlock the door to prosecution in Madison County. Kuba had thought over the weekend that he'd be relieved to be done with the case, to drop it with honor in light of the grand jury washout. But now he knew that was not possible.

Weber approached his next suggestion gingerly. He wanted Katherine Howes and probably some of the other girls to take lie-detector tests. Not to challenge their honesty, but to give them and the charges against Van Hook more credibility, while neutralizing his claim to have passed one. Victims of sexual assaults often were polygraphed; the results weren't admissible in court, but a test by a good examiner could offer substantial support for the victim's story. In this case, polygraphs would give Weber needed assistance in dealing with the public and a school board that already were buying into Van Hook's story of innocence.

Klein understood the reasoning and said she was sure the girls would agree. She had found Weber's approach to the case refreshing after what everyone had endured in St. Clair County; he didn't have to be convinced the girls weren't lying. And Klein couldn't help but wonder what Van Hook would think when he learned it really wasn't over yet.

Kuba reached over and popped a jelly bean into his mouth. He glanced back at Klein and Weber and said, "Let's get on with it."

Weber interpreted the agent's response to be confidence that a victim meeting Weber's demands was out there, waiting to be found. That surprised him; he didn't see how Kuba and Klein would be able to bring him what he needed. But he was sure the investigators had departed his office with a realistic sense of his criteria. He would have to have a solid case—not perfect, but solid enough to win once he filed charges.

It would be a blind tiptoe through a minefield. No matter where Weber stepped, something was likely to explode in his face. Prosecuting a popular teacher in the town where he grew up would be difficult enough, just on the legal issues and the burden of proof needed to convict—beyond a reasonable doubt. Weber also would face serious political repercussions from Van Hook's friends and family, and the well-organized teachers' union. The whole case would be hard for everyone. The prospect of proceeding on this one was not something Weber relished.

After the investigators left, his secretary, Denise O'Neill, stepped timidly into his office and asked, "Were they here to talk about that teacher, Richard Van Hook?"

Weber shook his head; weren't there any secrets in this office? "Yeah, why?"

"Because he used to teach at Edwardsville Junior High School when I went there, and all the girls thought he was a real pervert then. I never saw anything, but there were a lot of rumors. We all tried to stay away from him."

That certainly fit the pattern, Weber thought. How long had this been going on? How many victims were out there?

Two hours later, he walked across North Main Street to a drugstore and picked up a copy of the *Collinsville Herald* for Monday, February 22. The Van Hook case screamed at Weber with two stories by Ed Gurney bannered across the front page. The first recounted the grand jury's decision and said Van Hook was expected to return to class on Tuesday, the very next morning. The president of the Board of Education, Dick Cain, told the *Herald* he was satisfied there had been no sexual misconduct and that there had been no hesitancy to return Van Hook to the classroom after the board heard a report on the investigation the night of the grand jury's decision. Van Hook had attended the meeting in the company of David Chase, a representative of the statewide teachers' union called the Illinois Education Association.

State's Attorney Baricevic was quoted as saying his office had thought there was probable cause to believe Van Hook had committed crimes serious enough to be felonies, but wanted to get the grand jury's opinion before deciding whether to boost the charges beyond the misdemeanor level. Instead, Baricevic explained, the grand jury said no to everything. Even though he could have pursued the misdemeanor charges without grand jury action, he decided to accept the panel's conclusion that no charges were warranted and its recommendation to drop the misdemeanors. Reacting to criticism of his decision, Baricevic said he did not want to argue with the parents over what had happened. He said he could understand why people who did not deal with the justice system regularly would be confused.

Double-talk, Weber thought. He dealt with the justice system all the time, and he was confused by what had happened.

The president of the Caseyville School PTA, Linda Raby, told the *Herald* she was confident Van Hook was innocent and added, "The majority of the people I have talked to didn't believe it to start with. Most of the people I've talked to during the whole ordeal feel like I do." Her son was in Van Hook's class, and was looking forward to the teacher's return to school.

But an unidentified mother of a victim offered a different view; Weber guessed correctly that it was Sheila Howes. She tearfully and angrily explained that her daughter was likely to suffer serious mental problems because of what had happened. "My daughter appeared before the grand jury and went through pure hell. This man says he has been through hell. We've been through it, too," she said. She also announced that she and other parents were considering a lawsuit against Van Hook and the school district, and that some of the parents were refusing to return their children to school at Caseyville.

Weber felt a real sense of outrage for the first time. Still standing at the newsstand in the store, he could feel his stomach tightening. Had the school board really felt no hesitancy to return Van Hook to class so promptly after such serious allegations from a dozen girls? Weber was aghast. Returning Van Hook to class would be a calamity for the girls still in that school. Surely the cautious and proper avenue to take was, at least, to transfer him to another assignment for a while.

Weber read again the comment from board president Dick Cain, a lawyer who now was confident there had been no improper conduct. How the hell did he explain what these girls were saying?

Weber was glad some of the parents were thinking about taking their children out of the school rather than letting them face Van Hook again. At least they were trying to protect the children; obviously no one in any official capacity was concerned about them. Who was presenting the case from the kids' side? Weber wondered.

He also was infuriated by Barcevic's anemic explanation blaming the grand jury for his decision to dump the case. No prosecutor ever would let a grand jury dictate the resolution of misdemeanor charges; the panel had absolutely no input on such a decision. The union official's attendance at the school board's meeting with Van Hook made Weber wonder if the politicians had undergone some serious lobbying by the union.

Then he read the second story in the *Herald*, the personal "sidebar" as such pieces are called by reporters. It sent him through the roof.

"Richard Van Hook said he is not bitter," the story began. " 'No, I'm more relaxed that it's over and grateful I had a chance to go before the grand jury and show my side of the case,' Van Hook said."

In an interview at the office of Van Hook's lawyers, Bill and Bob Gagen, the teacher went on to explain, "I can't have any ill feelings. I feel very positive toward the state's attorney's office because they're the first ones to give me a chance to give my side ... When the first articles came out, I felt completely destroyed. I went through a period I would consider as close to hell as you could be. Then, all of a sudden, I saw a light there. The letters from my students this year I'll put someplace special."

He said he was anxious to return to his class. "These are the kids I'm trying to mold and I hope they haven't been affected too much. I believe that's where I belong."

He said he had been pleased to learn how many friends and supporters he had among fellow teachers and others. "Finding out you've got this many friends, before your own wake, is very special." What an odd thing to say, Weber thought.

When asked if his innocence would have been demonstrated more convincingly if he had been cleared by a jury in a trial, Van Hook seemed upset. Bill Gagen answered for him, saying the grand jurors found no probable cause to believe a crime had been committed, and that stopped the charges well short of the burden of "beyond a reasonable doubt" needed to convict in a trial. Bob Gagen added, "I don't give a damn what the Caseyville police think or don't think."

Weber wanted to explode. The Van Hook case suddenly took on a new sense of urgency and purpose.

Later that evening, a furious Pam Klein burned her copy of the *Herald* in the fireplace. The stories were the latest insults added to injuries. The phone at her house had been ringing at all hours; Pam's children often picked it up to hear the caller rant about what a bitch their mother was, or to have the receiver on the other end slammed down without a word. Within a few days, Pam would have a trap installed on her phone to try to trace the source of the calls. Although she could deal with the harassment, she refused to allow such an assault on her family.

But on Monday night, as she fed the newspaper into the fire, Pam could only scream, "Damn it, enough is enough!"

For reporter Ed Gurney, the interview with Van Hook had been another surprise in this bizarre case. Van Hook was a pleasant young man, obviously relieved the ordeal was over. Gurney had wondered if he would face an angry man, perhaps as resentful of the *Herald*'s coverage as his supporters were. But Van Hook spoke throughout the interview in a calm voice that showed very little emotion, let alone outrage over what had happened to him. He did not look like most people's idea of a child molester—the scary, trench-coated miscreant hiding in the bushes. Van Hook looked like what he and his supporters said he was—a dedicated teacher who was a fine man with a wonderful family.

Gurney had also talked to the cops, though, and he knew more than the average citizen about the charges. His journalistic objectivity had taught him to avoid leaping to any conclusions or letting suspicions influence a story. But he also had developed the typical journalist's cynicism; there seemed to be a lot of evidence and it was hard to understand why those charges were dismissed. Gurney wondered if the active style of politics practiced in St. Clair County had played any role.

Van Hook was a nice fellow, but he had not persuaded the journalist in Ed Gurney that he was an innocent man.

Kuba and Klein began their search for more victims and set a polygraph for Katherine Howes for Friday, February 26. Kuba arranged for Clinton Cook, a polygrapher with the Illinois State Police to administer the test, as requested by Weber; Cook was about the only polygraph examiner Weber really trusted for accurate results.

In the meantime the prosecutor decided Van Hook's return to the classroom amid such an outpouring of support required countermeasures. On Tuesday, Weber called school superintendent John Renfro and tried to persuade him that returning Van Hook to the classroom was a bad idea; the investigation was continuing, and considering Van Hook cleared on the allegations was premature. But Renfro said there was little else the school board could do. The grand jury and prosecutor had absolved Van Hook in St. Clair County, and further steps against him by the district could lead to legal action by the teacher and his union.

That reply was unsatisfactory; such rationalizations by the school district completely ignored the damage being done to the children. Weber decided public pressure was the only weapon he could wield at this point. On Thursday, he told reporters that he believed the case had been mishandled in St. Clair County, and that there were allegations of sexual misconduct in Madison County, too. Weber didn't reveal the Maxwell case as the basis for that, or discuss the statute of limitations problem. But he said he was reviewing the case, and believed he might be able to claim jurisdiction over the incidents in St. Clair County, too, because the school board's corporate office was in Madison County.

The stories turned up the heat under a pot that already was bubbling. True to their warnings, ten parents started picketing the Caseyville School Tuesday morning; they would brave the cold and the stares for four days. Jim and Sheila Howes were joined by other parents carrying signs and marching in a small circle in the parking lot. "Are ALL our children liars?" one sign asked. Others echoed that question with, "Are our children the guilty ones?" and "Wouldn't you believe your children?" One mother marched with a sign that asked, "Are our little girls safe in Caseyville School? Sixteen girls cannot be wrong." Other signs commended the Caseyville police, the DCI, and the Rape and Sexual Abuse Care Center because they believed. One asked, "Did our state's attorney really care?" The Howeses—who even let their blond daughter march in the line one day—sent their messages with signs that said, "No True Bill does not mean innocent," and "We are not against teachers." The war of words was on.

Katherine bravely trooped down to the state police forensic laboratory in Fairview Heights and took the polygraph test on Friday. The week had been a nightmare, but she was eager to take the test. She had no doubt she would pass, and she hoped that might convince people she was not lying. How could they believe she would lie about something like this? She drew a laugh from Pam Klein when she said she thought she would get a T-shirt that said, "I passed the polygraph. Did he?"

It was one of few bright spots in Katherine's week. The rest of the time, matters seemed to be going from bad to worse. Everyone at school looked at her as if they knew all the things Van Hook had done to her. She felt they all were staring at her as she walked down the hall or sat in class. She tried to shut them out, ignore them. But that was hard to do. She could feel her heart pounding and her face getting red. That angered her more. She wasn't sleeping much, and felt ill most of the time. She really was sorry she ever told anyone what had happened. When she heard Susan Williams telling other

girls all about what had happened, Katherine became so
angry that she hit Susan and they ended up in a fistfight.
The principal called Katherine's mother to tell her what
had happened.

Reporters from television stations in St. Louis had been
calling her parents, asking if they could interview her.
Her father was getting letters asking how such a Christian
man could have raised such a liar of a daughter. Some of
her friends' mothers suddenly had decided they couldn't
play with her anymore.

But the most painful blow fell when one of her little
brothers came home from school and asked her mother
what a "slut" was. He had heard one teacher call his big
sister that while talking to another teacher. Sheila Howes
burst into uncontrollable tears. Katherine had to run over
to the church to get her father to come home. She was
afraid her mother was never going to stop crying.

After that, her mom and dad went to the school board
office to see if the board would meet with the girls' parents to discuss some way to protect the girls from such
continuing abuse at school. Instead they came home even
more upset. Not only had the board rudely refused to
meet with the parents, but the Howeses had been told that
Katherine had perjured herself before the grand jury. The
Howeses had been given such a false and perverted account of the grand jury testimony that they couldn't believe their ears. The school board's version was that the
DCI had told the girls that Van Hook had passed a polygraph, and all the girls began to cry and refused to testify.
Nothing else could be done about Mr. Van Hook because
the board had to protect its employees under the union
contract.

Katherine and some of the other girls had started seeing counselors at Pam Klein's crisis center. Katherine
liked the woman she was seeing. Group sessions with
some other girls who had been sexually abused made
Katherine feel better, too; it helped to talk to other girls
who understood.

She had started to hate Mr. Van Hook. She realized that
he had used her, without caring about her at all. He said

all those things, and he never really cared about her. Now he was lying about it.

So Katherine didn't hesitate to take the polygraph. Pam explained that the test could help reopen the case with a more aggressive, more sympathetic prosecutor who might be able to get Van Hook convicted. Although Mr. Weber could not file charges over the crimes Van Hook had committed with Katherine, her case could be used to strengthen other charges. She still could be part of the effort to bring Van Hook to justice.

So Katherine sat there Friday, wired to the strange machine, as Clinton Cook explained the procedure. As the needles wiggled across the graph paper, she answered the prying, biting questions again.

"Last year, did Richard Van Hook put his penis in your vagina while at the Caseyville School?" Yes, she said.

"Did Richard Van Hook put his penis in your vagina?" Yes.

"Did Richard Van Hook put his mouth on your bare pubic area?" Yes.

Dennis Kuba called Weber later to advise him of Cook's conclusion. He had found no indications of deception in Katherine's answers, and he would file a report stating his opinion was that she was being truthful when she answered the questions. Weber nodded; okay, he had the first check mark on a long list of unlikely developments that had to happen before Richard Van Hook could be prosecuted in Madison County.

Klein and Kuba were working hard to check off the rest of the list, even when that meant working late hours on the weekends. On Saturday afternoon and evening, February 27, they talked to two 18-year-old girls who had brushes with Van Hook at Collinsville High School, in Madison County. The first girl was a senior in 1981 when Van Hook made some "weird" comments to her: he asked if she was "of age" yet, and leered that he would like to get her behind the bookshelves in the library. He even mentioned that he thought sixth-grade girls were really "built."

Van Hook had made his now familiar moves on the

second girl, Allison Hayden, when she was a freshman during the 1978–1979 school year. She was not his student, but he took her into the room where he taught history, and then closed and locked the door. He grabbed her and French-kissed her, and she fled the room. She told Kuba she had detested Van Hook after that.

At 8:10 on Sunday night, the investigators met with a 19-year-old woman whom Van Hook had asked to baby-sit for him when she was in his eighth-grade history and geography classes in 1977–1978 at North Junior High School. She declined because she always felt uncomfortable around him. He once asked her if she knew how many virgins there were in the school, and he always was asking girls for a kiss. Despite those telltale signs, she hadn't seen or heard of any improper contact between Van Hook and a student.

The agent called Weber on Monday to get his reaction to the new evidence. Weber said the comments to the first and third girls were not criminal conduct. Van Hook had, on the other hand, committed a crime in Madison County by kissing Allison Hayden. Unfortunately, the incident had occurred too long ago to be prosecuted. Weber decided, however, that Allison Hayden should take a polygraph; she could provide valuable testimony about an incident of sexual molestation that fit Van Hook's pattern, and this time it had happened in Madison County.

Weber was surprised Kuba and Klein had found three witnesses so quickly; that seemed to support their confidence about the numbers of girls among Van Hook's victims still waiting to be found.

And Weber had another surprising reaction to the first girl's story. When he heard that Van Hook thought sixth-graders were built, Weber suddenly remembered the slightly older Dickie Van Hook who had been dating girls Weber's age when they were kids. For the first time Weber could put a face on the name he was hearing so much about. He now remembered Van Hook—who was two years ahead of Weber in school—hanging around the sixth-grade girls in Weber's class. Weber shook his head; even then, he thought, even then.

* * *

On Monday, March 1, the Reverend Jim Howes finally broke his public silence. His simple and powerful letter to the editor of the *Herald* ran under the headline, "My little girl still cries."

"My little girl cried again last night. It is not the first time. But I don't know how to stop the hurt. She is one of the girls who accused a teacher of taking advantage of her in school. The charges have been aired in the press.

"People want it to go away. But my little girl still cries—still has nightmares—still cringes with fear.

"The principal and teachers tell the children to shut up and don't talk about problems. The letters to the editor make the teacher come out sounding like a saint. The school superintendent says unless there is more evidence, he can do nothing. The P.T.A. isn't interested. The School Board doesn't seem to be able to do anything about the problem. And my little girl still cries.

"What should I do? Does anyone believe that all twelve of these girls are lying about this whole situation? Would my little girl pace the floor, lock herself in the room, cry half the night for the sake of a lie?

"Are the doctors and counselors wrong about what she has been through? Does her hurt about feeing dirty, about being used, and fearing adults have to be compounded by being told that the adults who have responsibility in our community think she's lying?

"Can anyone do anything? I am admittedly angry. I want to deal with my own anger lawfully. But, my little girl still cries.

"Signed, A concerned father, James Howes, Caseyville."

Pam Klein read the letter, and had to take a very deep breath. How could anyone not be touched by that? How could anyone with a heart read that and not understand? How could so many people in the community continue to abuse these little girls?

Dennis Kuba and Pam Klein still were weary from the interviews over the weekend when the first of the week rolled around. But their efforts were about to pay off. On Tuesday night, March 2, the investigators talked to two girls, 12 and 13. The older one reported only that she hated Van Hook because of an incident when she lived near him in Collinsville. He accused her and some other kids of destroying some of his property, and called the police. She never had anything to do with him after that.

The younger one, Connie Hill, had been kissed on the forehead by Van Hook when she was in his sixth-grade class at Caseyville School in 1981. Van Hook had taken her into his library twice and closed the door for private conversations, but nothing sinister had happened. She remembered two occasions when she saw Van Hook and Katherine Howes go into his office and close the door. Don Weber would say later that her story was valuable because it corroborated Katherine's.

But the third interview of the night, set for 8:30, held more promise. When Kuba had called a 19-year-old girl named Sarah Louise Cramer earlier that day and told her he wanted to talk about Mr. Van Hook, she had asked with great surprise and intensity, "How did you find me?" Kuba wanted to leap through the phone; he knew a loaded response when he heard one. He explained that some other girls had suggested she might know something about Van Hook. Could she see him and Pam Klein that night? Okay, was the reluctant answer. Kuba's investigative instincts told him this girl could unload a bombshell.

The apartment was in a relatively new building on the south side of Collinsville, just across the street from an old catsup factory whose water tower formed the shape of a Brooks catsup bottle. As he and Klein hurried through the dark, cold parking lot toward the building, Klein spotted a penny glistening in the reflection of the distant streetlight. She quickly picked it up and grinned. "Well, what do you know about that? Finding a penny is supposed to be good luck, right?"

"Lord, I hope so," Kuba moaned as he rang the doorbell. He and Klein could hear footsteps coming down a stairway before a soft voice asked warily behind the closed door, "Who is it?" Kuba identified himself and Pam, and explained that they wanted to talk to Sarah Cramer. When the door opened, a slim young woman with dark brown hair and dark eyes asked for identification and studied Kuba's badge closely under the light. Apparently satisfied of her visitor's authenticity, she directed them up the stairway and through the door that led to the apartment living room. They were met on the stairs by the cute four-year-old daughter of the woman who had greeted them.

Klein and Kuba were startled to find another young woman and a burly young man sitting there, seemingly quite protective of their friend. The woman was tiny and slender, dressed in a T-shirt and jeans that hugged her small hips. She had a lovely face with fine features. She picked up a bottle of Pepsi and curled up in a ball in one corner of the couch. "Sit down," she said. "I'm Sarah. These are my friends, Belinda Barnett and Mark Richter."

Pam Klein glanced quickly around the room. It was compulsively neat and tidy, and very homey. The furniture was not expensive, but it seemed almost new and well kept. Klein sat next to Sarah Cramer on the couch, and Kuba sat on a chair directly across from her as he opened the conversation.

"Sarah, we would like to know if you have anything to tell the police about Mr. Van Hook and yourself."

The young woman looked back at the agent intently and asked, "What would happen if I did?"

Another loaded response, Kuba thought. His eyes shot to Klein briefly as he remembered the penny in the parking lot. Klein returned a knowing glance.

"What do you mean, Sarah?" Kuba asked.

"Well, if something had happened and I decided to tell you about it, what would happen then?"

"I would take a report on what you said, and then I would show that to the state's attorney to see if it was something he believed was a crime that Mr. Van Hook should be prosecuted for."

She wanted to know more, and she was watching

Kuba's face closely. "Would my name be in the newspaper?"

"Not if this was something that concerned a sexual offense. The papers don't print the names of victims of sexual offenses. But you should know, Sarah, that there is every possibility that people may find out who you are, and you would have to cope with the repercussions of that."

Kuba always was honest when he talked to a victim, and now he held his breath. He could tell she still was thinking as she took a long drink from her soda bottle; she needed more answers.

"Would I have to go to court and testify?"

That was a good opening for Klein. "Sarah, that's why I'm here with Dennis. My center and I are prepared to counsel and support you through the entire legal process and anything else that comes up. You will have a lot of people there for you."

Sarah's eyes flashed and her voice betrayed anger. "From what I read in the paper, it didn't sound like many people came through for those girls from Caseyville," she snapped.

Klein gulped; Sarah had nailed them with that observation. But Pam forged ahead. "I know it must look like that, Sarah. But we're still hanging in there for them, and we're still trying to straighten this out for them. Can you help us?"

Sarah sat quietly for a long time, taking another slow drink of Pepsi. Finally, she sucked in her breath and said softly, "All right, I'll help."

Klein felt herself relax, but she was anxious to hear what this girl had to tell them.

"Mr. Van Hook was my teacher in eighth and ninth grades at North Junior High," Sarah began slowly. "I had him for history and geography. While I was in the eighth grade, in 1976, he asked me to baby-sit for his kids." She paused, obviously giving careful thought to what she was about to reveal.

"See, I grew up in State Park Place. You know how most of the people there feel, like they're low class or something. And my mom was really proud that my teacher, someone like Mr. Van Hook, had asked me to †baby-sit for him. It was like it was a real honor for me and my family. She wasn't going to let me baby-sit until she found out Mr. Van Hook had asked me."

Sarah was beginning to look for excuses, Klein thought. Whatever was about to be disclosed, Sarah already was looking for a way to explain it, to rationalize it. She was embarrassed and ashamed, and she was afraid these two strangers would judge her harshly for what she was about to reveal.

"So I told him I would do it. It was on a Saturday, sometime before December 12. That's my birthday. I was 13 that year. He picked me up at my house late that morning and drove me to his house in Maryville. Just before we got to his house, he told me to lay down on the seat of the car, to duck my head down as we pulled into his garage. I didn't understand why he wanted me to do that, but I did it, anyway. He was my teacher, and I did what he told me to."

Sarah was about to become the Madison County version of Katherine Howes; Klein and Kuba could feel it. Klein was struck by the premeditation involved. Van Hook had planned this so carefully he even had her hide in the car so none of his neighbors would see her as they pulled into the garage.

Sarah quietly related how Van Hook took her into his family room, folded out a sofa bed, and asked her if she wanted to lie down; she said no. She asked where his wife and kids were. He said they were out somewhere; she couldn't remember where. He turned on the TV, and she watched *American Bandstand* for a while. He asked if she wanted something to drink and she said no again. But she smoked a cigarette he offered; in the meantime Van Hook went through some papers on his desk on the other side of the room.

When she was finished smoking, Van Hook startled her by kneeling in front of her and kissing her on the cheek. He played with her hair for a moment, and then began unbuttoning her blouse. She froze; she couldn't believe what was happening. He stood up, took her by the arm, and led her down the hall to his son's bedroom. He took off her clothes and then his, and then pulled a prophylactic out of his wallet. He even mentioned that when he bought it, the pharmacist made a joke over the fact that it was colored—yellow; the pharmacist had said something about Van Hook's wife having a good time with that.

But then Van Hook put the condom on and, suddenly, he was on top of Sarah, performing sexual intercourse with her.

She couldn't believe it. This was her teacher who was doing these things. She just couldn't believe it. And she was terrified; she didn't know what to do. She just laid there like a zombie, afraid to move or speak. He kissed her on the neck and cheek, but she was frozen in fear. She hoped she would wake up soon and realize it had been a bad dream. But it wasn't.

After what seemed like a long time, he got up and went into the bathroom. She dressed and sat there—on her teacher's son's bed—and tried to figure out what had happened. When he came out of the bathroom, he showed her around the house, as if nothing had happened. He even took her into his bedroom, and had the gall to open the drawer in the nightstand and show her the towel he said he and his wife placed on the bed when they had sex while she was menstruating. Another bizarre tidbit amid such a horrible experience. She had no idea how important that line would be.

As he drove Sarah home, he gave her five dollars so her parents would think she had indeed baby-sat. He also gave her a warning: if she told what had happened, no one would believe her, and the other teachers would gang up on her and give her a hard time at school. She went straight to her room, too frightened and too ashamed to tell anyone what had happened. But the next day, she told her best friend, Belinda Barnett—the young woman sitting at Sarah's elbow.

Corroboration, Klein and Kuba thought immediately. At last one of Van Hook's victims had told someone right after the molestation occurred. Someone besides a victim now could vouch for the story.

But Sarah's story was not complete yet. Van Hook had not approached her the rest of the year. But they both moved to Collinsville High School the next year, 1977—Sarah as a ninth grader and Van Hook as a new high-school teacher. One day in September, right after school started, he asked her to meet him in his classroom after school and said he would give her a ride home. She was concerned, but thought perhaps this was what she had been waiting for—perhaps Mr. Van Hook was going to apologize and explain why he had done that to her. That was what she really wanted now, a way to understand why he had done that.

When she arrived at his room, he gave her a little bag that contained two small bottles of liquor—a premixed whiskey sour and a screwdriver. He said he wanted to talk to her, but they couldn't do it there. He drove her to his parents' house at 1123 Constance Street in Collinsville, just a few blocks from the high school. They parked in front, went in, and sat in the living room until he got up and went into the bedroom. He called to her, telling her there was something he wanted to show her. He lifted the corner of the mattress and showed her a pile of condoms he said were his father's. He made some weird comment about his father still playing around even at his age, and then leaned Sarah back onto the bed. He took off his slacks and put on one of his father's condoms, and then pulled off her jeans.

She couldn't believe it was happening again. After she had been willing to meet with him again to hear his apology, it was happening again. How could she have been so stupid? she wondered.

Just after he began to have intercourse with her, they heard footsteps on the front porch. Sarah was terrified that someone would discover them, and everyone would find out what had happened. But Van Hook peered out of the window almost against the edge of the bed, and assured her it was just the mailman. Then he returned to the activity so rudely interrupted by the heavy footsteps.

When it was over, Van Hook took her home as if nothing had happened. The next morning, on the bus going to school, Sarah and a friend drank the liquor Van Hook had given her. Another witness for corroboration, the investigators thought.

Sarah said she also had told Belinda Barnett about that rape, and Belinda confirmed that to Klein and Kuba.

Pam Klein asked if Sarah had told anyone else. Her eyes shifted toward the large young man sitting across the room. Klein looked at him, too, and could see barely controlled anger in his face. Mark Richter knew. Sarah said that about a year ago, she had told him about both of the incidents with Van Hook. Richter confirmed that and, more important, said he had told his shop teacher, Charles Wandling, right after Sarah had mentioned it. Another witness, Klein and Kuba thought, and this time a teacher.

Pam Klein looked at the young woman almost cringing in the corner of the couch, and saw more than another victim to prosecute Van Hook. She was looking at another wounded little girl—inside a young woman now, but still a wounded little girl.

"How are you feeling right now, Sarah?" Pam asked.

"Scared to death," was the quiet reply.

Sarah's daughter came running back into the room, and seemed to sense the tension among the adults. She crawled onto the couch and squeezed up close to her mother. Sarah smiled and put her arm around the girl. "This is my daughter, Amy," she said.

Sarah looked over at the investigators and her face grew even more serious. "I've been expecting you to find me," she said softly. "I don't know why. I've been lying awake at night waiting for you to ring the doorbell. I guess there was a part of me that wanted someone to find me, to find out what happened—especially after what happened to those other little girls. I mean, I was young enough when it happened. But now he's picking on girls who were even younger than I was.

"I even started to call the police one night to tell them that the girls were telling the truth, that they had to keep going with the investigation. But I couldn't do it. There's no way to tell you what it's been like. I couldn't tell anyone what he had done. I was so humiliated and ashamed. I couldn't tell my parents. I'm adopted, and they're so protective of me. They're older than most parents, and I'm all they have. I'm still afraid this will kill my mom if she finds out. She was so flattered that such a nice teacher would ask me to baby-sit for his children. She was proud of that for me. She's like that about me, you know."

Klein asked if Sarah had said anything to Van Hook after the first time he forced her into intercourse. She looked embarrassed. "This may sound strange, but I remember asking if his wife and children were coming home. I still was wondering if I was going to baby-sit for him. I guess I was in shock. It was all so strange, so weird. He just said no when I asked him that. He was real strange, too; he was very crude about it. He never really said anything. I think that's why I kept expecting him to apologize the second time. It sounds crazy, but I was just a kid, and I kept trying to make sense out of it somehow."

Kuba asked if Sarah could find the houses where Van Hook took her again. She was sure she could. "I've tried to put a lot of this out of my mind, to try to keep it all a secret. But parts of what happened seem like they are engraved in stone. That house is something I'll never forget."

Kuba said he would pick up Sarah the next day so she could take him to the houses—proof that she had been in both of those places before, just as she said.

The reality of what was happening was sinking in on Sarah as Kuba made the arrangements for the next day. Klein sensed a combination of long-simmering rage and intense embarrassment. She asked how Sarah was feeling.

"Well, it's too late to turn back now, I guess. I have some mixed feelings about it. I don't really want to get involved, but I can see that he's really sick. All these years I thought maybe it was just something about me.

But now I can see that it's him, and something has to be done."

She looked into Pam's eyes. "I wonder how many other girls there are." Pam nodded.

Klein and Kuba said their good-byes and walked down the long stairway without exchanging glances. They said nothing until they got into the car, and Klein almost shouted, "Yes! Yes!" She and Kuba finally looked at each other and nodded. They headed for the nearest place to get a beer.

"Dennis, this s.o.b. is worse than we thought. He not only violated his position of trust as a teacher, but he violated this girl's trust as a baby-sitter. What a slime! How low can someone get? It was all I could do to sit there and maintain my professional demeanor when she described this guy having sex with a 13-year-old student on his parents' bed."

Pam thought about the courage it took for Sarah to talk to these two strangers tonight. She was a young single mother who had a lot to lose by involving herself in this case. She knew it even could cause her mother great pain. But Sarah had chosen right over comfort. She had thought Van Hook finally would be stopped and punished when she read about the investigation in St. Clair County. But then he beat the rap there, and the other girls suffered so much vocal criticism from so many people. Sarah really felt for those other girls; Klein could tell that. When the police finally showed up at Sarah's door, she made an intelligent, well thought-out decision to help the girls who had come after her. But telling the investigators what happened had reopened old wounds. Pam thought that, by the time Sarah was done telling her story, she also was doing this for herself.

Kuba was worried about the statute of limitations. Both of the incidents took place more than three years ago. That could prevent Van Hook's prosecution for them, too, just like all the others.

But Klein shook that off; she suddenly felt a new confidence. She and Kuba had done their jobs, against great odds. Surely God wouldn't let this go for naught again.

The first step had been taken, and Klein found her faith that everyone else would do what was right this time.

"That's Weber's job, and he'll come up with something. I just know it."

They looked at each other again and grinned. "But Weber's gonna go ballistic when he hears this," Pam said.

CHAPTER 8

Don Weber was standing at the windows in his office early on Wednesday, March 3, looking absentmindedly at the intersection of North Main and Purcell below. As he waited for Kuba to arrive, Weber still was turning over in his mind the information the agent had provided in the phone call late the night before. Kuba and Klein had found a victim in Madison County, just as Weber had challenged them to do, and the facts rivaled the abuse suffered by Katherine Howes. Sarah Cramer had been forced into intercourse two different times at two different locations, about five and six years ago. Both incidents were outside the three-year statute, but they fit the other two requirements Weber had set—serious abuse, in Madison County. By the time he hung up, Weber had decided he would have to make the statute of limitations fit somehow. He wanted to sleep on it, and he asked Kuba to come in first thing the next morning.

But Weber knew already that his decision was made. The violation of Sarah Cramer could not go unpunished. It had happened in Madison County, where he was sworn to prosecute those who violated the law. This case was a "go," Weber knew as he stared at the busy streets below. He could feel his adrenaline pumping.

Kuba's report that morning confirmed everything Weber's instincts had sensed the night before. They went into great detail about the Cramer case. Weber was amazed by what she had given the police to check out. Had Van Hook been her history and geography teacher? Did he have a sofa bed in his home? Did the Van Hooks have a towel in their nightstand for marital convenience? Did his father keep condoms under his mattress? Did the mailman routinely arrive at the home of Van Hook's parents sometime after school would have let out for the day? Would the girl Sarah shared the little bottles of booze with remember? All of this was circumstantial evidence that would be very damaging in front of a jury. There was a lot to do.

Weber agreed with Kuba's plan to have Sarah Cramer direct him to the two houses later that day; that would provide good support and credibility for her story. Weber added the idea of having her draw the floor plan of the home of Van Hook's parents. And, Weber decided, he would put Sarah on the polygraph, too. It was solely a public relations move; no one doubted her veracity. But another victim passing the polygraph would give Weber more ammunition against public opinion that still was raging in Collinsville; the girls deserved as much vocal support as the authorities could provide.

Weber got a call later from an upbeat Kuba. Without a misstep, Sarah had taken him and Klein to the house where Van Hook lived in Maryville, and then the house where his parents lived in Collinsville. And she had drawn a crude little sketch of the floor plan of his parents' home, even showing the location of the furniture in the living room and bedroom.

Sarah also had remembered that she baby-sat for Van Hook a few weeks after the first intercourse. She was sure it was close to Christmas of 1976 because she recalled holiday stockings hanging on the door. She had been suspicious of Van Hook's motives when he asked, and made him show her the tickets to the event that he and his wife were attending. She knew it sounded odd that she would go back to his house and baby-sit after what had happened the first time. But she needed the money, so she took the chance. The baby-sitting job on a Saturday night had gone off with no problem. She had met his nice wife and had baby-sat his two nice kids. Van Hook drove her home and nothing was said between them, especially about what had happened before.

As an added bonus, Sarah gave Kuba another witness for corroboration. When she had become pregnant with

Amy four years ago, she had told her boyfriend, Jay Carr, about Van Hook. She was having Jay's baby, and she thought he deserved the complete truth. Jay, who still lived with Sarah, had been so upset that he cried. She thought Carr even talked to Mark Richter about it.

Kuba also had some news of his own to pass along. DCI Agent Gary Lemming had snagged a tasty tidbit during an informal chat with Joseph Kurtak, a former member of the Collinsville school board. Kurtak had received two anonymous calls while he was on the board from parents who were concerned about reports that Van Hook had improper sexual contact with some kids.

"Okay," Weber said. "Keep up the interviews with all the other witnesses Sarah has given you and get me the reports as soon as possible. We want to move on this as fast as we can, Dennis. I'll review everything and figure out where we go from here."

Kuba's enthusiasm had been growing since he talked to Sarah, and now he could feel a new burst of energy. Early the next morning, Thursday, March 4, Kuba headed for Collinsville High School to interview Charles Wandling, the teacher Mark Richter had told. Kuba radioed Jimmy Bivens and asked him to come along as a partner. The ever ready Bivens replied, "You got it, good buddy."

Wandling, a husky man with a pleasant face, was surprised when Kuba and Bivens spoke to him just before nine o'clock. He confirmed Mark Richter's account of their conversation in 1981. An upset Richter had said he was going to beat up a teacher named Richard Van Hook at Caseyville Elementary School because he had forced a friend of Mark's to have sex when she was only 13. Van Hook had tricked her into thinking she was supposed to baby-sit at his house, but instead he had sex with her there, Mark had charged. Wandling took no action on the report because he wasn't sure of its validity. But when Van Hook's name appeared in the papers recently, Wandling had called Mark Richter again. Richter said he had learned that Van Hook actually had sex with this girl twice, the second time at his parents' house.

Despite Wandling's candor, he didn't want to get involved. He had known Dick Van Hook for ten years. He was a very popular teacher who was being supported by many of their colleagues. In fact, Van Hook was something of the "fair-haired boy" in the district, and Wandling didn't want to get on everyone's bad side by going against him. Before ending the interview, Kuba warned Wandling not to tell anyone that he had been questioned about Van Hook, especially the school district's administrators.

Kuba knew how valuable Wandling could be as corroboration for Sarah Cramer and Mark Richter. Another teacher would be able to confirm that Mark Richter had told the same story in 1981 that Sarah told police a year later.

Kuba didn't know, however, what the new information would mean to Weber. The agent was somewhat surprised by the prosecutor's tone when he called the next day.

"Kuba, I want to go all out on this as fast as possible. I want to lock in everything we can before Van Hook knows we've found Sarah. I've just drawn up subpoenas for all of Van Hook's records from Collinsville High School and Edwardsville High School, and I've included letters appointing you as an agent of the state's attorney's office to receive the records. Later on, we'll prepare a search warrant for his parents' house. I'll want to get everything lined up so we will have the bases covered when we go to the grand jury. I want to do that next Thursday, March 11."

Kuba groaned. "Weber, I don't believe this. I won't be here. Joanie and I are on vacation; we're going to Hawaii this weekend."

"Oh, great," Weber sputtered. "Well, it can't be put off any longer. Just do what you can before you leave, and brief someone else on your reports and interviews so they can testify for you at the grand jury. And set up polygraphs before the grand jury for Sarah, Allison Hayden, and Barbara Maxwell. I'll call them and Katherine Howes to testify for the grand jury, and probably some of the other girls, too. And I'll want to interview Sarah myself. Also, interview that school board member Joe Kurtak; I want to know what he has to say about those phone calls he got about Van Hook. And tell Klein I'm going to want her to testify before the grand jury as an expert witness on child sexual abuse."

"Slow down, Weber. Let me get a list of all this written down. Which girls do you want to testify?"

"Well, let's call the same girls who testified in St. Clair County, as well as Elizabeth McBride and Sally Morton. I want the grand jury to hear what all of the girls have to say. They all provide corroboration for each other. And I'll have a big list of other things I'll need you to do when you get back in town. I'm going to want you to go to the stores and look for colored condoms like Van Hook showed Sarah, and I'll want you to go to his mother's house and look under the mattress."

Weber took a breath. "It'll be a whole different ball game here, Kuba. This is going all the way."

Weber hung up and leaned back in his chair. This had become an investigation driven by the prosecution now. He wasn't looking for evidence to uncover a crime; he was looking for proof to convict a man before a jury. Those were two different propositions, and Weber knew it was crucial that the investigation from this point on be monitored very closely. He couldn't think of anyone he would rather have doing that kind of detailed, precision work than Dennis Kuba. He was disturbed that Kuba would miss the grand-jury session; he had great credibility with grand juries, and he could have delivered this case to them on a silver platter.

The change in the focus of the investigation also shifted the case into high gear—an exciting moment, but one that also carried some very heavy baggage with it. This was an extremely serious and sensitive case, and Weber knew he was going to face massive criticism in his own hometown. He would be taking on another popular hometown boy, a school system, and a well-organized group of teachers. There would be a lot of heat.

And it would all start soon, too, because he was planning some public statements to let everyone know where matters stood. Not only was the public entitled to know that this case had not died, but some schoolgirls who had been crying themselves to sleep needed to know the system was not completely bankrupt.

He also had to consider some weighty legal issues. The first was the problem with the statute of limitations. Weber had developed two theories to extend the statute beyond three years so he could prosecute Van Hook for the assaults on Sarah Cramer five and six years ago. First, he could argue that the proper prosecuting authority was unaware of the crime—a circumstance the law said could extend the statute. But that raised more legal issues, too. Weber was a proper prosecuting authority, obviously, and the police probably were, too. But could the school principal be a prosecuting authority? Perhaps even teacher Charles Wandling? Weber worried that someone who might meet the criteria had been told within those three years. It was a technical point, but it could prohibit a prosecution of Van Hook if a smart lawyer found the loophole.

Weber liked another approach better. The law allowed the statute to be doubled to six years if the person was a public employee who used his official position to commit the crime. Van Hook had used his position as a teacher to molest all of these girls. It was his position of trust and authority that gave him access to them, and allowed him to manipulate them, abuse them, and then intimidate them so they would not tell anyone—to commit and cover up the crime. Weber was unsure whether earlier court decisions in Illinois would support such an application of the "official position" law. He knew it usually was applied to the tax assessor who stole tax money or the court clerk who fixed tickets. This use of the law was not so direct, but it certainly seemed appropriate.

He called the State's Attorney's Appellate Service, the agency that handled appeals for prosecutors, and ran his idea past one of the attorneys there. The colleague agreed with Weber's interpretation, and promised to help do some research on the point. He would call back in a few days and give Weber some cases to support the idea.

Weber also was delving deeply into prosecution and

trial strategy. As a backup to the sex charges for the crimes against Sarah, Weber decided to use a technique favored by many federal prosecutors. He would put Van Hook on the witness stand before the grand jury, and ask him if he had molested the girls in St. Clair County. If Van Hook denied it, Weber could charge him with committing perjury in Madison County because he had lied to the grand jury. It was something of an end run around the jurisdictional problem, in effect giving Weber the right to try Van Hook in Madison County for his conduct in St. Clair.

Weber was confident it would work legally, and strategically. He carefully had read all the newspaper stories in which Van Hook claimed absolute innocence. Van Hook certainly had held fast to that claim before the grand jury in St. Clair County; he even had said how much he appreciated the chance to tell his story there. He apparently had been able to talk—to lie—his way out of it before the panel. But he couldn't know the authorities in Madison County had found Sarah, and he would have no idea what Weber's frame of mind was; he had dealt only with the prosecutors to the south. Everything Weber had learned about Richard Van Hook suggested the teacher would waltz into the grand jury and try the same song there. But this time he would pay dearly for those lies.

As he reviewed the case, Weber realized that Van Hook had to go to prison; so many victims of abuse required serious punishment. The perjury charges might seem a convoluted way to get at Van Hook, but Weber was sure the public would understand. He couldn't let Van Hook skate again. The perjury counts would be insurance in case a legal technicality prevented prosecution on the more serious sex charges.

On Friday, March 5, Weber decided to inform the public on the new developments. In an interview with Charlie Bosworth, the reporter who covered Madison County for the *St. Louis Post-Dispatch,* Weber disclosed that lie-detector tests were being administered to several girls as part of a new investigation into allegations of students being molested in Madison County. One already had passed and the others would take the tests soon, Weber explained. The tests were to buttress the girls' credibility, since the grand jury in St. Clair County had refused to indict. Katherine Howes's parents told Bosworth she had passed the polygraph, and that they would continue to push for more investigation of the allegations leveled by 12 of the 16 girls the police had contacted.

When the story ran in the newspaper's Sunday editions, Van Hook was not identified as the suspect because he had not been charged, and Katherine's name was withheld to protect the identity of a sex-abuse victim; that was the *Post*'s policy. The suspect's attorney, Bill Gagen, expressed confidence that further investigation would produce no new evidence. Addressing the allegations of sexual activities at the school, Gagen said flatly, "It couldn't have happened."

On Saturday, March 6, with only hours left before Kuba departed for Hawaii, he and Agent Lemming paid a visit to Joseph Kurtak, who had been on the school board from 1979 to 1981. In April or May of 1980, he got anonymous calls at home from a woman and a man complaining about Van Hook. The woman said he was physically abusing her daughter at the Caseyville School, and she wanted to know what action she could take against him. She refused to identify herself or her daughter, and said she would not go to the school board for fear the girl's name would be marked forever. Kurtak advised her to write a letter to the board and to contact Superintendent Renfro about the allegations.

Soon thereafter, Kurtak got the call at home from a man who said Van Hook was "taking liberties" with the man's daughter at school. The man said his daughter had to be treated for her nerves because of what had happened. Kurtak offered the same advice.

Kurtak discussed the calls with some other board members, but they told him there was nothing they could do without documentation.

* * *

Pam Klein had been counseling a few of the girls at the crisis center, and their moods were beginning to improve as the investigation showed promising signs. They were starting to have some hope of vindication for themselves, and justice for Van Hook. For the first time in weeks, the girls and their parents were cautiously optimistic.

But Katherine Howes was reluctant to get involved again. After all, she had been damaged the worst, and she had been regressing emotionally under the strain of all that had happened in the past two months. She became terribly upset when Pam called and explained that Weber wanted her to testify before his grand jury. She remembered the humiliation and the pain when she told her story to a roomful of strangers before. Why would she want to risk that again, even if everyone was promising it would be different this time?

But the other girls were more open to the idea, especially if it would help bring the proper punishment for Mr. Van Hook. All of the girls shared similar feelings about what had happened. They felt something was wrong with them; Klein could see it in their solemn attitudes that betrayed the emotional scars beneath the surface.

As Don Weber dedicated the first part of the week to preparations for the grand-jury session on Thursday, he got some unexpected aid. Assistant State's Attorney Randy Massey offered his services in whatever capacity his boss needed. Massey—who towered over most people at six-foot-five, topped with thick black hair and a mustache—had been in the office about 18 months, almost all of that time in juvenile court. He desperately wanted to move up to trial work and felony cases, and sitting in the second seat behind Weber on the Van Hook case was the perfect opportunity. And Massey cared about these cases. His experience with abused kids—the part of the job he carried home each night—would be useful in this case. So Weber welcomed him aboard; few people were lining up to help on this one.

As Weber finalized his plans for the grand jury, the day was taking shape as a marathon event; he planned to call about 15 witnesses. Eight girls, including Katherine Howes and Sarah Cramer, would testify. Weber would call Allison Hayden to establish Van Hook's "M.O.," his method of operating. Sarah and Allison were not contemporaries of the girls in Caseyville, and their similar stories helped prove Van Hook's persistent perversion.

Weber would call Charles Wandling to the stand to recount how he had been told an accurate version of Sarah's encounters with Van Hook a year before the police found her. DCI Agent Larry Trent would stand in for Kuba, and Klein would give the grand jurors a social-psychological foundation for understanding what had happened to these girls and why they had kept their silence for so long.

All of that testimony would be relatively simple to present, but the four witnesses Weber could call from the other side of the case would require careful planning and skilled questioning: Richard Van Hook; his wife, Sandra; his mother, Stella; and his colleague and defender, Maria DeConcini.

Richard Van Hook presented the greatest challenge. He had to deny the allegations from St. Clair County to leave himself liable to perjury charges. And he had to be surprised enough when confronted with the allegations by Sarah Cramer that he would lock himself in with statements and denials; that would keep him from suddenly developing an improved memory and a good defense story down the road.

Weber planned to spring a number of specific details on Van Hook on the stand. Weber assumed Van Hook would deny all of Sarah's allegations, especially involving the trip to his mother's house. If he fell into that trap, Weber would demand an explanation for how Sarah knew about the interior of his parents' house. The prosecutor also looked forward to grilling Van Hook about the towel in the nightstand; that cute little comment would come back to haunt him. It was one of the tidbits that made Sarah's story so irrefutable.

But Weber was planning to hold out one detail; he would not reveal that he knew about the condoms under the mattress. He wanted the police to search Stella Van Hook's house later, and he didn't want to tip off the family.

From Sandra Van Hook, Weber simply wanted confirmation of some of the details, especially the towel, the arrangement of the furniture in her house, and confirmation that Sarah had baby-sat for their children. He expected Sandra Van Hook to be hostile, but he hoped to avoid a confrontation that would cast her in a sympathetic light with the jurors.

Maria DeConcini was being called mostly as a political gesture, to let her have her say in Van Hook's defense, and to blunt any criticism that Van Hook was not given a fair hearing in Madison County. The woman had become a strange player in this case. Mrs. D., as many of the students called her, was one of Van Hook's most zealous defenders, and she had been the teacher assigned to instruct Sarah Cramer at home while she was pregnant.

While Weber planned for the grand jury, other aspects of the investigation continued. The first part of the week, Kuba got a tip from a deputy sheriff and called a 19-year-old woman who was a sophomore when she was in Van Hook's class in high school. The next year, when Stephanie Knight was a junior, Van Hook had transferred to Caseyville School. She visited him there after school, and reluctantly told Kuba that Van Hook had kissed her a few times in the library. Weber didn't think he could prosecute that one, either, but it gave him another name and another victim to use against Van Hook.

The rest of the events that week were more promising. On Tuesday, March 9, Allison Hayden's polygraph by examiner Clinton Cook showed she was being truthful when she said Van Hook had French-kissed her. The next day two more victims passed. Cook found no signs of deception when Sarah Cramer said Van Hook had intercourse with her at his home and his parents' home, and that he used a condom retrieved from under the mattress. Then Barbara Maxwell became the fourth girl whose allegations rang true on the lie-box. She said Van Hook rubbed her leg during diving class and kissed her when he drove her home.

By the time the word of Cook's conclusions reached Weber on Wednesday, the prosecutor already was drafting a unique document. If the grand jurors agreed with his assessment of the case, he would present them with an indictment that was the most comprehensive and innovative bill of charges he ever had drawn up. It took hours and hours of painstaking attention.

That process was interrupted Wednesday afternoon when Weber's secretary told him that David Chase from the Illinois Education Association was there to see him. Weber recognized the name immediately; after the St. Clair County case had been dumped, Chase had accompanied Van Hook to the school board meeting to be sure he was returned to the classroom. Weber had wondered how much lobbying of the prosecutors had happened in St. Clair County; maybe he was about to find out. If that was Chase's purpose, Weber wanted a witness. He had seen DCI Agent Jimmy Bivens down the hall discussing a case with one of Weber's assistants, so he asked his old friend to step into the office for a few minutes.

Chase was ushered in and took a chair in front of Weber's desk. Chase was a pleasant-looking young man with light brown hair and a neatly trimmed beard. His voice was soft and controlled, but Weber's suspicions were proven correct.

"Mr. Weber, the teachers in Collinsville are watching this investigation in Madison County very closely," he said. Weber was surprised that Chase would be that blunt. The attorney quickly adopted a mealymouthed persona to avoid telegraphing his intentions to Chase, and therefore to Van Hook. Weber smiled and said something about his mother being a teacher in Collinsville.

Chase said the teachers did not care for the new investigation Weber had started, and added, "The teachers are very well organized in Collinsville. We hope things come out well for Mr. Van Hook tomorrow. If they don't, there will be serious political repercussions."

The implication was clear: If Weber screwed with Van

Hook, the teachers' union would use its substantial political and financial influence against Weber in the next election. Weber glanced at Bivens, whose face was turning bright red as the muscles in his jaw tightened. Weber repressed his comparable anger and slipped into a pleasant, deferential tone.

"Oh, I don't think you have to worry. I'm sure everything will come out okay tomorrow."

Chase smiled, said, "Fine. We hope so," and left.

Weber hoped he would tell Van Hook everything looked good, that they had it wired in Madison County, too. Weber didn't want Van Hook too wary to testify before the grand jury.

As the door closed, Weber looked at Bivens, who was about to rip the arms off the chair. Weber grinned and asked, "Do you think that was meant to be intimidation?"

Bivens said angrily, "Damned near, I'd say."

Pam Klein gathered a gaggle of girls around her early Thursday, March 11, as they sat on the wooden benches that lined the walls on the third floor of the Madison County Courthouse. She watched with a mixture of sympathy and gentle amusement as the girls dealt with their combinations of fear, nervousness, and excitement. They were less naive this time, and they really wanted the people on the grand jury to believe them. Their agitation kept them moving in and out of the small conference room Pam was using as their headquarters for the day. Sometimes they sat in the room; sometimes they sat on the benches in the hall. They fidgeted and chattered and sat and stood and paced.

They all seemed awed to be in a courthouse as participants in something much more profound than a class visit to a government center. They gawked at all of the oak and marble along the walls and floors of the 70-year-old building, and carefully approached the railing around the atrium that rose through the center of the three-story building. From any vantage point along the iron banisters, the girls could watch the activities on the two floors below as people scurried back and forth, in and out of doorways, offices, and courtrooms. The girls were taken with the bronze statue of President James Madison at the center of the ground floor, a focal point for everyone gazing over the railing.

The assembly of schoolchildren was sobering to Weber as he met them that morning. He had known they would be there, but to see the victims gathered together for the first time was a wrenching experience. They were all just little girls, just kids. He had known that intellectually, of course. But to see them there, looking more like a Brownie troop than a group of sex-abuse victims, drove the reality home. Van Hook had to be prevented from claiming any more innocent victims.

Klein introduced Weber to the girls, and he said a brief hello before heading for the large courtroom where the grand jury would convene. He hoped he was warm enough to offer them some reassurance. But he was wound pretty tightly because of the day he faced, and he wasn't sure he could be very chatty. Later, he would spend a few minutes privately with Katherine Howes after Klein told him how upset the girl was as she awaited her turn before the grand jury. Tears rolled down her cheeks as she told Weber how scared she was. He promised her that this time would be different. She would be among sympathetic people who would believe and support her. Katherine trembled and sobbed as she said she didn't think she could tell her story all over again. Weber reassured her. He would do most of the talking; all she had to do was confirm the details.

The group of girls also was being watched closely that morning by DCI Agent Larry Trent. As the father of a girl, as well as two boys, Trent had great empathy for what the kids down the hall obviously were enduring. They clustered around Pam Klein, scared and anxious, sometimes holding hands and whispering as children did. But Trent knew that an important part of their childhoods had been stolen, never to be replaced. At this age they should not be dealing with such experiences and concerns. The good memories of childhood, that part of being an innocent kid, had been destroyed. That made Larry Trent angry.

He was Dennis Kuba's supervisor, and he had been keeping up with the Van Hook case through Kuba's written reports and almost daily conversations. A week earlier, a grinning Kuba had walked into Trent's office with one of those "good news-bad news" situations. The good news was that the Van Hook case was going to the grand jury in Madison County; the bad news was that Kuba was going on vacation to Hawaii, and Trent would have to fill in at the grand jury. He was the most familiar with the case, and it was his responsibility as squad leader.

So Larry Trent sat in the courthouse hallway reviewing the thick file assembled by Dennis Kuba, and watching the emotion-charged scene only a few feet away.

Weber wasted no time beginning the day's work. He called in Trent to run through Kuba's reports on all the interviews and the evidence, giving the panel a solid foundation on which to build the rest of the case. Klein followed him to offer expert testimony about sexually abused children, and to confirm that they rarely told anyone about the abuse—not their parents, not the police, not school officials, not even their best friends. Many people had difficulty understanding and accepting this phenomenon, but it was true. Kids were too embarrassed, too shy, too frightened, too uncertain about what had happened.

Then Weber turned the grand jury over to the girls. He started with Van Hook's victims from Caseyville School—Paula Birch, Elizabeth McBride, Sally Morton, and Lori Parker. He followed them with the case he found to be the worst—Katherine Howes. Although she had been so nervous that she vomited in the stairwell when she was called to testify, Weber thought she did pretty well. Sarah Cramer then took the stand to tell a story quite similar to Katherine's, a story that Weber hoped would be the focus of the grand jury's charges against the perpetrator. The last victims to testify were Allison Hayden and Barbara Maxwell, two girls who didn't quite fit the pattern of Van Hook's other prey, but who came from families whose social position in town lent extra credibility to their accounts.

Teacher Charles Wandling was called next for two reasons. First, he could support Sarah Cramer's story, recounting how he had heard of Van Hook's sexual advances on Sarah a year before she told the police. Second, his appearance before the grand jury would lock in his testimony under oath, making it impervious to pressure from other teachers.

Weber also called a teacher to confirm that Van Hook once had come to his class to call Lori Parker and Sally Morton out of the room for a conference. That was the day the girls said Van Hook took them into his library office individually and kissed them, sending them in tears to the rest room. That had, in fact, precipitated the investigation in the first place.

The girls were considerably less traumatized by this grand jury than they had been before. It wasn't that bad, each said as she finished; they actually were able to smile about it. And they wanted to know if an indictment would be handed down that day. Klein couldn't predict what would happen, so the girls insisted they wanted to stay through the afternoon to see what would happen, even though that meant facing Van Hook, his wife, and anyone else who showed up to support him during the session after lunch. Klein admired the girls' dedication and courage, and agreed to stay with them. This was a turning point for them, a good day for them after so long. Klein was just glad she had Mary Free and Mary Sudholt from the crisis center to help her handle her young group; these victims still were little kids.

Weber was pleased with the way the evidence was developing. The girls seemed to be well received by the grand jury, helping ease the nagging uncertainty he had about taking them before the panel of citizens. After all, this case had been washed out by such a group before. Of course, the way a prosecutor leads a grand jury has a strong impact on the results. This group also was experienced, having heard a series of major cases, and the panel was led by an intelligent foreman, Phil Curry of Edwardsville. But once the prosecutor left the grand jurors alone to deliberate, they were on their own.

And Weber was unsure just how the adversarial witnesses he had subpoenaed would do. What about Richard Van Hook made people believe he couldn't do these heinous things? After all, he had an incredible amount of support in the community. Would he walk in and win over these grand jurors, too?

Van Hook arrived at the courthouse after lunch, accompanied by his wife, his mother, and Maria DeConcini. The girls at the end of the hallway saw him come in and began to whisper as he walked toward the grand-jury room. He saw them, but gave them no real notice and walked on without any reaction. Klein saw that as smugness, an air of arrogance that could explain how he really viewed those girls. They didn't even warrant a second look after he had finished with them.

The nasty looks came from Sandra Van Hook and her mother-in-law, Stella. They shot stares at the girls that Klein thought definitely were meant to intimidate. The glaring would continue through the afternoon.

Weber was fascinated by the scene on the Van Hooks' bench. Stella and Sandra hovered over Richard; it went beyond being protective to a point Weber thought was ridiculous. Maria DeConcini—a bulldog of a woman with short black hair—appeared to have assumed the role of captain of the guard.

Before the Van Hooks testified, Weber called two witnesses to give the inquiry some balance. Gus Viviano, the custodian at Caseyville School, testified that he had seen nothing unusual involving Mr. Van Hook and had found nothing in the trash to support the girls' accounts of dirty magazines and condoms. And Weber allowed Maria DeConcini to drone on for 30 minutes about her team-teaching arrangement with Mr. Van Hook, and what a fine man he was.

Then it was time for a flurry of activity that would lead to the day's finale. As an opening gambit with the Van Hook family, Weber called Sandra. She was an attractive woman with short, medium-blond hair, a fair complexion, and an incredibly confident air. She unabashedly confirmed the location of the towel and its purpose, and said Sarah Cramer indeed had baby-sat for them on a Saturday. In those brief comments Sandra had inadvertently provided important credibility for Sarah's testimony.

Weber had anticipated the meeting with his next witness, Richard Van Hook, for some time. Accompanied by his attorney, Bill Gagen, Van Hook walked into the room with little apparent nervousness. He wore a blue business suit, and was neat and well groomed. The witness seemed sure he was about to talk his way out of it, just as he had before.

But Weber moved almost immediately to a carefully drafted series of questions from a list on the podium in front of him. Using the language from Kuba's reports of the interviews with the girls, Weber asked pointed questions.

Did Van Hook caress the breast of Paula Birch? Did he unzip Elizabeth McBride's jumpsuit and put his hand on her buttocks? Did he have intercourse with Katherine Howes? Did he perform oral sex on Katherine Howes? Did he kiss Lori Parker and put his tongue in her mouth? Did he kiss Sally Morton and squeeze her buttocks? Did he force himself on Barbara Maxwell, kissing her and touching her thighs and buttocks? Did he kiss Stephanie Knight, his former student at high school who visited him at Caseyville?

Richard Van Hook calmly and firmly denied each accusation. Weber guessed Van Hook was thinking this was just going to be more of the same stuff he had deflected before. He had no inkling of perjury charges.

The first surprise for Van Hook came when Weber mentioned Sarah Cramer. It was not a grand reaction—just a flash in the eyes and a tightening of the jaw. Weber saw it, and he and Van Hook locked eyes. The teacher had not seen that coming.

As Weber had expected, Van Hook flatly denied Sarah's allegations. She had been at his house two or three times to baby-sit, but Van Hook insisted he never brought her there on a Saturday morning, especially to have sex with her. And he was sure she had baby-sat after school, not on a Saturday night.

Weber bore in deeper with more unexpected information. What about the towel in the dresser in the bedroom? Van Hook showed no reaction as he coolly answered that there was no towel in the dresser. Weber wondered if he was hearing the trap door clanging shut; Van Hook could not know that his wife already had told the grand jury all about the towel.

The next move was designed to keep everyone off balance. Weber sent Van Hook out of the room, with instructions not to talk to his wife, and then called Stella Van Hook as the next witness. As Weber stepped into the hallway, everyone watching could tell he was less than pleased to see Richard and Sandra conferring in hushed tones at the end of the hall.

Weber brought in Stella Van Hook quickly to get her denial that Sarah Cramer ever had been in Stella's house. Of course, Weber knew that gave more credibility to Sarah's story, since she had been able to describe the floor plan of the house; she was there sometime, obviously on a day when Stella wasn't home.

Then Richard returned to the hot seat. But now, after the hallway conference with his wife, he remembered the towel and what it was for. Weber was not surprised; Van Hook had no choice but to backpedal. Weber asked him point-blank if he had talked to his wife. Van Hook admitted they had talked, and said she reminded him that there was a towel in the nightstand, not the dresser that Weber had mentioned before. Weber didn't think that scored any points with the jurors, and it still didn't explain how Sarah knew about the reason there was a towel at all.

"Did you ever tell Sarah Cramer about the towel?" Weber insisted.

"Not that I know of," Van Hook said cautiously but calmly.

"Did you ever discuss your wife's menstrual cycle with Sarah Cramer?"

"I'm sure I did not."

"Did you ever tell Sarah Cramer that towel is there for the reason that it's there?"

"Not that I know of," he repeated.

"And there's no way she could have known about that towel and its use, is there?"

"None that I know of."

Good, Weber thought. Van Hook was locked in; he couldn't come back later and remember telling Sarah why the towel was in that drawer. He had denied a fact Sarah could have known only from an intimate conversation with him. How could there be an innocent construction for that?

Weber played out the hand with more tidbits. Did Van Hook take Sarah to his parents' house? Never. Did he give Sarah liquor? No.

Now it was time for a tactical move, the kind Weber especially liked to spring on witnesses who thought they were good at the game. Since Van Hook claimed to have taken a polygraph test before, would he take another one? Of course he would, was the answer. Weber smiled; Clinton Cook, the state police polygrapher, was set up and waiting in the room next door. Still interested? After Van Hook conferred briefly with his attorney, he changed his mind. There would be no lie-detector test this day.

Weber ended his questioning of Van Hook, and the teacher left the room. But now he was visibly shaken as he walked over to meet with his family, DeConcini, and David Chase of the teachers' union. Richard, Sandra, and Stella huddled together, their arms around each other as they talked.

With the reference to a polygraph test ringing in the grand jurors' ears, Weber called Clinton Cook to explain how the tests worked, what their value was, and especially, how well the four girls had done on the tests he administered. Weber hoped the grand jury caught the contradiction. The girls had passed tests from the cops; Van Hook had just said no thanks. Who had credibility now?

Weber's last move was to call Sandra Van Hook back to the stand for more forthright testimony. She was certain she never had discussed her and her husband's sexual habits during her menstrual cycle with Sarah Cramer; she never had told her about the towel. But Sandra offered an unsolicited speculation about that last point. Sarah could have been snooping through the house while baby-sitting, found the towel, and surmised its use.

Weber didn't think that was a very convincing alternative to what the jury already had heard from Sarah, and it ended his presentation of the evidence. He walked out of the grand-jury room about 4:15, leaving the jurors to deliberate on what they had heard from 18 witnesses that day, and on a special document Weber had presented.

The tension in the hallway was felt by everyone, including the half-dozen reporters covering the event. They spent a lot of time watching the opposing camps polarized at the ends of the hall. While the grand jury deliberated, Maria DeConcini approached the journalists to berate them for recklessly publishing unfounded allegations and trying to ruin a fine teacher's career and life. Why were Weber's nasty comments reported in detail while Van Hook's side of the story never was told? she demanded to know.

Finally, Charlie Bosworth of the *Post-Dispatch* told DeConcini that he and his colleagues would be more than happy to print Van Hook's side, except that the only comment from him and his attorney that day had been "No comment." In fact, Bosworth said, if Deconcini cared to go on the record, the reporters would be glad to quote her view of the case as one of Van Hook's colleagues and supporters. She agreed, and went on in an angry voice to denounce the girls' allegations as preposterous. It was ridiculous to believe that all of these sexual activities occurred at school without being detected. And DeConcini doubted that any girl suffering such abuse would keep that a secret from her parents for so long.

Thirty-five minutes after the grand jury began deliberating, foreman Phil Curry called Don Weber back into the room and gave him the panel's decision: Richard Van Hook had been indicted on all 17 counts.

Weber felt a rush of gratification; this was the first big

turning point in what probably would be a thorny case. After a sigh of relief he quickly arranged for Circuit Judge Andy Matoesian to accept the indictment formally in the courtroom. Then Weber motioned to Agent Larry Trent. As soon as the indictment was returned, Weber explained, he wanted Van Hook arrested and taken directly for booking at the county jail, a block away.

Pam Klein announced the news to the girls; they were stunned for a moment as the gravity of it all sunk in. The tears started, and the girls began to hug each other and Pam. It was a deeply emotional moment for some kids who had suffered injustice upon injustice, and Klein felt that witnessing the girls' first step toward restoration was a reward for her work with them.

In the courtroom, a shaken but controlled Richard Van Hook stood at the table with his attorney as Judge Matoesian announced that the teacher had been indicted on 5 felony counts of indecent liberties with a child, and 12 felony counts of perjury. The judge explained that the charge of indecent liberties carried a sentence of 4 to 15 years, and perjury was punishable by 2 to 5 years. The reporters quickly calculated that the total of the maximum, consecutive sentences was 135 years—a number too absurd to report. At most, they figured, Van Hook would face the combined maximums on each category, 15 and 5 for a total of 20.

Weber made no recommendation on bail, and the judge set it surprisingly high—$30,000. That meant Van Hook had to come up with $3,000 in cash to secure his release from jail. Weber had expected the judge to release Van Hook on a recognizance bond—his promise to appear in court later. Van Hook told the judge he did not have the cash to make bond then. Weber looked at his watch; it was a few minutes after five o'clock. He wondered if Van Hook might have to spend the night in jail because it was too late for someone to get to a bank.

Trent was joined by Sergeant Dennis Fischer from the county Sheriff's Department as he asked Van Hook and his family to step into a conference room off the courtroom. Trent announced that Van Hook was under arrest and would be taken directly to jail for booking. Although Van Hook seemed calm and offered only a resigned "Okay," his wife and mother were visibly angered.

Then Trent pulled out his handcuffs. Bill Gagen seemed surprised and said quickly, "That's not necessary; you don't need handcuffs." Trent shook his head. "It's our policy to place handcuffs on a subject after they've been arrested and until they get to the jail."

Sandra and Stella Van Hook were getting angrier. "That's not necessary at all," they said in unison. But Trent explained firmly that he had no choice; the policy protected everyone from any unfortunate incidents. The handcuffs would be removed as soon as they got to the jail.

Van Hook turned around slowly and held his hands behind his back. To Trent, the click of the cuffs symbolized the righteous performance of the criminal-justice system, and it sent a wave of satisfaction through him. He had read the reports in this case, had been shocked by the grand jury's decision in St. Clair County, and had no doubt Van Hook was guilty. Dennis Kuba deserved to be present for the arrest, but Trent was glad to be there in his stead to see all that hard work—and good police work—come to fruition.

As Trent escorted Van Hook into the hallway, the scene was unlike anything he had witnessed before, and the atmosphere was more emotionally charged than he had expected. As Sandra and Stella Van Hook looked on in outrage, some of the girls at the other end of the hall broke into self-conscious but sincere applause.

Sandra Van Hook turned toward the girls, and Weber who stood near them, and spat out, "You dirty, filthy—"

Before she could complete the thought, Bill Gagen took her by the arm and led her away. "No, Sandy, no. Not now," he said.

But Maria DeConcini exploded into bellicose ranting and raving that filled the hallways and stunned everyone. She charged awkwardly toward the girls, almost convulsive with fury and shaking her fist in the air.

"You little tramps, you little sluts. How dare you go through with this," she bellowed.

Weber never had seen anything like that before, and at first he thought DeConcini was aiming her venom at him. As he heard the words "tramps and sluts," he realized she was shouting past him to the group that stood behind him. In amazement he thought, she is shouting those epithets at a group of schoolgirls! Weber could understand why the Van Hook corner would resent him; he had just taken the first step in a process that could put Van Hook behind bars. But surely a teacher would not assault her own students with that kind of savagery.

Pam Klein gathered the startled girls under her arms like a protective mother hen, and she and Randy Massey began shooing them toward the conference room as DeConcini's wailing continued. Klein immediately reprimanded herself for not anticipating that kind of assault from Van Hook's vocal supporters.

Of all the girls, Sarah Cramer was wounded the deepest by DeConcini's outburst. While Sarah had been pregnant, Mrs. D had been her homebound teacher; Sarah thought they had nurtured a real friendship during those visits at her home. Now Mrs. D was calling her those names. Sarah was shocked and hurt; it was the worst thing that had happened to her yet.

As DeConcini finally stormed out of the building, her tirade drove home an important point with Weber and handed him another bit of trial strategy. He turned and mused to Virginia Rulison, the coordinator of the prosecutor's victim-and-witness program, "That's who these girls were supposed to report Van Hook to? Wait until the jury sees that!"

Virginia nodded; her job and nature had given her keen instincts about these situations. "Maybe people will believe the girls now when they say a teacher said the girls should be painted red like fire hydrants so dogs can pee on them," she said.

But Pam Klein saw another dynamic at work in DeConcini's unrestrained invective. Her use of the words "tramps and sluts" showed that even this woman had the

mind-set of an offender. This female teacher was sexual-
izing these girls in the same way as the male teacher who
had victimized them. The girls weren't just liars or con-
spirators. No, they were sluts who shamelessly used their
sexuality for evil, who used their bodies to ensnare and
degrade others. How bizarre to assign that kind of
sexually-driven motives to kids!

Long afterward, Klein and the others would hear that
DeConcini had expressed her outrage at the girls in more
than words. A reporter would say that DeConcini had
confirmed that she made a list of the girls who appeared
before the grand jury that day, and circulated it among the
teachers and the other schools so they could "protect
themselves" by knowing which girls were involved.

And more was still to come.

On the block-long walk to jail, the sullen Van Hook
surprised Larry Trent by saying, "I'm going to beat this."
This peculiar comment was expressed very matter-of-
factly, Trent thought. He would have expected Van Hook
to protest that he was innocent, or that the indictment was
a terrible injustice. But instead of challenging the accu-
racy of the charges, Van Hook had chosen to say he
would beat them. Trent thought the message in that
choice of words was obvious.

Within moments, his gaze still fixed on the sidewalk
and his voice quietly controlled, Van Hook said again,
"I'm going to beat this . . . I'm going to beat this." Trent
would not let it pass this time. "I don't think so," he said
in a voice equally as controlled and even more determined. "But you will get your day in court. Then we'll
see."

Don Weber was exhausted, but he had to face the reporters so they could tell the public the real story. He offered as many details as was proper, crediting Kuba and
Klein for their work in finding evidence of crimes in
Madison County. And he said he had doubts about the
way the case was handled in St. Clair County. And then

Weber offered a heartfelt explanation for why he reopened a case so many thought was closed.

"This case cried out for prosecution. That's why I did it. I couldn't have slept at night if I didn't."

Some of the parents credited Weber and the investigators with seeking justice denied their daughters elsewhere. "I felt that Mr. Weber was a scrapper; Mr. Baricevic is not," Sheila Howes said.

The Hawaiian rain still was pounding against the window in the hotel room, for the second afternoon in a row, when the telephone rang about two o'clock. Dennis Kuba was sure it was the news from the grand jury back in Madison County; it was six o'clock at home, time for the fateful decision to have been made. He could tell from the sound of Larry Trent's voice that the news was good.

"They indicted him on 17 counts. You should have been there when I snapped the cuffs on him," Trent said with a grin Kuba could feel 5,000 miles away. Van Hook's family had come up with the $3,000 in cash for the bond within an hour, so he spent almost no time at the jail. But hammering him with 17 felony counts by a grand jury was good enough, Kuba thought.

Klein called only minutes later to congratulate Kuba, too, and to remind him that Don Weber had a lot more work for them to do. With the indictment locked in, Kuba knew he would return with renewed vigor. He ordered exotic Hawaiian drinks from room service, and he and Joanie toasted Don Weber.

The tropical sun came out the next day, and the rest of Kuba's vacation was fabulous.

CHAPTER 9

In compiling the indictment, Don Weber had designed a multilayered trap to ensure Richard Van Hook would be punished. The five most serious counts were for indecent liberties with a child, the charge formerly called statutory rape because it applied to sexual activities with children under 16. Four of those counts referred to Van Hook's despicable violations of Sarah Cramer: two for having intercourse with her in December 1976 and again sometime between September 1977 and June 1978; and two for performing acts of lewd fondling on those same occasions. Weber hoped drafting those counts that way might give skeptical jurors a compromise; if they weren't convinced of the intercourse, but thought Van Hook had at least made advances, they could convict him of fondling her.

The fifth indecent-liberties count charged Van Hook with lewd fondling for kissing Allison Hayden. Weber brought her into the more serious charges because her family's social status and stable life added credibility to all of the allegations.

There was careful strategy behind the 12 perjury counts, too. Five referred to Van Hook's denials before the grand jury that he sexually molested Sarah. But the other seven applied to the girls from Caseyville School in St. Clair County. That way Weber had gained at least some jurisdiction over those incidents.

And he was proud of the indictment because he had found two paths toward extending the statute of limitations to six years, giving him jurisdiction over crimes that might have slipped past a less tenacious prosecutor.

Weber hoped the indictment would be powerful enough to force Van Hook into a guilty plea. That would allow

Weber to avoid the considerable risk of losing a difficult case at trial, and letting down those girls again while Van Hook eluded justice one more time.

Although Weber believed the evidence was strong, he was concerned about some of the legal issues, especially the question over the statute of limitations. If Van Hook pleaded guilty, Weber might even be persuaded to recommend a minimal jail sentence while allowing Van Hook to request probation. Weber's primary goal now was making sure Van Hook never taught again or had access to schoolgirls.

But more evidence would make such a beneficial outcome even more likely, so Weber ordered Kuba and Klein back onto the streets to look for more victims or witnesses in Madison County.

On Monday, March 15, John Baricevic called Weber's assistant, Randy Massey, and proposed a meeting to discuss the case. That gesture gave Weber some hope that Baricevic would be willing to file charges in St. Clair County to increase the pressure on Van Hook to plead guilty, and perhaps to allow Baricevic to save some face; that would be fine with Weber.

Weber, Randy Massey, and another assistant, Keith Jensen, drove to Baricevic's office in Belleville that afternoon. Weber had begun to explain the new evidence against Van Hook when Baricevic abruptly asked why Weber had told the newspapers that Baricevic's office mishandled the case. From the tone of the question, the purpose of the meeting was clear: to take Weber to the woodshed for criticizing Baricevic. The meeting degenerated rapidly after that, and the two prosecutors soon were disagreeing in extremely loud voices. Weber decided that his office didn't require him to tolerate such attacks; he stormed out, leaving his stunned assistants in his wake. So much for detente.

Weber discussed the meeting frankly with reporters later, saying he felt Baricevic's sole intention had been to berate him. Baricevic told the press he had asked for the meeting to exchange information, and thought it had been productive. He wouldn't comment on his personal relationship with Weber. But he said the DCI was continuing its investigation of the incidents at Caseyville School by looking into allegations that surfaced after the grand jury dismissed the case.

Weber later received a brusque letter from Baricevic stating he would not submit more allegations to his grand jury because another "no true bill" there might hurt Weber's case. If it was good, Baricevic said, there was no need for more charges.

The meeting with Baricevic was the second rebuff for Weber that day. He had offered to attend the Collinsville school board's meeting that night to discuss the case against Van Hook so the board could decide what to do with the teacher while he was charged. Van Hook was taking a few days off, and Weber was insistent that it would be a mistake to let him return to the classroom or stay in any school attended by the victims or witnesses. But Weber's offer was rejected flatly by board president Dick Cain. He said the agenda for the meeting that night was full, and he didn't have time to contact the other members to see if they wanted to add Weber. The prosecutor got the hint; the Van Hook matter was not a priority.

The board already had discussed its options in a closed session Thursday night, just hours after the indictment; it delayed a decision until Monday night. The district's attorney, Jack Leskera, said the board had a limited right to suspend Van Hook, but had to be careful not to interfere with the criminal investigation while trying to get information about the new charges.

Despite hopes that the community would ease back from some of the rhetoric until the charges were resolved, Van Hook's supporters seemed to step up their activities on Monday, too. The teachers' union announced that a union lawyer from the state capitol in Springfield would represent Van Hook over job matters before the school board. David Chase added that the union was "doing some support types of activities I can't go into."

Chase's meeting with Weber before the grand jury was mentioned by Ed Gurney in the *Collinsville Herald,* and

Chase denied it was improper. He had simply wanted to indicate the union's concern about Van Hook, not try to persuade Weber one way or the other. Weber disagreed, calling the meeting with Chase "very improper."

When the school board met Monday night, the audience was packed with Van Hook supporters who sported big orange lapel buttons with slogans such as "We need more teachers like Mr. Van Hook." The board went into a closed meeting to discuss Van Hook's status, and more than 40 of his supporters were still waiting when the board reconvened in public about 11 o'clock. The board decided that Van Hook would be removed from the classroom and assigned to the district's educational center for nonteaching duties, such as library activities and planning projects. The board said Van Hook had agreed to the reassignment because he preferred to be out of Caseyville School until he was acquitted.

The decision was not popular with the skeptical crowd, and some Van Hook partisans wondered aloud whether the board was assuming Van Hook was guilty. The crowd already believed that was the assumption by the reporters, who obviously were set on trying him in the press. Maria DeConcini said Van Hook's reassignment implied the board thought he was guilty. One man defended Van Hook by saying flatly, "The man, to my personal opinion, is not guilty of any wrongdoing." Kathy Hanke, president of the local of the teachers' union called the Collinsville Education Association, said she had heard that Van Hook did not want to return to Caseyville School because he and his students had been threatened.

Van Hook's corps of advocates began its labors in earnest after that. Signs appeared in classroom windows and elsewhere declaring "We Believe Mr. Van Hook" and like sentiments. Bumper stickers announcing "We Support Mr. Van Hook" showed up on cars. His church sponsored a mostaccioli supper to raise money for his legal fees; it was the same Methodist church attended by Klein's mother.

There were less public efforts, too. There were anonymous hang-up calls at Klein's house at 3 A.M. every morning; bags of trash were dumped on her front lawn. A teacher at the high school told Klein's daughter that her mother was a bitch, and she should be ashamed of her. Other teachers approached Weber's mother at her school, patted her hand condescendingly, and said, "Well, we don't blame you for what your son is doing." Weber's father, a salesman, began getting the cold shoulder.

Letters continued to appear in the *Collinsville Herald;* some of them criticized Weber and accused him of seeking headlines instead of justice. One man's letter suggested that the situation had snowballed from a simple hug or squeeze of the hand. "Everyone has a right to his opinion," the man continued, "but public slander against a person who hasn't had his day in court is not anyone's right. Mr. James Howes has had a lot of press coverage with his condemnation of Van Hook. Even though Howes may have been called by God to the ministry, that doesn't mean he had God's power to judge. It seems to me a minister should be the first person to exercise the Golden Rule."

The victims fought back occasionally. One girl's father wrote a letter to the editor criticizing a woman teacher he said had stood up in class and named the girls who made allegations against Van Hook.

But the tide seemed overwhelmingly in Van Hook's favor. In the same edition of the *Herald,* a brief story announced that a Van Hook defense fund had been established. "A spokesperson said money received would be used to help the Van Hooks pay defense costs and other extra expenses relating to charges brought against the teacher in Madison County. The spokesperson said the idea for the fund developed out of a desire to show Van Hook that people in the community want to offer their support."

Weber, Klein, and Kuba were outraged, as were the parents of the victims. Never once had anyone in the community offered any support, even a kind word, to the girls. Where was the girls' defense fund? No one in the school district had voiced any sympathy, let alone an offer to get them counseling or other assistance. But it seemed the "community" couldn't do enough for poor Mr. Van Hook.

The indictment fanned the flames of panic, anger, and resentment among the teachers. Not only could Pat Shahini see it, but a different teacher, who never really liked Van Hook, was watching in awe as some of her colleagues became increasingly hostile. A few teachers, who normally were kind and caring, were throwing around words like "sluts, bitches, and sleaze," as if these girls were five-dollar whores along the Stroll in St. Louis instead of sixth-graders in their own school district. Van Hook was being railroaded, these teachers insisted. And a publicity-hungry prosecutor—out to add another notch to his gun—was destroying all the teachers in Collinsville in the process.

This other teacher was afraid to say anything; this was the wrong time to be going against your colleagues. But she had always thought Van Hook was weird. He was too "touchy-feely" for her; she didn't like his habit of slipping his arm around women in the halls or touching them lightly on the arm and elbow. In fact, as she watched him join in the gossip with the women, and wiggle his behind down the hall, she wondered if he wasn't secretly gay. Her reaction to the charges had been surprise, but mostly because he was supposed to be involved with girls. He talked much too much about swimming and diving, about how he used to model nude for art classes, and about how someone was always trying to pinch his butt. He was a nerdy nuisance to this woman, and she usually reacted to his conversation with a polite smile and a nod, and then a hike.

She even had been put off by Van Hook's pride in the note of encouragement he got from Superintendent John Renfro after the decision by the St. Clair County grand jury. The note said something to the effect of, "Glad to have you back. Keep up the good work." But Van Hook showed it to everyone and talked incessantly about it, as if it had been the Teacher of the Year Award.

And amid the rancor, the kids got lost. Many of the

teachers were so preoccupied with the potential ruination of a teacher that little thought was given to the girls. The teachers were too close to this, and there was the ever-present fear that, if they could do it to him . . .

It was late March before Klein and Kuba geared up to resume their search for victims and witnesses. They had two interviews on Tuesday, March 23. At 3:45 that afternoon, a 14-year-old girl said Van Hook was a good teacher and she never had seen him do anything improper. But at seven that evening, Kuba and Klein visited Stephanie Knight, the 19-year-old who had said earlier that Van Hook had kissed her a few times. In her small apartment in Troy, just north of Collinsville, the slim, brown-haired young woman sat in a chair and looked forlornly at the investigators.

"I was kind of relieved when you called me," she said quietly. "I've really been upset by this whole thing."

Klein and Kuba traded glances, feeling one more time that something dramatic was about to break loose.

"What happened to me is going to sound strange, but it was really just a schoolgirl crush that got out of hand. See, I never really dated much or had a boyfriend, and when Mr. Van Hook started coming on to me, it made me feel special, like I had something over the other girls. It was always real hard watching everyone dress up for the boys and go to the prom and stuff like that. I wasn't very comfortable with boys, and when Mr. Van Hook started acting like he had fallen in love with me, it seemed like a romantic fantasy. The next thing I knew, it all had gotten out of hand."

Stephanie Knight told the investigators she had been a high school sophomore in Van Hook's geography class for the 1978–1979 school year. The next year, Van Hook transferred to Caseyville School, and she started visiting him there after school in September of 1979. She had a crush on him, and he allowed her to use the library to work on a project; it seemed like a pleasant arrangement. After two or three weeks Van Hook began locking the library doors and taking Stephanie into his little office.

Sometimes she would file library cards for him there. But soon he began kissing her; she was surprised, but she didn't resist. After all, she really liked him. The innocent kisses soon became French-kisses as he fondled her breasts. Before long, he was removing her clothes, kissing her breasts, and inserting his finger into her vagina while they lay on pillows on the floor. Although he kept his clothes on, sometimes he put her hand on his penis.

That didn't surprise Klein and Kuba at all, but Stephanie's next disclosure was a bizarre development that added another layer of odd perversity to the story. She said Van Hook called his penis "George," and said all men named them like that. Klein marveled at this new and even more adolescent twist in a case the investigators had thought couldn't get any stranger.

Van Hook was using his standard lines on Stephanie, too. He told her she was the sweetest virgin he ever knew, and wondered how she still could be pure at 17. He said he and Stephanie couldn't date publicly because he still was married, but claimed he and his wife were having arguments and might get divorced. He gave Stephanie gifts—a small pewter statue of a little girl and a gold-colored necklace with the initial "S" on it.

Then he began to pressure Stephanie to have intercourse. He had a doctor friend who could get birth-control pills for her. But that was too much; she decided the relationship was getting too serious, and she stopped visiting him. She hadn't told her parents what happened, but she had confided a bit in a friend, Nancy Seally, without giving her too many details.

Stephanie Knight had believed Van Hook loved her until she read the newspaper stories about the other girls. She realized he was doing the same things to them at 11 or 12 that he had done to her at 17. She remembered how confused she had been at an age when she thought she knew what she was doing. She knew Van Hook could do strange things to a girl's mind. She didn't want to get Van Hook in trouble, but she felt sorry for the other girls. When she was deciding whether to tell what had happened, she wondered how she would have felt if Van Hook had done those things to her little sister.

The next day, Wednesday the twenty-fourth, Kuba and Klein interviewed Stephanie's friend, Nancy Seally. She was 22, worked with Stephanie, and they had become roommates. When they moved in July 1981, Stephanie misplaced a necklace and became quite upset; she said Van Hook had given it to her. Stephanie said she cared a lot for Van Hook, and he cared for her. Her glowing comments about her former teacher were so continuous that Nancy began to suspect she was carrying a torch for him.

Nancy had shown Stephanie the newspaper stories about Van Hook and the girls at Caseyville School, but Stephanie refused to admit anything improper had happened to her. Nancy noticed, however, that her friend became very upset over the news that the grand jury in St. Clair County had refused to indict Van Hook. When Nancy was being interviewed by an assistant prosecutor over an unrelated incident at work, her concern about Stephanie surfaced. Nancy told the prosecutor that Stephanie should be interviewed about the Van Hook case. Nancy had not known what really happened until after the investigators had talked to Stephanie the day before. Stephanie told her all about it after that.

For Don Weber, the evidence from Stephanie Knight about another incident in St. Clair County was more valuable than Klein and Kuba thought. It was powerful support for Weber's plan to invoke the "doctrine of other crimes," the legal theory that allowed testimony about crimes unrelated to those on trial. He wanted the jury to hear testimony from as many victims as possible, even though Van Hook probably would be tried first on charges dealing with only one or two girls.

Under state law, a prosecutor trying a person for one crime is barred from using evidence about other illegal acts unless they fall under specific exceptions. One of those is crimes establishing a "modus operandi"—an identifiable method of operating that can be linked to the M.O. in the case at trial. Weber had become an expert in the M.O. argument, having refined it during a murder case against a man who killed his own father with poisoned doughnuts to get his hands on the inheritance. In a legal brief, Weber argued that the man was linked to several deaths from poisoned pastries, a common thread that should allow the use of those other cases as evidence in the father's murder. Weber won over the judge, and the stories about a whole assortment of deadly doughnuts helped convict the man. The Illinois Supreme Court later affirmed Weber's M.O. theory.

In the Van Hook case, Weber would use the same argument. The list of similarities was growing: the kinds of acts Van Hook committed with the girls, where he took them, what he told them, the gifts. All of those perverted peccadilloes could provide powerful evidence to prove the charges involving just one of the victims. Using several witnesses to establish this blatant M.O. was a cornerstone in Weber's case.

But Kuba still had work to do that Wednesday after talking to Nancy Sealy. He executed a search warrant at Stella Van Hook's house at 1123 Constance Street in Collinsville. It was not a job he looked forward to, thanks to Weber's insistence on one specific point: Kuba had to look under Stella Van Hook's mattress to see if any of the condoms Sarah Cramer had learned about so unwillingly still were there. When Weber told Kuba that, the agent's face fell and he mumbled, "Oh, no." He expected that to be a terribly embarrassing moment, if not downright humiliating.

At four o'clock, Kuba arrived at the little house with crime-scene technician Louis Reddo and Assistant State's Attorney Dan Schattnik. Stella Van Hook sarcastically submitted to the search with a wave of her hand and "You're Weber's puppet. Just do what you want to do." Lou Reddo took photos while Kuba drew a rough diagram of the floor plan to show how accurate Sarah's drawing had been. Kuba and Reddo walked out to the car while Reddo loaded another roll of film, and he asked, "Did you look under the mattress yet?" Kuba cringed. "I couldn't do it." Reddo laughed and shook his head. "Weber wants you to do it; you have to do it."

Kuba reluctantly went back into the house and told the owner that he had to look under her mattress for prophylactics. "Just go ahead and do what you want," she snapped. As Kuba reached for the corner of the mattress, Stella said, "Wait a minute. If you find any under there, that's where my husband used to keep them." Kuba wanted to hug her; he asked again if that was where her husband normally had kept them. Yes, she said, and then added, with no hint of embarrassment, that she and her husband had not needed them for some time because of their age. And he had been dead for almost a year, she explained.

Kuba lifted the mattress; there was nothing there. But he and Reddo smiled anyway; Stella's confirmation was worth it.

Don Weber was thrilled with the day's results, and shared a chuckle with Kuba over the mattress. On the serious side, Stella Van Hook had not understood how devastating it was to confirm the mattress as the repository of her husband's condom supply. She had verified Sarah Cramer's knowledge of a second bit of evidence that no one could have guessed out of the blue, and no girl would have known without good reason. Dick Van Hook's chatty explanations to his victim about Dad's condoms and the towel in the nightstand were coming back on him with ruinous consequences.

Most of Klein's and Kuba's waking thoughts were consumed by the Van Hook case, and they had to struggle to keep up with the daily activities in their jobs and personal lives. Pam had to keep the crisis center going for the sake of all victims of abuse, and Kuba had to track cases that had nothing to do with little girls in the Collinsville school district. But every free minute the investigators could squeeze out was spent trying to track down more potential victims of Van Hook and to arrange interviews to be conducted in what Klein and Kuba jokingly referred to as their "off" hours. The worst part of the time-consuming search was that it kept them away from their families so much. Pam's daughter was a model in the high-school fashion show, and was upset that her mother had to miss such an important event. Dennis's young son wondered why Dad wasn't around to play with in the evenings. Most nights, Pam and Dennis found themselves grabbing greasy meals in fast-food restaurants on the way to interviews. To get a spirit-lifting laugh and try to make the trail less of a grind, Klein even brought along a pair of candlesticks to adorn the Formica table at McDonald's one night.

Over the next three weeks, Klein and Kuba would stagger through what seemed like an endless series of interviews—24 girls and 2 boys in just 22 days. Fourteen of the girls said they never had seen anything unusual involving Van Hook; one of them added that he was a very nice person and she didn't believe the allegations against him.

But ten of the girls did have information about Mr. Van Hook. No incidents of abuse like those with Katherine Howes or Sarah Cramer came to light, but several episodes fit the now-familiar pattern practiced so expertly by Van Hook. He seemed to have been testing some of these girls to see if he could become more aggressive on them later. He had kissed a 12-year-old on the cheek as a reward for improving a grade while he was her teacher two years ago; she returned the favor later with a kiss on his forehead for his birthday. He once took her into his library office and asked her what she would do if he started kissing her. She became frightened and said she would run from the room. She learned later he had played out the same scene with one of her friends.

Another ninth grader who baby-sat for him said he had kissed her several times and invited her to watch pornographic movies with him. She also had seen porno magazines at his house.

That stash of magazines and movies was in a closet, according to a 21-year-old woman who had baby-sat for the family when she was in school. She remembered that Van Hook obviously favored his female students over the males, and always talked about how attractive one of the other girls was.

The other incidents reported by the girls were mostly suggestive. A 19-year-old girl said she was in the ninth grade when he wrote her a juvenile note saying, "If you meet me behind the door, I'll give you an A and you won't have to take the test." She took the test and never met Van Hook behind the door. She remembered that he often made comments about girls' physical attributes.

An 18-year-old said she remembered sitting with Stephanie Knight in the library and talking to Van Hook when he surprised them by saying, "I just ought to take you girls into the back room and let you beat me." The girl had no doubt the comment was sexually suggestive, and Stephanie was so upset that she immediately left the room.

Van Hook once took another ninth-grade girl out of class, stood her in a secluded hallway, and leaned toward her until his body almost touched hers. Then he lectured her about how to behave in class. It was a frightening, intimidating experience she learned later had been shared by one of her friends.

Another former student remembered that Van Hook wrote notes to some of the girls in his class, calling them either "Charlie's Angels," after the popular TV show, or "Richard's Angels," his own collection of girls. Van Hook once berated the girl in front of the class after he saw her kissing her boyfriend; Van Hook threatened to photograph them if he saw the offense again. Jealous, Klein assumed.

The 19-year-old daughter of one of Collinsville's leading families offered support for diver Barbara Maxwell's story about Van Hook kissing her in the car. The new witness also had been a member of Van Hook's diving team in grade school and high school, and she remembered Maxwell being hesitant to be alone with Van Hook in his car. The witness had no problems with the teacher, but she added that she wasn't surprised at all when she heard about the allegations against him.

The two boys who were interviewed offered no useful information, but both of them remembered that Van Hook always preferred the girls; he showed an almost active dislike of boys.

During the hectic run of interviewing, Kuba got a call from Sarah Cramer asking him to stop by her apartment to see something she had found. She presented him with her yearbook from high school with a revealing message from Van Hook among the normal scribblings and autographs from other students.

"Sarah, Here's wishing the best of everything to the best baby-sitter I ever had. (You weren't a bad student either.) I hope I see a lot of you in the future. Always, Dick V.H."

Interestingly, and revealingly, Van Hook had underlined the words "best" and "ever had." What easily could have been a sweet, innocent inscription from a favorite teacher carried a darker, almost sadistic meaning to the girl Van Hook twice had forced into intercourse. ". . . the *best* baby-sitter I *ever had* . . ."

By the time Klein and Kuba halted their interviews in mid April, they had talked to 54 girls in three months. Twenty of them said they never had experienced anything out of the ordinary with Van Hook. But 34—the number was staggering to Klein, Kuba, and Weber—34 of them either had been molested by Van Hook physically or verbally, or knew something else about the abuse that could make them witnesses against him.

Don Weber couldn't use much in that last string of interviews, but the sheer numbers confirmed that Richard Van Hook was a serial child-molester, and a very dangerous man. As the investigators presented Weber with the last of the reports, the three colleagues sat quietly in his office and let the inescapable conclusion sink in.

They would never have a real count of Van Hook's victims until they talked to every girl he had been close enough to touch.

CHAPTER 10

Richard Van Hook's assault on the case against him began barely two weeks after the indictment. On Wednesday, March 24, his lawyers filed a motion for substitution of judges, exercising his right to one automatic change. Circuit Judge Andy Matoesian had been assigned to the case, which had made Weber more than happy. He had tried a lot of cases in front of Matoesian, and he liked the judge's style. But Van Hook got one free move, so Matoesian was out and another judge would be brought in. That maneuver disappointed Weber. Matoesian's removal was not a good way for Weber to start this complicated and sensitive case.

The defense's next move also caught Weber off guard. The Gagen brothers added two cocounsels to the team—John Gitchoff and his young associate, Jim Wallis. That quickly changed Weber's outlook on the case. John Gitchoff—known to everyone as "Gitch"—was a fascinating character who knew his way around the courts in Madison County like few others. Weber never had faced Gitchoff in a courtroom, but the young prosecutor was more than aware of the old pro's reputation.

At 56, Gitchoff had spent 30 years honing the practice of law to an art. He had developed a strong private practice before serving six years as a circuit judge, two of them as the chief judge. When he tired of the bench in 1977, he returned to practice all aspects of the law, from criminal to personal injury. Gitchoff was well connected to the Democratic machine that controlled politics and almost everything else in Madison County. He had a wide variety of clients; he was a "player" who knew the system inside and out. He had learned long ago that the most effective law sometimes was practiced far outside a court-room. He masked shrewdness and killer instincts with an open, avuncular style that kept people off balance. He usually called women "hon" or "sweetie" with an ingra-tiating innocence that kept him from sounding conde-scending or offensive. He had a lively and natural sense of humor that made him entertaining, and he carried all of those traits into the courtroom. With his easy manner, his dark hair combed back, his slightly slouched posture, and thick middle, Gitchoff could slide from kindly uncle to master attorney before a hostile witness or opposing counsel knew what hit them.

As a judge, Gitchoff had run an unconventional court-room. He often surprised spectators by announcing that they could smoke in his courtroom, because he certainly would. It was not unusual for him to lean back, his black robe unzipped, and prop his feet up on his bench. If he became restless or tired during testimony, he sometimes would stand behind his chair and lean his elbows on the back in a relaxed pose. There was little formality in his presence on the bench. Once, after DCI Agent Jere Juenger had taken the witness stand and spelled both of his names for the court reporter, Gitchoff sent ripples of laughter through the room by asking, "Wait a minute. If your last name is spelled J, U, E, N, G, E, R, and is pro-nounced 'Yenger,' and your first name is spelled J, E, R, E, why isn't it pronounced 'Yery'?"

Gitchoff took that same relaxed view of most aspects of the job. One legendary story said that he had been pre-paring for a long and troublesome hearing on a motion by a prison inmate when the judge learned the real intent was just to get the man back to the county so he could see his wife. The savvy Gitchoff gave the couple 30 minutes alone in his chambers, which was equipped with a couch. When the man emerged, smiling, he dismissed the motion and contentedly returned to prison.

Weber's older brother and legal mentor, Philip, had known Gitchoff well for years. Philip had worked for a firm that handled a lot of cases on referrals from Gitchoff while he was a judge. Phil Weber often referred to

Gitchoff with the title of "the don," a nod toward his position of respect in legal circles and among his friends
and family, and the reputation of some of his clients.

Weber knew much less about Jim Wallis—a short,
round, bespectacled lawyer who had handled a few small-
time criminal cases without developing any particular
reputation. Wallis might be little more than a flunky for
Gitchoff, Weber thought, or he could be picking up valuable tricks while working at Gitchoff's elbow.

With all of that in mind, Weber knew he would have to
be careful every step of the way. On April 15, he answered the defense request for a list of potential witnesses
with an incredibly comprehensive roll—78 names of
girls, school officials, teachers, police officers, doctors,
crisis-center employees—everyone who had anything to
do with the case. But Weber made sure that standard procedure for lawyers was followed—he scrambled the
names in no logical order. He wasn't going to give any
extra consideration to what could be a formidable defense
team.

In late April, Sheila Howes called Pam Klein with a bizarre, disturbing story. On a school day the week after
Easter, her sons were playing basketball in the driveway
of the family's mobile home while she was preparing supper. It was a comforting, typical American scene, until
one of the boys ran in to tell her that someone had parked
across the end of their driveway and was sitting there,
watching the kids. With the harassment Katherine and the
family had endured since January, this mysterious visit
was cause for alarm. Sheila looked out of the window and
saw a green car with a Missouri license plate; it was, indeed, blocking the driveway and a woman with black hair
was sitting behind the wheel. Sheila was concerned
enough that she called and asked a neighbor to look out
and confirm this driver's odd choice of a parking place.

Sheila said she recognized the intruder, and it made her
blood boil. The woman lurking in her car and watching
the Howeses' children was Maria DeConcini, Richard
Van Hook's bombastic colleague who so carefully had

taken down the names of the girls who testified before the grand jury in March.

What an outrage, Sheila fumed, that this woman would now invade Katherine's privacy. Surely the child had suffered enough, being called a slut and subjected to similar abuse from teachers, students, and even some kids she had thought were her friends. But apparently, some other people felt more harassment was in order.

Sheila Howes called the police, but DeConcini had driven away by the time an officer arrived.

Jim Howes was furious at this latest violation of his home and family, but wanted to be sure his wife's identification was accurate. He and Sheila drove to the Caseyville School the next day and waited until the teachers arrived for work. As the hefty woman with the coalblack hair got out of her green car, Sheila Howes picked her out. Maria DeConcini definitely was the unwelcome visitor the day before.

And there was more. Sheila told Klein that DeConcini had returned several days later, parking in front of the mobile home next door. She slid over to the passenger's side of the car and glared angrily at the Howes children again as they played in their own yard. After 15 minutes she drove away.

Once again Klein was dumbfounded by the intensity of the resentment against the girls, and the depths to which some of Van Hook's supporters would sink. Klein advised the Howeses to keep a careful eye on their children, and to call the police immediately if it happened again.

Not only was the episode unsettling, it confirmed again for Klein something that had become very important for her: the girls in the case were showing more courage and maturity than some of the adults in Collinsville.

The next brush fire for Don Weber came when Associate Judge Edward C. Ferguson was assigned to the Van Hook case. The prosecutor viewed Ferguson—a barrelchested man with a salt-and-pepper beard—as a defenseoriented liberal with the potential to wreak havoc on Weber's unusual legal theories in the case. Weber stewed about it until May 28, and then took bold, perhaps dangerous, action in an unprecedented motion asking Ferguson to remove himself because he was too prejudiced to give the prosecution a fair trial. There was, of course, no provision in the law for that request, and Weber could offer no factual support for the allegation. Ferguson denied it on June 18. But Weber hoped his rather brash effort had, at least, put the spotlight on Ferguson when he decided the technical issues later. Weber also hoped he hadn't angered Ferguson too much. If he had, he may have shot himself in the foot.

While Weber worried over courtroom strategy, essential bits and pieces of the case still needed to be assembled by Dennis Kuba. As he had expected, Weber sent him out to look for more witnesses. But other directives from the prosecutor were somewhat more surprising and, in some cases, distressing. Kuba was especially annoyed in June when Weber had him return to the Bear's Cave at Caseyville Elementary School to answer a critical question—was the little room big enough for two people to have sex on the floor? At Weber's order, a humiliated Kuba lay down so another agent could take a picture to prove there was enough floor space. The result was a painfully comical photo of a prone Kuba, dressed nattily in a leather sports coat and stretched self-consciously between some empty five-gallon buckets at his head and a trash can at his feet. As he lay there, Kuba couldn't help but remember the exchange between him and the prosecutor in St. Clair County, who wondered if people really could have sex in that little room. The photograph became something Kuba would despise forever, a memento from an assignment he would never let Weber forget.

But if that was embarrassing, the next assignment was infuriating. Weber sent Kuba on a tour of pharmacies and stores in the area to find out where Van Hook had purchased the yellow prophylactic he used with Sarah Cramer at his house. Kuba was so upset he called Klein to rant and rave about the asinine chore. But he did his duty, hating every minute as he went to eight pharmacies in Collinsville, Caseyville, and Maryville. No one remembered Van Hook being a customer.

But the ninth pharmacist completely changed Kuba's attitude. With a smirk that demonstrated his scorn for Kuba and his mission, the pharmacist explained that Dick Van Hook was his neighbor, and that the Van Hook family had been customers at the store for years. With irritating condescension the pharmacist guided Kuba to a condom display that covered a wall behind the cash register.

"Here they are, right here," the man snapped. "You can look at them. You can take photographs of them. You can write down the names of them. You can do anything you want."

Kuba decided to ignore the sarcasm and the attempt to embarrass him. He nodded patiently and said, "Well, I'm just interested in whether you sell colored prophylactics."

"At one time I did. Three or four years ago I carried a line that were black, red, yellow, and green. I used to take them to parties and amuse people with them. But I don't stock them anymore."

Kuba smiled. This brief, chafing encounter had just convinced him that he had found the source of Dick Van Hook's yellow condoms. Kuba now had a different view of the assignment, and he walked out of the store feeling much better. It wasn't worth much as evidence, but at least Kuba had answered the question.

A series of interviews by Kuba in June and July also brought out some useful information that supported the victims' stories. Debbie Weaver, a friend of Sarah Cramer's, remembered splitting some little bottles of whiskey sours with Sarah on the school bus; Sarah told her they were gifts from Mr. Van Hook.

The postal worker who had delivered the mail at Stella Van Hook's house for 15 years confirmed that he dropped it in her mail box between 2:30 and 2:45 P.M. every day, with no more than a 30-minute variance. That fit perfectly the time frame when Sarah remembered the mail arriving.

Stephanie Knight's story also drew new support. Her

mother had ordered her not to visit Van Hook again after she mentioned a kiss from Van Hook. A friend recalled Stephanie saying he got "fresh" with her, and another said Stephanie talked about Van Hook giving her a necklace and kissing her several times. The second girl said she believed Stephanie was in love with Van Hook, and was thrilled about being so close to him.

A couple of miscellaneous memories didn't help the case, but certainly fit Van Hook's pattern. A 19-year-old woman said Van Hook asked her to join his swimming and diving team because he thought she had pretty hair. A woman, who was 25 now, said she had been in Van Hook's class at Edwardsville Junior High School, and he already had the reputation as a flirt who passed out good grades to girls who submitted to his passes. She wouldn't acquiesce to his demands, so her grades weren't so good. She and a friend even complained to a school counselor about Van Hook's teaching methods.

A neighbor and former friend of Van Hook's offered some interesting recollections, too. The woman said the families' relationship had been terminated about six weeks ago because of continued disagreements between the children. Richard Van Hook was disliked by most of the kids in the neighborhood, in fact, because of his aggressive behavior toward them.

Then the woman delivered one of the most startling tidbits collected so far. She said Van Hook led several of the boys from his swimming team in a surprising activity—peering into the girls' locker room while the girls were changing clothes.

That set Kuba back a bit. Even for the Richard Van Hook who Kuba thought he had come to know, that seemed like amazingly juvenile and reckless conduct—especially drawing in some boys who could let slip word of the disgraceful peeping.

Before long Kuba heard another account of the locker-room voyeurism. A 21-year-old man who had been on Van Hook's swimming team in high school said Van Hook had told team members about locations they could use to watch the girls in their dressing room at the Gaslight Bath and Tennis Club in Collinsville, including a little peephole. How pathetic, Kuba sighed.

The young swimmer also described how Van Hook had entertained team members on the long drive to a swimming meet with descriptions about his sexual activities with his wife, including details about their favorite sexual positions. He monopolized the conversation with stories of his further sexual adventures with college girls and the positions used then, highlighted by a sexual encounter in an elevator. It was well beyond the normal locker-room stuff.

The young man's father also remembered a comment from Van Hook during a conversation at the Gaslight Club. A woman who walked by in a bikini drew an appreciative stare from Van Hook, who said she was starved for affection and would get it if she rolled over on her back. The man said he thought then the inappropriate comment betrayed an unusual attitude about sex.

By the time the summer of 1982 ended and a new school year rolled around, the Collinsville district had lost one of its families. Jim and Sheila Howes had decided that the survival of their children, especially Katherine, required an escape from the community that had turned its back on some of its own. The Howeses moved to Kentucky. They still could not believe how much criticism, even contempt, had been shown for Katherine and the other victims. The really nasty assaults had come from a small but very vocal number of teachers, parents, and others. But the number of people who offered support and encouragement was even smaller. Jim and Sheila Howes had waited for someone in the school district to offer an apology, just some small token of concern, caring, or sympathy for what they had been through. But that never came.

The Van Hook case erupted for Weber again at the end of August, when he learned that the school district had sold the Miller Educational Center, the building where Van Hook had been placed to keep him away from students. The scuttlebutt was that the district was about to

assign Van Hook to library duties at Webster Junior High
School, where some of the victims now attended classes.
Irate, Weber immediately called school board president
Dick Cain, who said the story was not quite as Weber had
heard. The Miller center had been sold, and the district
was thinking about assigning Van Hook to the "media
distribution center" at Webster. But there was a separate
entrance, and Van Hook was not expected to come into
contact with any students.

The prosecutor had attended Webster and knew the lay-
out well. The school board's idea was not good enough,
he replied tersely. Van Hook still could run into the victims or witnesses in the halls or cafeteria, and that was totally unacceptable. Van Hook could not be around victims
or witnesses for valid legal reasons, and prudence certainly suggested he shouldn't be around female pupils at
all. The solution was simple, he insisted to Cain. "He's
not going to be in a building with any girls."

The renewed controversy over Van Hook's assignment
hit the front page of the *Collinsville Herald* hours before
the school board met on August 26 to make a decision,
once again under public pressure and scrutiny. After another closed session, Cain announced that Van Hook
would work in the board's administrative offices, process-
ing paperwork for books and periodicals.

Weber was satisfied with that, but it was irritating to
have to intervene in these matters at all. Didn't anyone
else in authority understand what was happening here?

The hubbub had barely settled down when Weber was
rocked by the first of what would be a torrent of motions
by the defense attorneys. On September 30, Jim Wallis
asked for dismissal of the charges in a pair of motions
that were well researched and astutely written. He argued
that the grand jury had no jurisdiction to indict Van Hook
because some of the alleged crimes happened more than
three years ago, and the rest happened outside Madison
County. In what would become recurring themes, Wallis
challenged the extension of the statute of limitations and
the classification of Van Hook as a public employee.

In an intriguing twist, he also suggested that the victims had "a legal duty" to report the crimes against them; their failure to tell the police within three years prevented any extension of the statute of limitations.

Weber now had his answer about Jim Wallis; he was a clever, intelligent, and resourceful defender who would be unrelenting in his efforts on behalf of his client.

Weber's response to the motions was direct and forceful. That Richard Van Hook was a public employee was abundantly clear. He was a teacher in the public schools, performing the constitutional function of educating children. He had exploited his "fiduciary relationship," a position of trust and authority. State law even declared that teachers "stand in the relation of parents and guardians to the pupils."

Weber also returned fire against Wallis's suggestion that the young victims in this case had a legal duty to report the crimes. The courts had defined a person with a legal duty as the director of a government department, division, or agency, or a designated subordinate—not a schoolgirl. And, Weber wondered, to whom were the girls supposed to report sexual abuse? Their teacher? The one abusing them?

Weber filed his response, and that should have been enough to ease his mind. But it wasn't; he still was uneasy about the points Wallis had raised. After researching the law with a more critical eye, Weber was not quite as happy with the indictment. The more he thought about it through early October, the more he leaned toward exercising one of a prosecutor's ultimate powers—the ability to tip the chessboard and start the game over.

On October 21, he convened a new grand jury and presented testimony from Dennis Kuba and Phil Curry, the foreman of the previous grand jury that indicted Van Hook. Then Weber offered a completely revamped set of charges, drafted with a meticulous eye toward the technical points in the law and Wallis's objections. The grand jury returned the new indictments, and Weber dismissed the previous one.

Since the focus of the prosecution was Van Hook's exploitation of the girls during the performance of his official duties, Weber made that the warhead for the new indictment by adding felony charges of official misconduct. He had another good reason to apply that charge; a conviction required that the official forfeit the post. If convicted, Van Hook automatically would lose his job and would be prohibited from teaching in Illinois again. That would eliminate any more wrangling with the school board over Van Hook's status, an exercise Weber had found infuriating.

The result of this new attack was a complicated pair of indictments designed to hit even harder, while answering Wallis's complaints. The first document was a double-barreled blast—four counts of official misconduct and five counts of indecent liberties with a child. The misconduct charges carefully followed the law to explain that Van Hook was a public employee who committed forbidden acts—spelled out in 14 subparagraphs listing the sexual molestation of Katherine Howes, Sarah Cramer, Sally Morton, Lori Parker, Allison Hayden, Elizabeth McBride, Ellen Spanos, Tammy Pauley, and Carrie Vernon, the library worker who quit after one kiss from Van Hook. Weber added a fifteenth—Van Hook had called Katherine and tried to intimidate her into silence.

That indictment included the same five counts of indecent liberties Weber used before, beefed up now by adding that Van Hook had "exploited his official capacity and the fiduciary position of confidence and trust reposed therein as a teacher" by committing the acts against Sarah Cramer and Allison Hayden.

In the second indictment, Weber pared the perjury charges down to 10 from the 12 he had used before.

Weber hoped he had covered all the bases this time. The charges of official misconduct and indecent liberties were the most threatening, but held the most legal problems for the prosecution. The perjury charges were a good move as a backup, since Weber was sure there was little that Wallis could do to challenge them.

On October 25, Van Hook calmly entered a plea of "not guilty" to the new indictments.

* * *

Sarah Cramer was bowling with some friends one evening when she turned around, and was shocked to see Jim Wallis watching her from the back of the bowling alley. Was he following her? She was horrified, and it was then that the full impact of this case on her life sunk in. Some of the young men with her charged back to confront Wallis, who denied he was following Sarah or conducting surveillance of her. But Sarah was convinced that was exactly what he was doing. Van Hook's attorneys were shadowing her, hanging over her the way their client's actions had haunted her. When would this end? she wondered.

Another blizzard of motions from Jim Wallis swept across Don Weber's desk on November 9. Two motions to dismiss the new indictments restated essentially the same old complaints. But Wallis added new weapons to his attack by claiming that the testimony by Dennis Kuba and Phil Curry was insufficient to justify the indictments.

There was more—an aggressive motion asking the judge to order Weber to provide in detail the dates, times, and locations at which Van Hook was alleged to have performed the acts. Motions like that always irritated Weber. No good prosecutor ever supplies that kind of minute detail. It was available in the police reports already provided to Wallis; that was all he would get.

The fourth motion filed that day was something new. Wallis wanted the victims' medical reports, as well as any reports about the victims by Pam Klein or staff members from the crisis center. Klein was outraged. Richard Van Hook had manipulated these girls cruelly, taking advantage of their trust in him in the worst way. After he got what he wanted and moved on to new conquests, he left his young victims to wonder what was wrong with them that their teacher would do such things to them. They would be searching for years for ways to deal with what had happened, and why it cast such a dark cloud over their lives. And now Van Hook and his attorneys brazenly wanted access to these girls' innermost thoughts about the damage he had inflicted. He wanted to know what these girls were telling their trusted counselors, even the details that went well beyond the issues before the criminal court. Klein feared that could set back the treatment of sexual-assault victims for years, perhaps even discouraging women from reporting crimes and seeking counseling.

When Klein told the girls, they were understandably concerned and confused. One more time the adults were trying to invade their privacy and hurt them. The telephone calls to Klein from the girls and their parents—mostly the parents—had continued unabated while the case inched through the courts. They wanted to know what was happening and why it was taking so long to get to trial. The parents wanted reassurance that the authorities were going to secure the conviction and that Van Hook would go to jail for his crimes. Even the parents of girls involved only slightly, or who had not even been touched by Van Hook, wanted to keep up on the case.

Many of the girls told Klein they felt they were in danger from Van Hook as long as he was free. Some of them still were having trouble at school; others were not sleeping well. The move to Kentucky had not helped Katherine Howes; she still was on an emotional roller coaster.

Weber was optimistic that state law would protect the center's documents. It said any statement by a victim of sex abuse to a counselor or employee of a rape-crisis organization could not be disclosed without the victim's written permission. But, ominously, there was an exception for court cases; a judge could inspect the material to determine if it was needed as evidence, and order it turned over if necessary.

Weber was glad Klein had turned for legal help to a friend and colleague, Stephanie Robbins, who was a board member at the crisis center. Robbins and Weber had been assistant state's attorneys in the late 1970s. They had prosecuted several sex cases together, including those loathsome gang-rapes.

When the next hearing for arguments on the motions was held on November 22, Wallis also asked for the notes

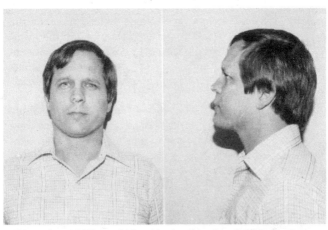

Mug shot of Richard Van Hook taken by the Illinois State Police in January 1982.

The Caseyville Elementary School library wing on the back of the building. Richard Van Hook's private office was just to the left of the windows.

The "Bear's Cave," the small room in the center of the bookshelves, was Van Hook's private office in the library in the Caseyville School. (Alva W. Busch, Illinois State Police)

The storage room Van Hook used as his office. (Alva W. Busch, Illinois State Police)

Agent Dennis Kuba stretched out on the floor of the "Bear's Cave." (Illinois State Police)

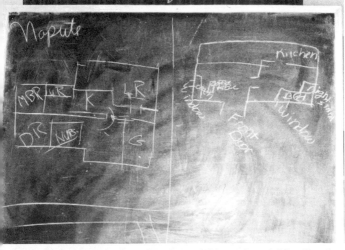

A blackboard drawing used as an exhibit at the trial for Sarah Cramer to show the floor plans of the houses where Van Hook took her—his house on Napute Street in Maryville, left, and the home of his mother, Stella Van Hook, on Constance Street in Collinsville, right.

Stella Van Hook's house.

Demonstrators protesting the dismissal of charges against Van Hook in St. Clair County walk picket lines in front of the Caseyville Elementary School in February 1982. They marched for four days in bitter cold. (Courtsey of the *Collinsville Herald/Journal*)

Richard and Sandra Van Hook leaving the courtroom under media scrutiny during his trial in Madison County in February 1983. (Courtesy of the *Collinsville Herald/Journal*)

The investigative team: Pamala Klein, director of the Rape & Sexual Abuse Care Center, and Special Agent Dennis Kuba of the Illinois State Police Division of Criminal Investigation.

Agent Kuba enters the Caseyville Police Department at the Village Hall, where the Van Hook investigation began in January 1982.

Associate Judge Edward C. Ferguson of Madison County Circuit Court, the trial judge in the Van Hook case. He later became chief circuit judge.

Defense attorney John Gitchoff, the former judge and veteran lawyer tapped by Van Hook to represent him. (Courtesy of Drew Gitchoff)

Prosecutor Don Weber answering questions from reporters outside the courtroom after long deliberations by the jury. Girard Steichen of the *Belleville News-Democrat* is in the center, and Special Agent Larry Trent of the State Police is behind Weber. *(Edwardsville Intelligencer)*

In the courthouse hallway after the verdict, Agent Dennis Kuba comforts two of the girls who accused Van Hook of sexual misconduct; Agent Trent (left) watches the crowd. *(Edwardsville Intelligencer)*

and any other documents used by Phil Curry in his testimony before the second grand jury.

By then the exchanges between Weber and Wallis were showing signs of increasing conflict. Wallis turned petulant as he complained about Weber allowing Phil Curry to tell the grand jury that five of the girls had passed polygraph tests, while Van Hook had refused to take one when he testified. That was inadmissible in court. Weber matched Wallis's tone and shot back that Van Hook's attorney, Bill Gagen, had been allowed to testify before the grand jury to explain that he did not believe in polygraphs.

That drew another peeved protest from Wallis, outraged that Weber was disclosing grand jury testimony to news reporters in the courtroom. Judge Ferguson shrugged and said that the reporters knew testimony about polygraphs was prohibited in trials.

Wallis then turned to the new ground, arguing that the reports from the crisis center should be disclosed because the staff had made itself part of the case by participating since Day One. Stephanie Robbins argued passionately that the crisis center was not a governmental agency over which the judge had jurisdiction, and he could not order that sensitive material turned over to the defense without some proof of its relevance. Ferguson delayed a ruling until later.

Wallis also contended that the defense could not prepare its case without much more specific information about times, dates, locations, and other details from the prosecution. How could Van Hook defend himself against allegations that he had sex with Sarah Cramer sometime between September 1977 and June 1978, or that sometime in September 1980 he supposedly fondled Katherine Howes?

Ferguson was unconvinced; he agreed with Weber that the information was in the charges and the other documents already supplied. Ferguson withheld his ruling on Wallis's motions to dismiss the indictments until he could review the law. That did little to end Weber's anxiety about which way the judge would rule on these crucial points.

After the hearing, reporter Ed Gurney from the *Collinsville Herald* asked Wallis about the polygraph issue, and got instead a threat of a lawsuit if he even mentioned that in his story. Gurney was shocked; he responded that the press was entitled to report anything that was said in open court. Gurney wrote a complete story—including the defense attorney's warning—and never heard any more about it.

A week later, Weber sent Wallis 12 specific responses to some of his questions. Weber had decided to play it safe, especially in light of the uncertainty about Ferguson's inclinations.

By Thanksgiving, Weber had begun to develop serious concerns about convicting Van Hook. The prosecutor hoped he was overreacting to the unrelenting attacks by Wallis and the uncertainty of how Judge Ferguson would rule on the essential issues. But those factors were highlighting something he had known all along—this delicate, unprecedented case against a popular teacher could crumble in the courtroom if everything didn't go exactly right. And a jury's acquittal of Van Hook, after everything his victims had endured, would do more damage to them than anyone could estimate. Weber winced every time he thought of the look on the face of a victorious Van Hook.

With that in mind, Weber called in Pam Klein and Dennis Kuba for a serious conference. They shared Weber's fears, so he made a modest proposal. What if he offered to let Van Hook plead guilty to one count of indecent liberties for having sex with Sarah Cramer, with the punishment to be probation and permanent revocation of Van Hook's teaching certificate? Although all three believed that Van Hook deserved prison time for his crimes, they agreed he had a good chance of escaping a sentence even if he were convicted. After all, he was a respected teacher with no prior record, overwhelmingly supported by the community against charges that many refused to believe. A judge would take all of that into account.

Weber had decided that Van Hook had become less important than giving the victims a sense of justice and vindicating law enforcement on the rumors circulating throughout the community that the investigators and the girls were part of some despicable conspiracy to frame an innocent man. If Van Hook admitted having sex with a young student, the public finally would understand that he had not been hounded over some innocent and misunderstood pat on the fanny and a benign kiss on the cheek.

If Richard Van Hook was placed on probation and never could teach again—confessed and disgraced—Weber thought everyone could feel that justice was done. Klein and Kuba agreed.

Weber called John Gitchoff and presented the offer. Gitchoff's voice betrayed little reaction, but he sounded sincere when he said he would take the offer to his client. Weber and Gitchoff met on the third floor at the courthouse in Edwardsville on a sunny day about two weeks later and leaned against the railing as Gitchoff delivered the response.

"Don, I talked to Dick about it. He was flexible and listened to your offer. But his mother and his wife would not hear of it. They absolutely put their foot down. Dick said he might plead guilty to showing Sarah a *Playboy* magazine in exchange for probation, but that was all he would agree to."

Weber was disappointed. He shook his head slowly. "That won't do it, John. He has to plead to a sex charge."

Now Gitchoff shook his head. "He won't do that, Don."

"Okay. That's it, then. We go to trial."

As Weber thought about it later, he saw the quagmire that trapped Richard Van Hook. He couldn't admit guilt because of the way his family, friends, colleagues, and others were supporting him. His wife didn't want a child molester for a husband, and his mother didn't want a pervert for a son. His colleagues couldn't accept a teacher who had illicit sex with students, and the community residents didn't want an upstanding citizen they trusted to turn out to be such a threat to their own children. Richard

Van Hook was under such tremendous, almost crushing pressure to vindicate himself that he had no room to negotiate.

On December 8, Wallis launched another barrage of motions asking for dismissal of the charges; they were too vague to allow defense attorneys to prepare a case without the extra details denied by the judge. Another motion complained that there was so much duplication that the charges should be dismissed, or Weber should be required to limit the counts he would prosecute at one time. But one of the motions really grated on Weber. It accused him of misconduct for the way he handled the grand jury in October, saying he misled the panel about the evidence by calling only Dennis Kuba and Phil Curry to testify.

Another surprising court document was filed on December 10, but it didn't come from Jim Wallis. Sarah Cramer filed a civil suit against Richard Van Hook and the Collinsville school district, seeking damages for being sexually abused by her teacher in "acts of extreme and outrageous conduct." The suit echoed the criminal charges, alleging that Van Hook had "exploited his official capacity and the fiduciary position of confidence and trust reposed therein as a teacher for his own advantage." He had "unlawfully, wrongfully, and indecently assaulted, debauched, lewdly fondled and kissed, and carnally knew Sarah Cramer against the consent and will of Sarah Cramer." As result of those violations, she had suffered "great mental anguish, shame, humiliation, and embarrassment."

The suit, filed by attorney Elizabeth Levy of Caseyville, also charged that the school district failed to investigate charges of sexual misconduct against Van Hook, specifically in the reports by Sarah's friend, Mark Richter, to teacher Charles Wandling, and in the anonymous calls to school board member Joe Kurtak. As set out by state law, Sarah asked for unspecified damages in excess of $15,000 on each of four counts.

Officials with the school district had no comment when contacted by reporters.

Weber knew the suit was coming; he had held several conversations with Elizabeth Levy. But he was less than happy that it was filed while Van Hook's trial was pending. The suit gave Van Hook the right to a sworn deposition from Sarah, perhaps providing him with valuable information to use in his defense against the criminal charges. But Weber understood the timing; the suit had to be filed before Sarah's twentieth birthday, just two days away. Waiting would have created an intolerable irony; she would have been barred from suing because of the statute of limitations.

All of Don Weber's fretting about Associate Judge Edward Ferguson was for naught. On December 21, the judge delivered a wonderful Christmas present to Weber, the investigators, and the girls. Ferguson rejected all points in Jim Wallis's challenges to the indictments in forceful language that left no doubts, and validated all of Weber's theories.

Most important, Ferguson approved the extension of the statute of limitations to cover Van Hook's activities. There weren't any prior cases on point, but the judge said it was obvious the legislature intended to treat public employees differently.

He also validated Weber's use of a grand jury in Madison County to review events in St. Clair County. Nothing in the law prevented that, Ferguson said, and he thought a grand jury in one county even could return an indictment concerning acts in a different county. The legal remedy for that was transfer of the case to the proper county, not dismissal of the indictment; Wallis had not sought a transfer. In fact, Ferguson added, proof of crimes in other jurisdictions might be admissible at trial for some purposes, including "modus operandi." Bingo, Weber thought. Here was the first clue that his plan to use several of the girls' testimony under an M.O. argument just might get the judge's approval. Ferguson was quite a good judge after all, Weber nodded.

None of Wallis's arguments fared any better. Ferguson said sufficient evidence existed to justify the indictments, and the language was specific enough to allow Van Hook to prepare a defense. And there was no prosecutorial misconduct by Weber

In the only bone thrown to the defense, however, Ferguson ruled that two of the counts of official misconduct and the five counts of indecent liberties were duplicative; Weber had to choose which counts he would pursue at the trial. Fair enough.

Ferguson set the trial for January 17.

Weber was ecstatic. Not only had his conduct of the case been vindicated, but Ferguson had given the prosecutor powerful weapons to wield against Van Hook in the courtroom—weapons Weber knew he would need to overcome the teacher's seemingly invincible credibility. For some inexplicable reason people seemed to want to believe Van Hook and reject the girls. Weber would need an overwhelming case when he faced jurors from that same community and tried to convince them of Van Hook's guilt beyond a reasonable doubt. With Ferguson's ruling, Weber finally felt he had a fighting chance when he walked into the courtroom to slug it out with Richard Van Hook.

It was time for Van Hook to take on an adult.

CHAPTER 11

The loss of all of the substantial motions by the defense attorneys did little to deter them. There still were surprises in store from the pugnacious Jim Wallis and the crafty John Gitchoff. On January 3, Bill and Bob Gagen filed a motion to withdraw from the case, turning the reins over entirely to Gitchoff and Wallis. Bill Gagen had accepted an appointment as a prosecutor in a nearby county, creating a conflict of interest. The legal team had discussed the situation with Van Hook the day before, and it was decided that the Gagens would pull out.

Gitchoff and Wallis filed a formal entry of appearance, explaining that Gitchoff would be the lead counsel at trial and Wallis would continue to handle preliminary motions. Since Gitchoff was unfamiliar with the file, he would need additional time to acquaint himself with it and to interview witnesses. Complicating matters even more was his role as chief defense counsel in a murder trial set for the first week of February. With all of those factors converging, Gitchoff asked Ferguson to postpone the Van Hook trial until March 14. The judge set a hearing for January 6.

Weber was furious. The girls had spent the Christmas holidays on pins and needles, anxiously awaiting mid January as the final chapter in their long and painful story. Now Van Hook wanted to prolong their agony another two months. The delay would be almost as difficult for Weber. A prosecutor has to get "up" mentally for a big trial, and too many delays saps the determination. An old saying among prosecutors is that a delay always benefits the defense. There always is the fear that even a strong case can fall apart if it ages too long. This one—

based on events from more than three years before, populated by young and scared witnesses, and powered by unconventional legal theories—was not the strongest Weber ever had built, anyway.

Klein, the girls, and their families were furious, too. Some of the parents were beyond the point of rationalizing a delay and a perpetuation of their families' upheaval. And it almost was a matter of basic survival for the girls. They wanted Van Hook in jail right now, because some of them were sure that was the only way they would be safe.

One girl had started sleeping with a baseball bat and her parents would find her up in the middle of the night, double-checking the locks on doors and windows. Many of the girls were spending hours and hours crying, unable to sleep. Katherine Howes combined those symptoms by crying herself to sleep every night.

For others, the impending trial had meant withdrawal into a protective shell of quiet, even depression. The younger ones seemed more agitated and were having trouble in school again.

Wallis opened the court hearing on January 6 by dropping four more motions onto the heap. One asked the judge to order Weber to produce all reports on medical or psychiatric exams of the girls. The other three motions had a common theme. Wallis wanted all charges referring to activities in St. Clair County transferred to the courts there. He wanted charges involving different girls tried separately. And he wanted Weber barred from mentioning any girl's allegations while trying the charges involving a different girl. That would neutralize Weber's M.O. argument.

At the hearing, an angry Weber turned his attention to the defense's intolerable delaying tactics. He wasn't even willing to go along with the Gagens's motion to withdraw, let alone the request to put off the trial until March. Judge Ferguson seemed somewhat impatient himself. He granted the change in attorneys, but the request for the delay got a cooler reception. The judge compromised with a trial date of February 7, depending on the murder trial Gitchoff expected to try the week before. Ferguson ordered all additional motions to be filed by January 13, in time for a hearing on the seventeenth.

Weber was impressed again; Judge Ferguson was reining in the defense in a reasonable and judicious manner, giving attention to the rights of the victims as well as the defendant.

In his written response to Wallis's attempt to separate the charges, Weber insisted that they were part of a continuing course of conduct. To prove any count, the testimony of other girls was admissible as evidence of a "modus operandi." Weber attached a graph on which X's spread across 17 categories, even more detailed than the chart used by Agent Dennis Kuba before the grand jury. In what Weber saw as an incredibly persuasive document, 15 X's marked the tactics used on Sarah Cramer; 16 were used on Katherine Howes; 15 on Stephanie Knight; 9 on Lori Parker; and 4 on Sally Morton.

Finally, Weber argued, the charges from activities in St. Clair County should be tried in Madison County because that was the location of the main office of the Collinsville school district—the source of the authority that gave Van Hook such corrupted control over these girls.

The paper flood from the defense continued; on January 13, Wallis filed seven more motions, including his eighth, ninth, and tenth attempts to get the charges dismissed. There was little surprising in any of them, but Weber was disturbed by a request to provide the defense with information about any criminal records or juvenile-court records of the victims. He hoped that wasn't an indication that the defense intended to put the victims on trial.

Richard and Sandra Van Hook attended the hearing January 17, perhaps hoping to see at least some of the charges thrown out. But Judge Ferguson's only nod their way was a ruling that Van Hook would be tried first only on charges involving Sarah Cramer—four counts of taking indecent liberties with a child, two counts of official misconduct, and four counts of perjury. Those acts occurred in Madison County, the judge noted, and limiting the trial to them would avoid confusing jurors. The other charges would be tried later; but the judge delayed a ruling on whether to transfer some of them to St. Clair County.

Those decisions were fine with Weber. The counts involving Sarah were the strongest, and he still hoped to convince the judge that testimony from several other girls would be proper as evidence of Van Hook's M.O.

On February 1, an event Weber had hoped could be avoided came to pass. John Gitchoff had demanded that Sarah Cramer submit to a sworn deposition in the civil suit she filed against Van Hook and the school district. Now Gitchoff would get a detailed preview of Sarah's testimony at Van Hook's criminal trial—a test-drive without obligation, to see how their cross-examination should run.

Weber attended the deposition at the office of Sarah's attorney, Elizabeth Levy, in Caseyville. Her husband, Mark, also a respected attorney, sat in with them. Lawyer Bill Gagen still defended Van Hook on the civil suit, and he was accompanied by Gitchoff's son and investigator, Drew Gitchoff. The Collinsville school district was represented by attorney David B. Stutsman of Belleville.

The only surprise in the crowd was Richard Van Hook. It was extraordinary for the defendant to sit in for a deposition; in this case, it struck Weber as strange beyond that.

Weber was impressed by the young woman who walked in and sat down at the table in the small conference room. This Sarah Cramer was a relatively confident young woman, dressed in a nice jacket and slacks. She wore just a slight touch of makeup and her hairstyle was just sophisticated enough. She looked exactly her age, and she carried herself well. She sat in the center on one side of the table, flanked by the Levys. Weber—little more than an interested observer today—sat off to one side. Gagen was directly across the table from Sarah, and Van Hook sat calmly to Gagen's right, on the opposite corner from Sarah.

Before long the conflict that Weber and Elizabeth Levy had predicted began simmering to the surface. As soon as Gagen asked Sarah whom she lived with, Elizabeth Levy objected and instructed her client not to answer. That was the plan Weber and Levy had drawn up to counter what they assumed would be the defense tactic of concentrating on Sarah's sexual history, unwed motherhood, and cohabitation with the baby's father, Jay Carr. Weber was adamant that Van Hook be prevented from using that kind of information in his defense; it was improper legally and, Weber thought, morally.

Sarah also had warned Weber that she was opposed to any effort to involve Jay in the case. She was so insistent that Weber was convinced the issue could be her Achilles' heel; if she were attacked there, it could unnerve her so badly that she could unravel on the stand.

As expected, Gagen said the question of Sarah's living arrangements would be certified—presented to a judge with a request that Sarah be ordered to answer it. That was okay with Weber; the certification process would continue until well after the trial. As the biographical questioning continued, Gagen asked if Sarah had been married. Weber thought Gagen was getting close to dangerous territory again. When Sarah explained that she had received some schooling at home while she was pregnant, Gagen asked when her baby was conceived and the date of birth. Levy objected again; anything relating to the baby was irrelevant.

Weber felt ill when Stutsman responded, "I think anything that involves her sex life would be pertinent." Another black eye for the school district and more proof of its insensitivity to the girls abused by its teacher. Not only did the district's lawyer show no sympathy or understanding of this girl's trauma, but he wanted to delve into unrelated sexual activities. Way to go, school board, Weber thought.

Gagen's questions about the actual incidents elicited little new from Sarah. But Weber wondered why Gagen was so tenacious about getting exact dates for the incidents; obviously that was important to the defense. Sarah wasn't able to provide much assistance. The first time was around her birthday, which was December 12; the second time was during the Christmas season.

As Sarah began to describe the actual sexual activity, Weber noticed the first flutter in Van Hook's calm demeanor. He shifted his body a bit, leaned forward onto the table, and stared intently as the young woman described how her teacher surprised her by unbuttoning her blouse. Weber kept watching Van Hook, and the conclusion was inescapable—he was enjoying the testimony.

After Sarah completed the descriptions of the two incidents with Van Hook, she explained that she had received schooling at home in the tenth grade because she was pregnant—"homebound," the school called the program. And her teacher, ironically, was Maria DeConcini. Gagen asked if Sarah told DeConcini about the encounters with Van Hook, and she said no. Weber thought it was small wonder the girl had not confided in DeConcini. But the suggestion reinforced his secret plan for a special moment in the trial that would begin so soon.

Sarah's innocence shone through when Gagen asked why she hadn't told the police or someone in authority about Van Hook.

"Well, I didn't want to break up a whole family. My gosh, I thought it was all my fault." She paused a beat and then added firmly, "But it is not; I know that now."

The beneficial effects of counseling, Weber thought.

Gagen asked how the incidents had affected Sarah, and a quiet voice offered a sad, simple, and intimate portrait of a girl battered by a storm no child should be forced to weather.

"Well, it has affected me a lot, because I started withdrawing from people, and my whole life. It just changed my whole outlook on everything. I didn't like anything anymore. I couldn't stand people. I thought everybody was out to get me. I thought everybody was talking behind my back. I didn't care about school anymore. I couldn't stand teachers. I even felt suicidal after this happened. I was ashamed to tell anybody except my best friend."

Sarah went on to offer some insight into life with Dick Van Hook when she recalled that, while she was baby-sitting for his children, they brought out some magazines containing pictures of naked people. The kids asked if she wanted to look at them, adding, "Everyone else who watches us does."

Gagen ended his questioning by asking if Sarah was friends with anyone on a long list of names—mostly the other Van Hook victims. As Sarah explained that she did not know them, or knew them only slightly, Weber thought again how the lack of contact between the girls proved there was no Machiavellian plot by these kids to "get" this teacher.

Stutsman began his inquiries with the most important issue for the school district. "He never made any sexual advances toward you at the school, is that correct?" He didn't get the answer he wanted.

"That is wrong," Sarah said with firm simplicity.

"Oh, that is wrong? Okay, tell me about that."

"Because I was supposed to watch his kids, but it turned out to be something totally different. Right around Christmastime he gave me a pair of earrings, wrapped up in Christmas stuff, and he kissed me on the cheek."

"Where did this occur?"

"In his room. He got the package out of his closet."

Van Hook had even supplied a cute anecdote about the gift. He was buying the earrings for Sarah at the jewelry counter at a department store when his wife walked up. She thought the earrings were for her—a natural assumption for a wife—and she walked away to avoid ruining the surprise.

Stutsman asked, "Well, did anything happen that, more or less, shocked you?"

Weber could hear the anger and frustration in Sarah's voice. "Yes, the whole thing. The kiss on the cheek at school—my teacher. It shocked me."

She described telling some of her friends, and hearing that Mark Richter had told teacher Charles Wandling that a colleague was having sex with a student.

Stutsman asked, "Do you know whether Mr. Wandling would have any particular interest in that?"

Sarah seemed taken aback and retorted with incredulity, "Well, I should hope so, being a teacher."

Stutsman asked why Sarah had gone with Van Hook to his parents' house, knowing that the first time she had been alone with him had resulted in the sexual incident.

"I thought I could find out . . ." She left the thought unfinished and sighed again. "I lived for a year with it going through my mind almost every day. Why did this happen to me? Why did my teacher do this? And I just couldn't stand it. It was just too much for me to handle. So, I thought . . . he said there was going to be a talk. I thought he was going to tell me why it happened."

Weber watched Sarah intently, and it was painful. She had been 13 the first time Van Hook assaulted her. With a child's mind she had been searching for an adult answer to events she couldn't understand. The distance between the child and the young woman was driven home again in a surprising and revealing answer to another of Stutsman's questions.

"When was it you started dating boys, how early in life?"

"Gosh, I never did get to go out on a date until after I was pregnant."

Weber's disdain for Stutsman's stiff, unsympathetic demeanor continued to grow as the attorney's questions became sharper.

"Had you ever had sexual intercourse before the eighth-grade incident with Mr. Van Hook?"

Elizabeth Levy objected, and Stutsman altered course a few degrees to concentrate on Sarah's baby. There were more objections to his questions about the father's identity, the dates of conception and birth, and finally, whether Sarah had intercourse with other people. And in another long series of questions, he asked whether Van Hook ever threatened Sarah to keep her quiet.

"The way he threatened me was by telling me that if I told anybody, it wouldn't do any good. Nobody would believe me because I was just a kid and he was the teacher."

The same line used on Katherine Howes, Weber remembered.

Sarah said one of the reasons she had not offered forceful resistance to Van Hook's advances was because she had been taught to obey her teachers. Stutsman cried, "You mean you are supposed to have intercourse with them if they say so?"

Weber was furious. What an insulting question, and what an abusive thing to say to this young woman. Weber wondered how Pam Klein would be reacting to this, and an old phrase popped into his mind. "Just another crow."

Reinforcement for that opinion came quickly. Stutsman asked if Sarah felt bad about having sex with the father of her baby, as she had about the sex with Van Hook.

"No, not at all."

"What is the difference?" Stutsman queried.

"Because I was in love then."

Elizabeth Levy used her turn to question her client to draw out an interesting recollection. She asked Sarah how Van Hook treated her at school after the sexual incidents.

"Well, he used to always give me looks like you would give your wife or somebody, like, 'We have got a secret.' You know, seductive looks."

"How did that make you feel?"

"It made me feel very uncomfortable. I couldn't stand to be there, but I had to."

The deposition was over. Weber hadn't learned much about the defense tactics, except the obvious plan to try to portray the victim as sexually active and to use her teenage pregnancy against her. Weber hoped the judge would agree with what seemed to be an insurmountable obstacle to that approach. Under the law, the question of consent absolutely cannot be an issue in a charge based on the tender age of the victim. The law assumes minors were incapable of giving legal consent for sex. Even if a hypothetical victim enthusiastically beds the entire football team in full pads and helmets, a teacher who has sex with her still has committed a felony. Adults are supposed to know better, after all. Weber just hoped the judge would agree with that view of the law.

* * *

Later that week, he found himself facing the height of the pretrial barrage—a hearing on Friday, February 4, three days before the start of the trial.

The first order of business was a ruling from the judge on the use of the documents from the crisis center he had ordered Klein to submit the day before. She was relieved when the judge announced there was nothing the defense attorneys were entitled to see; the notes from counseling and therapy sessions were confidential and did not address the facts in the charges.

But John Gitchoff pressed further, asking the judge if the records showed any history of sexual activities by the girls, or any evidence of promiscuity. Weber flinched; that confirmed his fears about a strategy suggesting the girls were sexually active, perhaps even suggesting the ridiculous notion that these prepubescent girls had seduced poor Mr. Van Hook.

Fortunately, Judge Ferguson wouldn't budge on the issue. He ruled that the notes fell under the state's mental-health code that required a client at a crisis center to approve the release of such records. It was a temporary victory for Weber; he was sure the issue of Sarah's sexual history would be argued again later.

Gitchoff next trotted out a surprise; he wanted a delay in the trial date because of a segment of the *20/20* news program on ABC just the evening before, focusing on sexual abuse of children, mentioning teachers, Boy Scout leaders, and even prosecutors among the offenders, and pointing out that they rarely went to prison for the crimes. Gitchoff's humor emerged as he grinned and noted that judges and defense lawyers had not been included on the list, and added that he was willing to give Weber credit for arranging a scheduling deal with ABC. As a result the program could prejudice a trial starting on Monday.

Again, Ferguson agreed with Weber that such a motion was premature. The judge said jurors could be questioned to determine if they had seen the program and whether they could set aside any opinion they had formed. Motion denied.

Wallis then turned to the most serious issue remaining—Weber's request to use the M.O. witnesses. Wallis and Ferguson discussed holding private hearings with each witness before she testified to determine if her story was admissible. But Weber offered an alternative: a full hearing Monday morning at which he would present testimony from the four girls he had decided to call—Sarah Cramer, Katherine Howes, Stephanie Knight, and Lori Parker. They were the only witnesses who would testify about sexual incidents, Weber explained, although other girls would be called to add corroborating details, such as seeing the four victims in the Bear's Cave with Van Hook. Weber added a gibe at Wallis's complaint about that much testimony being confusing by sneering, "I don't think it will be confusing; I think it will be overwhelming. And I think that's what they are worried about."

Ferguson accepted Weber's plan, and denied the defense attorneys' motion to ban the supporting witnesses. Weber took it as a compliment from Ferguson when he said he was confident the prosecutor knew the bounds when presenting evidence to support witnesses in an M.O. case. Weber was starting to feel a lot more comfortable with this judge, after all. He was reading the law before the hearings and making sound, reasonable rulings.

The defense had a couple more rounds to fire. Drawing on details from Sarah Cramer's deposition, Wallis argued that the charges should be dismissed because some of her friends knew about the alleged crimes, but failed to report them within the three-year statute of limitations.

That irritated Weber. It was a faulty argument on an issue that already was settled. He read the definition of a person with a legal duty to report a crime, adding that it obviously referred to someone in an official capacity in a government agency. "That doesn't mean telling your girlfriend," he snapped with a condescending glance at Wallis.

Motion denied. But Wallis tried another tack, arguing that some of the perjury charges should be dismissed because Van Hook had responded with terms such as "Not

that I know of"—not exactly denials. Weber responded
that such an interpretation of the law would emasculate
perjury charges and allow everyone to lie under oath. As
Weber's frustration escalated, he popped, "I find it hard
to believe that Van Hook doesn't remember taking a girl
to his mother's house in September of 1977 and having
intercourse with her, and being surprised by the mailman.
But that's a question of fact for the jury."

Ferguson almost chuckled as he noted that the perjury
laws and previous cases were somewhat confusing and
added, "I will have a ruling for you Monday morning. I
am going to read some more cases and be further confused."

On the sixth, Weber violated his previously unbending
rule against working on Sunday; he thought God would
allow an exception for this. With the combined efforts of
Virginia Rulison, Pam Klein, and Dennis Kuba, he assembled all of the girls likely to be witnesses at the courthouse in Edwardsville. Virginia had scored a major coup
in getting a key to the building, and Klein and Kuba escorted the girls—trailing long scarves and dropped
gloves—to the small courtroom on the third floor.

The girls reacted almost as if they had entered a mag-
nificent cathedral. The unusual quiet of the empty courthouse left the girls wide-eyed, speaking in hushed tones,
and moving carefully, as if not to disturb some unseen but
powerful presence. They became even more serious as
they entered the courtroom and somberly awaited their
turns to climb onto the witness stand they had feared for
so long.

As the girls lined up on the benches, their feet swing-
ing slightly above the floor, Klein and Kuba described the
process as simply as they could. They tried to predict
what would happen and what the girls would be asked on
the stand. They explained what the judge's job was, and
where all the parties would be sitting—including Mr. Van
Hook. At that table, right there, the investigators calmly
told their young friends. All eyes turned toward the table.

From there, the girls filed over to Weber's office across

the street. One by one the prosecutor met briefly with them to renew their acquaintance and reassure them that he would try to protect them on the witness stand, and to keep their time there short and sweet. One girl asked what she should do if the defense attorneys yelled at her; another worried that she wouldn't know the answers to some questions. Weber was not particularly comfortable with children, so he was hoping these visits the day before the trial would build as strong a bond as possible. With the major witnesses, Weber took a few extra minutes to go over their statements again briefly, emphasizing the important points needed to establish the M.O.

As he talked to Katherine Howes, Weber stressed that she had to remember how Van Hook had told her that he dreamed about her and that she made him feel younger. She still was an emotional wreck, crying and shaking, dreading every minute of the time she would have to face another crowd and tell the story that so many adults seemed to disbelieve. She asked if she would have to talk about the sexual activity again, and Weber apologized for the certainty that she would. He hoped stressing those phrases would give her something solid to concentrate on. She deserved at least that much when she faced another battering.

CHAPTER 12

Monday morning, February 7, 1983. Don Weber knew this was a big day for many people, but his thoughts mostly were on a group of kids who should be out selling Girl Scout cookies instead of waiting to testify in a trial. These girls would never forget what was about to happen, regardless of the result. If Richard Van Hook were convicted, they would be able to return to their lives and their community with dignity and credibility; they would have their faith restored in an imperfect and cumbersome system; and they would see someone who had committed heinous crimes punished. But if he was acquitted, the girls' reputations would suffer even more, the acrimonious outcry against them in their hometown would increase intolerably, and their already fragile emotional conditions could be destroyed for life.

It was a big day for Don Weber, too. As an elected official pursuing an already unpopular prosecution, he had a great deal at stake. And, it was his hometown, too. He faced wily and determined opponents who would keep the pressure on him relentlessly as he struggled to prove a case based on intricate and sometimes confusing details, supported by a complicated theory about "modus operandi"—not exactly an everyday term to most people. Would a jury be able to grasp the subtle idea that a common theme in otherwise unrelated events helped prove these allegations? The hearing this morning could make or break this difficult case, and Weber was worried about how far this judge would go in support of the theories Weber had advanced.

And he couldn't help but think this morning about Richard Van Hook. He certainly arose today to face incredible pressure and strain. The day he once was so sure would never come had arrived, and there was nothing he could do to stop it. He had no choice but to sit in a courtroom and listen to a succession of girls tell the whole world about his secret weaknesses and bizarre practices with children, things most people surely would find perverted and sick. He would have to endure even more newspaper and television news accounts of these allegations, and even more stares when he tried to go about his business in public. And, most of all, he had to keep up his strength and his facade of innocence for his family, friends, colleagues, and community.

It was a big day for a lot of people. Weber hadn't counted, however, on how many of those people would show up at the courthouse in Edwardsville. In fact, he felt as if he had walked into the middle of a proverbial media circus. Spectators, relatives, and reporters were lined up several rows deep outside the double doors to Judge Ferguson's courtroom; Weber slipped through the side door to the judge's chambers.

Ferguson called the hearing to order as Weber and Randy Massey joined John Gitchoff and Jim Wallis before the bench. Wallis asked that the public and press be kept outside while Weber presented the testimony from the girls to support his M.O. argument. Since the whole point of the hearing was to determine if that evidence was admissible, Wallis argued, making it public before the judge ruled would be prejudicial and damaging to Van Hook. Weber objected, and Ferguson ruled quickly that the hearing would be open to the public. With some good-humored trepidation, Ferguson asked his bailiff to open the doors, and the crowd pushed noisily in.

Ferguson's courtroom was one of the smallest in the building, a 30-by-30 foot box with only two rows of short benches in the back for spectators and reporters. No more than 30 people could be squeezed onto the seats. But associate judges got the smallest accommodations; the huge courtrooms at the other end of the third floor were reserved for civil suits. That's where rich and powerful lawyers appeared before judges who often came from their ranks.

As the hearing began, Weber wasted no time going on the attack, ripping into Van Hook's plans for an affirmative defense based on his supposed belief that Sarah Cramer was married. One of the exceptions to the law prohibiting sex with a girl under 17 was if she was married. But, Weber said almost sarcastically, thinking the girl was married wasn't a recognized defense; the defense would have to prove she actually was married.

Gitchoff conceded nothing, arguing strenuously that Sarah's sexual activities before, during, and after her contact with Van Hook were absolutely essential to the defense. When Gitchoff said calmly, "We can prove that this girl was sexually mature for her years, prior to the dates of these alleged incidents," Weber knew the battle was joined.

Gitchoff noted that Sarah testified at her deposition that she met Jay Carr while she was in the eighth or ninth grades, within the period covered by the charges against Van Hook. Sarah's daughter was delivered in March 1979; that meant Sarah was sexually active in June 1978, the end of the time frame listed in the indictment.

With his wry, understated humor Gitchoff added, "Assuming that the pregnancy was not an immaculate conception, there would have to have been some intercourse."

Despite his flippant remark, he was quite serious about the legal point involving Sarah's relationship with the baby's father. "If they, in fact, had everything going in a marriage relationship but a marriage certificate, then I feel that's what the law intended. I don't think it's the marriage certificate that is the point; I think it's the activity and, in particular, the sexual activity."

Weber could feel his frustration rising as he responded. "First of all, Judge, the statute says that the child has been married; it doesn't say that the defendant reasonably believed she was. Second of all, Sarah has unequivocally stated that she met the father of her child after the last incident with Van Hook."

Making yet another trip around the bush, Weber said that a victim's prior sex acts or even her reputation for sexual behavior were not admissible in a case where consent was not an issue. And, he said for what seemed like the hundredth time, consent cannot be an issue in what essentially is a case of statutory rape.

Wallis jumped into the fray by noting that the father of Sarah's baby was listed as a witness, and the defense had to be able to define the relationship between Sarah and Jay Carr. That did it for Weber. Sarah already had warned him against involving Jay in any way, and she had become emotional at the mere mention of his name during her deposition. With the defense preparing to make Jay Carr an issue, Weber could see he had only one choice.

"Judge, I am not going to call him as a witness."

Gitchoff snapped that the defense might call him. Weber was starting to steam as he turned to the judge. "They want to subpoena him so they can get things in the back door that they can't get in the front door."

Judge Ferguson took over, and ruled in no uncertain terms. Prior sexual conduct was irrelevant to the charge of indecent liberties with a child because consent was not an issue. And, the judge added, married means married, pure and simple. Since the law referred only to victims who previously were married—not who previously were sexually active—Van Hook would be barred from using that as a defense because Sarah simply had not been married.

Weber grinned. The judge he had been so worried about—the one he had tried to force into stepping aside—was ruling for the prosecution right down the line.

Then it was time for the real challenge—the presentation of the evidence to determine if the four girls Weber wanted to use as M.O. witnesses would be permitted to testify. For this hearing, they would not have to give complete accounts of what had happened—just the details that were common to so many of Van Hook's lecherous teacher-student conferences.

Sarah Cramer was first. As she had at her deposition, she seemed poised and confident, easily the most mature

and strongest of the victims. Weber asked a few easy biographical questions to give her a chance to relax, and
then moved through her time as a student of Richard Van
Hook and to the visit to his home in Maryville for the
first sexual contact. As she began to describe the entire
incident, Weber decided to make it simpler for her as he
interrupted, "Did he have intercourse with you?"

"Yes, sir," she said firmly.

With that established, Weber took Sarah through the
litany of lines and little moves that defined Van Hook's
pedophilia. He told Sarah he wished she were older, and
that she made him feel as if he were back in high school.
He had dreams about being in a motel with her. He said
she was the only girl he was involved with, and asked if
she were on birth-control pills. He sometimes talked
about his wife, even showing Sarah the towel they used
at sexually inconvenient times. He asked Sarah to baby-
sit for him, offered her alcohol, and gave her gifts that included money and earrings. He told her not to tell anyone
what had happened, because no one would believe her,
anyway.

Sarah's innocent confidence came through with Weber's last question, when he asked if Van Hook had undressed her completely for these encounters. "Yep," she
snapped bluntly.

John Gitchoff's cross-examination zeroed in immediately on the date of the first incident, and he pushed her
for a definition of "around" her birthday. Two to four
weeks was around the date to her, she said. The rest of
Gitchoff's questioning focused on the dates involved in
all the incidents and comments cited by Sarah, while
barely touching on the M.O. argument. Weber again wondered why the exact dates were so important.

Stephanie Knight took the stand next—another slim,
dark-haired young woman who ran through the list of Van
Hook's comments and activities. Not only had he
dreamed about her, he said, but he once talked in his
sleep and called out her nickname, "Steph."

Gitchoff's cross-examination again dealt with the
dates, refusing to accept answers such as "late fall" and

narrowing that down to "September to November." Stephanie balked when Gitchoff asked her to demonstrate the kind of short kiss she described as "just a peck, you know." When she wouldn't do it, Gitchoff displayed his lack of self-consciousness, puckered up, and made a little smooching sound. That was it, she said.

When she seemed a little confused about the dates he was asking for, Gitchoff switched to his schmoozing style and said, "I don't want to confuse you, and I am not trying to trick you, honey."

Weber chuckled; Gitchoff absolutely was trying to confuse her, and it looked like he might be able to do it to all of the young witnesses.

Gitchoff surprised Weber by asking Stephanie, "Did he indicate to you that his penis had a name?" Why would the defense want to bring that kinky tidbit out on cross-examination?

"Yes," she said softly.

"Okay. What was that name?"

"George" was the matter-of-fact reply.

If Weber was somewhat surprised, the reporters sitting behind him were flabbergasted. This was the first they had heard of this penile peccadillo, and it struck two of the veteran beat reporters as so adolescently silly that, as they looked at each other in amazement, it gave them an uncontrollable case of the third-grade giggles. Two tough, cynical, trial-weary reporters were reduced to unrestrained snickering in the back of the courtroom. One finally spun off the bench and fled the courtroom; the wave of laughter could be heard echoing down the hall outside the doors. Judge Ferguson shook his head, grateful there was no jury to observe that display.

At the defense table, Richard Van Hook lowered his head.

Weber's third witness was Lori Parker, a 12-year-old who seemed incredibly cool for her age. She recounted how Van Hook took her into his little room and French-kissed her; told her that she made him feel younger, like he was in high school again; told her he didn't care if this got him fired, but didn't want her to think he was a rapist;

and offered to pay her a dollar if she stayed after school with him. She explained how she and Sally Morton, who had just endured a similar encounter, ran to the rest room to cry.

The recklessness of the activity by Van Hook that day suddenly hit Weber. Was this man finally out of control, after all those years of careful planning and calculated manipulation? Why had he risked everything, calling two little girls out of class for a chance to corner them, endangering a life and career for a kiss and a grab? The tragedy of this man's life began to sink in. Van Hook really was very sick; he needed help.

Lori drove home the innocence in the girls again during long cross-examination by Gitchoff as she described how Van Hook "touched my buttocks, or whatever you call it." And, as had Stephanie, Lori refused to pucker up and simulate a kiss for Gitchoff's convenience.

Finally, it was time for Katherine Howes, the witness Weber worried about the most. He had to handle her gently, and he tried to put her at ease by opening with, "Katherine, I know you are nervous, but do you remember your name?" His little joke didn't help much; she was shaking as she sat there, twisting some kind of little cloth in her hands, painfully reminiscent of the first night with Pam Klein and Dennis Kuba.

Weber hoped she would remember the important points they discussed, and he asked if Van Hook had said anything about their age difference.

"He wished I was older and he said that I made him feel like he was in high school again," the flat answer came back with mechanical memorization.

And what did Van Hook say about his wife while he was wooing this little girl? "He said that his wife said he wasn't as turned on to her as he used to be."

Had he warned Katherine not to tell? "He said that I shouldn't tell anybody because it could get him in trouble, and it could ruin my dad's reputation." That was the answer that made Weber's blood boil. Van Hook had pushed every button with these girls.

Katherine recited the list of gifts—three pairs of earrings, a couple of boards with slogans carved on them, a key ring with the word "love" on it, and finally, a folder with Winnie the Pooh on the cover and a five-dollar bill tucked inside.

Gitchoff again conducted a long cross, even with this shaky witness. As he got into detailed descriptions of the sexual encounters and intercourse, Weber finally offered an objection that was sustained by the judge.

Gitchoff's next question was, "Were there other occasions that he masturbated? Do you know what I mean by masturbate?"

"I think so. I don't know. I'm not used to all of these big words."

Weber loved those answers; they could come only from kids caught up in something they really didn't understand. No one would believe these girls were making this up when they didn't even know the terminology.

Gitchoff pushed on. "All right. Did he play with his penis in your company?"

"I don't know. I wasn't paying much attention to him. I was, like, frozen. I wasn't paying much attention to anything he was doing."

After Ferguson sustained several more objections to questions about the rude details, Gitchoff was done and Weber quickly excused Katherine; that completed his evidence on the M.O. issue.

Another of Gitchoff's young associates, Gregory Becker, handled the argument against the M.O. witnesses. In a long statement Becker complained that the effect of calling so many girls to testify about the "modus operandi" would be prejudicial, and devastatingly unfair to Van Hook. "It's too overwhelming," he said. Becker insisted that M.O. witnesses had to relate only to identity of a perpetrator, and identity was not an issue in this case. Weber looked at Becker askance and wondered where that came from. Indeed, identity had nothing to do with Weber's case, nothing to do with the M.O. that Van Hook had applied, and nothing to do with the legal use of M.O. evidence in a trial.

Becker said there were more differences in the girls'

stories than similarities that suggested "a common author." With Sarah Cramer, Van Hook was very secretive and careful, taking the girl to his home for some quick and blatant moves—no clever seduction, just "straight sex." Becker said bluntly, "He didn't ask her preference for sex; he just took it." Even to Weber, that sounded like an awfully harsh way for Becker to describe the actions of his own client.

With Stephanie Knight, Becker said, the allegations were that Van Hook had carefully seduced her, but had been reckless enough to risk being caught at school. Becker called the activity with Stephanie an affair, not indecent liberties.

The basic and numerous differences in the approaches described by the girls suggested totally different psychological makeups—the actions of two different men, not alternative sexual techniques by one person. Becker said a valid and significant M.O. point with evidentiary value would be if Sarah Cramer echoed Stephanie's memory of "George" as a nickname for Van Hook's penis. That would be devastating because even two fertile imaginations couldn't come up with a common fact like that independently. But Becker insisted that the "vast differences" in the approaches described by all the girls should eliminate them as witnesses at trial.

Weber stood slowly as he said he could agree with many of the descriptions of the evidence offered by Becker. But then Weber retorted, "I just don't think he was in the same courtroom that everybody else was in this morning." How could anyone argue that grounds for M.O. witnesses had not been established when Sarah and Katherine agreed on 17 points, Sarah and Stephanie agreed on 14, and Sarah and Lori agreed on at least 8? Of course, there were differences. "It took him different ways, in his capacity as teacher, to seduce these different girls," Weber snapped.

As Judge Ferguson leaned forward to issue his ruling, Weber's guts tightened; this was the defining moment for this case. The tension in the courtroom could be felt by everyone as they awaited the decision.

The judge noted that this kind of crime does not provide much evidence other than the recollections of the people involved. So any other proper evidence is valuable, and the jury must decide what it proves. There were enough common factors to outweigh the inherent prejudice against Van Hook and allow all four girls to testify. And Ferguson quickly denied the defense motion to dismiss the perjury counts.

Weber was jubilant; he had won the major points in a tough trial. He would have been happy with approval of three of the girls, but he had all four. He kept the M.O. evidence in and kept evidence about Sarah's sexual history out.

Now Weber's primary concern was handling his delicate witnesses in the increasing pressure of the trial. They were the most fragile witnesses Weber ever had presented, and the youngest by far. Other sexual assault victims had suffered as badly from the attack, but they hadn't had to face the added injury of a community that rejected their stories so hatefully.

The girls had told Pam Klein that testifying at the hearing had not been as bad as they had feared. Weber hoped they would hold up during what was to come.

Selection of the jury began after lunch Monday. Most observers were predicting a slow process of sorting out the people tainted by the massive publicity about the Van Hook case. But Weber's hunch was right again; only a few of the people had paid any attention, and most of them could remember few details.

Weber had picked a lot of juries and knew there really was only one important question, with only one acceptable answer. He looked each juror in the eye, pointed directly at Van Hook, and asked, "If I prove to you that Richard Van Hook is guilty, will you convict him?" The only answer was an unhesitating yes. Anything, equivocation or qualification of the answer, and that juror was disqualified.

Weber had decided to get as many men on the panel as possible. Experience had taught him a strange irony about

jurors on sex cases—women were tougher on the female
victims than men. He hadn't found a satisfactory explanation for that paradox. It seemed women should be more
sympathetic; they ought to be able to empathize with a
sexually abused woman. Wouldn't they want to send a
clear message that any man who committed that despicable act would be dealt with harshly? Or did they fear that
a charge like that could be filed against their sons or hus-
bands? Women were ready to impose the death penalty in
the blink of an eye, but sex cases were different. Were
they reluctant because convicting a man of exercising that
violent power over a female seemed an admission that all
women were vulnerable?

The men, on the other hand, were almost ruthless
judges of sex crimes. The male juror probably saw his
wife or his daughter as the victim, and felt a primal protective urge for vengeance. Weber figured the men also
wanted to send a message to women—don't judge all of
us by this beast's transgressions.

During the questioning of the jurors, only three choices
caused Weber some concern. The first was a former client
of Gitchoff's from a civil case; Weber left him on the
panel. When Gitchoff later asked why, Weber couldn't resist tweaking the old pro. "Because everyone who knows
you knows that all of your clients are guilty." For once
Gitchoff failed to see the humor in such a remark.

Another question arose over an administrator from the
Edwardsville school district, where Van Hook had taught
before going home to Collinsville. Weber certainly
wouldn't want any teachers on the jury, but the natural
conflict between teachers and administrators might work
in the prosecution's favor. As he approved the juror, Weber also wondered if the man had heard any rumors about
Van Hook from his time in Edwardsville.

The third question came up when one of the jurors was
identified as the uncle of Charles Bosworth, Jr., the reporter
covering the trial for the *St. Louis Post-Dispatch*. Like his
journalist nephew, Calvin Bosworth—known as "Pokey"—
had grown up in Venice and Madison, Gitchoff's home turf;
Pokey and Gitchoff had known each other all their lives.

During a recess, Weber asked Charlie Bosworth if there was a reason to disqualify his uncle. The reporter shrugged and said the only factor he could think of was that Pokey had three daughters and a granddaughter he worshiped and that the rangy, tough-as-nails railroader probably would rip limb from limb any man who messed with them. That was good enough for Weber; besides Pokey Bosworth probably was well acquainted with Gitchoff's reputation for guilty clients.

The panel eventually seated was very close to what Weber was looking for—11 men and 1 woman. There were no kooks—just solid citizens Weber hoped would be repulsed, and ultimately angered, by what had happened in the sanctity of the schoolhouse, between a trusted teacher and the children he was sworn to nurture.

CHAPTER 13

The tension in Richard Van Hook's face was obvious the moment he stepped into the hallway on the third floor on Tuesday morning, February 8. As he and his wife walked stiffly toward the courtroom for the start of the trial—shadowed every step of the way by television cameras—some people thought the look on his face seemed pained, anxious, maybe even frightened.

But that was not how Don Weber read it. Van Hook was nervous, to be sure, but his eyes still seemed challenging. "You can't prove it," the look said to the prosecutor. It wasn't defiance; it wasn't confidence. Weber thought it was, perhaps, just a solid belief that no one would reject the word of a respectable teacher and accept a bunch of wild allegations by some spiteful kids. It was that view that so many in Collinsville held so fervently. Everyone Van Hook knew had reassured him, patted him on the back, encouraged him, and vilified the sluts who accused him. No one, save John Gitchoff perhaps, had warned him that he might be in grave danger from Don Weber and the case he had assembled with that pack of traumatized little girls. On this morning, Weber could see a classic Greek tragedy unfolding. This man's own actions were dragging him down, finally beyond salvation.

The drama would play in front of another packed house. Bailiff Wes Edwards had to remind would-be spectators several times that seating was limited, and that they would have to remain orderly as they waited a chance to get a seat. Wes winked at the reporters, and promised to get them in first. It was a scene that would be replayed daily during the trial.

Weber had spent the night before trying to relax by

watching the television mini-series *Winds of War.* He had learned long ago that furious, last-minute preparations were fruitless; if he wasn't ready by now, it was too late.

But he was nervous as he faced the jury to present his opening statement. He started by explaining that the grand jury had indicted Van Hook on these charges, implying that the defendant was not the victim of some evil scheme by the prosecutor and the girls. Then he moved to the crux of the case; the evidence would show that Van Hook was a teacher in the public schools—a public employee—who exploited his position to take sexual advantage of the victims.

Then he stumbled, finding himself wide awake in the nightmare that haunts every trial lawyer.

"The girl who's on trial . . ." He sucked in his breath. Had he really said that? Damn! How do you repair that kind of slip? "Not the girl who's on trial," he said slowly. "But the girl at issue here—the defendant is on trial—is Sarah Cramer."

As his mind raced, he realized how psychologically telling that slip of the tongue really was. Everyone knew it was precisely the girls who would be on trial here. Anyway, there was no choice but to plunge ahead as if nothing had happened. He moved directly to the theory of "modus operandi," explaining that three other girls would support Sarah's testimony by telling incredibly similar accounts of sexual contact with Van Hook. He described the progress of the investigation, with each girl being sought out by the police rather than coming forward with information against Van Hook. Weber hoped that would let the jurors know immediately that this was not the result of a plot by a sinister bunch of scorned schoolgirls.

Next, Weber focused on the law against indecent liberties with a child, explaining to the jury that the issue of consent, and traditional ideas about rape, did not apply in this case.

"I want to emphasize to you that whether or not Sarah Cramer wanted to do this—and the evidence will be that she did not—she was not raped. She wasn't hit on the head. But she was 13 years old at the time of the first incident—14 at the time of the second. And that's the kind of girl the legislature meant for this law to protect—someone who, by law, is subject to indiscretion. And she's not responsible for that."

Weber described each incident completely, listing the specific details that made Sarah's account so believable. Even Van Hook's wife would corroborate a damning detail—the towel in the nightstand. That was proof beyond bare accusations, especially when viewed in light of Van Hook's convenient lapse of memory concerning the towel while testifying before the grand jury.

Then Weber approached a delicate point in the story—Sarah's return to Van Hook's house to baby-sit shortly after being forced into sex there. That could be difficult to understand for some adults—especially jurors unfamiliar with sexually abused children.

"You have to remember this in the context of a 13-year-old girl, after she had assured herself that there really would be kids there this time. Van Hook had shown her the tickets, so she knew this would be a legitimate baby-sitting job. Now, we're not saying at any point here that Van Hook broke her arm or threatened her with a gun or knife. What we are saying is that he's a 34-year-old man, and she's 13; and he's using his position of influence to lure her into his web, and to seduce her."

Weber followed that theme to explain the second sexual incident; Sarah was a confused child looking for answers to a painful question about a teacher she had respected. But he added that this encounter, too, would be corroborated by another Van Hook woman; this time Stella would confirm that prophylactics were kept under the corner of her mattress—a fact Sarah couldn't possibly have known unless she had been in that bedroom and was told about those prophylactics. Weber even offered a world-class understatement by saying Stella wouldn't be a willing witness.

He returned to the M.O. theory, this time invoking a familiar, comforting image. "We have in this case evidence of a design or plan—what Jack Webb referred to on *Dragnet* as the 'M.O.' Basically, the theory on M.O., in simple terms, is like this: If you have an animal that quacks like a duck, and it's got a bill like a duck, and it's got feathers like a duck, and it flaps its wings like a duck, then you can feel reasonably sure that you are dealing with a duck."

In this case, Weber explained, four girls who didn't know each other told similar stories about being molested by the same teacher who approached them at school, used the same lines, took them into the same little office, gave them the same kind of gifts, and warned them about the consequences if they told what happened. Ten to 15 M.O. points made this child molester look exactly like a duck.

Weber went into greater detail about the acts involving Katherine Howes than he would have normally in an opening statement. But he feared she might crumble on the stand, coming apart before she could tell her heartbreaking story. So Weber told it for her; at least the jury would hear it.

After that he began to argue his case—not exactly proper form for opening statements. But if Gitchoff let it slide, Weber would press the advantage until he drew an objection. Finally, that moment came as he urged the jurors to ask themselves how Sarah Cramer would know so many intimate details about the homes and lives of the Van Hook family unless she were telling the truth about what happened. Once Gitchoff objected to Weber's argument, the prosecutor wrapped it up. He had talked for about 20 minutes.

Gitchoff chose to reserve the opening statement for the defense team until the beginning of its case. Weber felt that tactic was a bad move, but he understood it. Some lawyers preferred to lay out the framework just before their witnesses filled in the blanks. But Weber believed that strategy gave the prosecution too many free-throws during the three or four days it would take to get through its case. The jury ought to have some idea of what the defense attorney's explanation was while the prosecution's witnesses testified.

The first witness for the prosecution was Dennis Kuba—another tradition for Weber. He had learned long ago to establish the credibility of the investigation, and the investigator, as early as possible. Kuba was a good-looking guy who connected well with jurors, and he had compelling evidence. He explained how he had found Sarah, taken her statement, and then corroborated her story with witnesses, including Stella Van Hook. Kuba also testified to another bit of evidence Weber always presented—the distance between the important locations. Kuba explained that it was just three-tenths of a mile, a two-minute drive, from Collinsville High School to Stella's house on Constance Street.

Kuba produced the earrings Sarah had received from Van Hook, and the yearbook the teacher had signed for her. Weber let the jurors wonder about the inscription; he would save that for a dramatic reading later.

Gitchoff's persona as the friendly uncle was engaged as he began cross-examining Kuba; the defense attorney addressed the agent comfortably as Dennis—even Denny—and got him to agree that it wasn't unusual for students and teachers to write in yearbooks.

"Did you ever do it, Dennis, when you were in school?"

"Yes, sir."

"So did I"—the affable defender grinned as he segued into another self-effacing little joke—"but I could never get anybody to say anything nice about me. But the fact that she has it in there is not really unusual."

Weber decided to wipe the grins off the jurors' faces and remind them this was serious business. "Your Honor, I'm going to object to whether it's unusual or not. That's for the jury to decide."

Ferguson agreed. "I'll sustain that. The jury will disregard that statement."

Weber was not opposed to a light moment now and then, but he knew better than to let the defense attorney laugh the prosecutor's case out of the courtroom with the first witness.

With the scene now set properly by Kuba, Weber called Sarah Cramer to the stand to recount what happened for the umpteenth time, but the one that really counted. He hoped putting her on so early would catch Gitchoff by surprise, perhaps before he really was ready. And an early appearance by Sarah gave Weber the rest of the trial to corroborate her story.

As the young woman stepped through the doors at the back of the courtroom and walked up the aisle surrounded by Van Hook's friends and relatives, she looked like she was running the gauntlet; Weber felt sorry for her. But she seemed ready. Weber walked to the end of the jury box farthest from the witness stand, so Sarah would have to speak loudly enough to be heard by the jurors and would be looking at them as she testified.

Sarah tagged all the bases in confident testimony that Weber was sure was effective with the 12 people in the box. She was consistent with all of her previous testimony, denying the defense any easy chances to impeach her on cross-examination. When Weber asked her why she ducked her head as Van Hook pulled into his garage that day, Sarah responded, "Well, because I was brought up that you are supposed to respect your teachers, and obey them." Perfect.

When Van Hook undressed her in his son's bedroom, did she try to stop him? "No, I was too afraid. I was just frozen." Just right again. Weber anticipated that the jury would hear that same description from Katherine Howes later.

Sarah's eyes were moist as she said later, "I couldn't believe it was happening. I thought I would wake up and it would be just a bad dream."

She supported everything with believable details. When Van Hook showed her the towel in the nightstand, he explained that there had been a chance his wife would be menstruating on their wedding night, so they asked a priest if it was okay to have sex.

"Did you think it was strange that he was talking about his wife's menstrual period with you?" Weber asked.

"Yeah, I was very embarrassed for her," was the genuine reply.

Why didn't Sarah tell school officials what happened? "I thought they would all just kind of gang up on me because I was saying something about another teacher," she said. Perceptive, thought Weber, given what had happened.

"Did you feel that Van Hook himself would do something to you?"

"Yes. I was afraid that he would flunk me."

To educate the jury on how this kind of abuse affected girls in the real world, Weber asked Sarah how she felt after the first incident. "I felt horrible. I was ashamed and embarrassed," Sarah said softly. Weber hoped the jury could see this was no casual quickie between a sexually precocious teenager and a popular teacher.

Weber wanted to be sure the jurors understood why a girl would baby-sit for a man after he had abused her. Weber had Sarah remind them she was in the eighth grade and had asked to see the tickets as proof to overcome her disbelief. Then he asked flatly why she would go back to his house. "Because I needed the money."

Weber also gave the jury a look into this girl's mind by asking why she was willing to talk to Van Hook, at his request, in his classroom a year later.

"Well, I always wondered why my teacher did this, and I always carried it around in my head, trying to figure it out. I was hoping he would explain it to me, and apologize, or give me an explanation."

As Sarah described the incident at Stella Van Hook's house, Weber had her walk to a blackboard in the center of the courtroom and draw the floor plan of the house, another effective bit of corroboration. She even explained that she was worried when she realized no one else was home. When Van Hook sat down on the couch, she sat down on the floor on the other side of the coffee table, keeping the table between them for distance and protection.

Her youth was apparent when she described her reaction to Van Hook showing her the packages of condoms under his parents' mattress. "I didn't know what to do. I just thought it was kind of gross." What was her reaction to Van Hook's joke about his dad still needing condoms at his age? "I just thought it was kind of sickening."

Weber glanced at Richard Van Hook. He wore a medium-blue suit and coordinating tie. His hair was combed neatly. He was listening with interest, but there was no real reaction. Weber interpreted the look on his face—perhaps a combination of pain and confused concern—as the mask so often worn by a perpetrator. A guilty man listening to the truth about his crime never knows quite how he should look; his guilt prevents him from being genuine. He has too much to protect. He is too worried about what the jury is thinking and seeing. An innocent man is less concerned about appearances. He reacts naturally because he knows something is wrong here, and he wants everyone else to know that. An innocent man reacts; a guilty man just acts.

Weber turned back to Sarah. What did she think when Van Hook pushed her back onto his parents' bed?

"Oh, my God. It's going to happen again," she said quietly.

After she described the repeat performance, this time interrupted briefly by the mailman's arrival on the front porch, Weber couldn't hide his disgust. With a cutting edge of revulsion in his voice, he asked, "What did he do when he was finished with you?"

"He took me home ... He dropped me off a couple blocks away so that my mom wouldn't know that he brought me home."

Sarah explained that she had told no one but her best friend, Belinda Barnett; her boyfriend; and eventually another friend, Mark Richter. She had shared the bottles of alcohol with Debbie Weaver, and told her where they came from.

"Now Sarah, did you ever go to the police with this story? Did you contact the police with this?"

"No, never," she said firmly.

"Why not?"

"Because I was ashamed of it."

Weber delved deeper into the pathology of child molestation.

"Did you think it was your fault that this happened?"

"I did at first."

"Do you now?"

"No."

As Weber sat down, he wondered how John Gitchoff would approach this witness. He had to tread a fine line. He couldn't let her off unscathed, but he couldn't batter her into tears and risk losing the jury's sympathy. He was faced with a good witness who offered no cracks of inconsistencies to chisel into chasms of doubt for the jury.

Gitchoff's tone was soft and friendly, and he called the witness by her first name. He immediately established that she was suing Van Hook and the school district for money, and then he wondered why she didn't file the suit six years ago, right after the "alleged" abuse.

"Because I was too ashamed about it then."

"Okay. And six years later, you were not ashamed?"

"That's right," she said almost defiantly. She was beginning to tense up a bit. She knew Gitchoff was the enemy, and she was growing wary again. Weber hoped she could withstand the pressure.

"Okay." Gitchoff smiled.

"Well, I still am. But I have told everybody now, so it really doesn't matter."

She never complained to anyone about what happened, Gitchoff wondered.

"I complained to my best friend."

"Well, did you complain to her, or did you just tell her what happened?"

"I told her, and I was crying, and trying to deal with it."

That was a new scene for Weber, conjuring up an image of yet another wracking moment pushed on this victim by that teacher—the one sitting right over there. Sarah was beginning to reveal more about the emotions that accompanied this abuse.

Gitchoff ventured into dangerous territory. "A little later on, you testified, you told your boyfriend?"

"Yes," Sarah said softly.

"And what's his name?"

"Jay Carr," was the response in a voice that was beginning to crack. Alarms began sounding in the prosecutor's head.

After Sarah said she told Jay almost two years after the first incident, Gitchoff asked, "Do you recall what the occasion was that you wanted to tell Jay Carr?"

Weber objected; that was too far and it violated the judge's earlier rulings. Ferguson called the attorneys to the bench. Weber said Gitchoff knew the answer was that she told Jay because she was pregnant; that was off-limits. Gitchoff argued that he had a right to ask what made Sarah decide to tell Jay. Gitchoff was reaching for the back door again, but Ferguson sustained the objection.

Seconds later, Gitchoff asked why Sarah chose to tell Jay Carr two years after the alleged incident. Weber's objection sent the attorneys into the judge's chambers for arguments outside the presence of the jury. Gitchoff said Weber's objection was premature because no one knew what Sarah's answer would be. Weber offered to bring Sarah into chambers and ask her, and Gitchoff angrily responded, "I don't want this stuff. I've got her on cross-examination now, Mr. Weber."

But the judge liked Weber's idea and had Sarah brought into the already crowded chambers. She was beginning to sob as she sat down between Weber and Gitchoff in front of the judge's desk; the tension was peeling back her resolve. The judge asked Sarah for her answer. She began to cry and mumbled, "We were just talking."

Gitchoff wanted to know why she would wait two years to tell Jay Carr, after protecting the secret she shared only with Belinda Barnett for so long. Sarah was crying harder as she said with absolute frustration, "Because I was pregnant and I thought he ought to know."

"Because you were pregnant?" Gitchoff asked.

Weber was losing his temper. "Because she was pregnant and she thought he ought to know," he spat out angrily.

Judge Ferguson allowed Gitchoff to make his record and ask a lengthy series of questions about the dates of the baby's conception and birth, information Gitchoff said he needed to get a specific date for the second incident. Sarah cried the whole time, and the defense was getting details Weber had hoped to keep confidential. Finally, Weber offered to amend the charge to reflect Sarah's answers and to restrict the time period to August through October of 1977—instead of August to June as listed in the indictment.

But that didn't satisfy Gitchoff. He returned to the same old saw about Sarah's sexual maturity being a valid issue because Weber had harped on her "tender years" when he questioned her. Ferguson rejected the third trip to the back door. But Gitchoff was relentless, arguing that Sarah's maturity could be used to impeach her testimony about the towel in the nightstand. Not an issue, Ferguson ruled for the fourth time. Gitchoff pushed harder. He might want to suggest that she was snooping around the house while baby-sitting for the Van Hooks, and found the towel; that could explain how she knew about it, and her sexual maturity would become an issue then. Ferguson shrugged; Gitchoff could ask if she found the towel that way. But the judge said forcefully that her maturity remained off-limits.

Sarah continued to cry during the whole conversation, and Weber's anger once led him to snap at Gitchoff, "Are you finished with her?" It was the same language Weber used when questioning Sarah about the abuse she suffered from Van Hook. Gitchoff was resourceful, relentless, fast on his feet, and he was protecting his record for appeal. But the victim still was being abused.

After nearly 30 minutes of arguing, the judge sent the lawyers back into the courtroom with a witness whose emotions were now like a raw piece of meat. Gitchoff pursued the course he had charted in chambers by asking why Sarah never told her mother. They weren't that close, Sarah said. Had Sarah started menstruating? Yes. Did she talk to her mother about that or did her mother buy her sanitary napkins or tampons? No, they didn't even talk about things like that.

Weber was drumming his fingers on the table. What

was the relevance of this? Was it necessary to delve into these personal matters with an emotional young woman?

"Sarah, you say you never told your mother what happened?"

"No, not until after it came out in the papers."

"Well, that's six years later, right?"

"Right."

"And after you file a lawsuit?"

Sarah was crying again as she mumbled, "Yes."

"Is that right?" Gitchoff hesitated. "Are you okay, honey? I mean, we are going to be here for a little while. Are you all right?"

Sarah nodded, and the questioning continued. More rehash about her decision to tell Mark Richter after he had seen Jay Carr crying; a long explanation of why she confided in Dennis Kuba when she never talked to the police before. As Gitchoff covered the part about Sarah directing Kuba to Stella Van Hook's house, the defense attorney asked if Sarah knew the way "because you say Mr. Van Hook took you there that day?"

Despite all she had been through, Sarah still wouldn't let that pass. She said firmly, "Because he *did* take me there, yes."

In a long discussion about the date of the first encounter at Van Hook's house, Sarah said the best time frame she could offer was a Saturday, probably after Thanksgiving and before mid December, since there were no Christmas decorations up yet. Gitchoff took great care to discuss how she watched *American Bandstand* on television at Van Hook's house that day; she agreed when Gitchoff suggested the show was broadcast about 11 o'clock or noon. She remembered the television as a 19-inch portable model. Weber wondered why Gitchoff was so interested in that.

Gitchoff also had Sarah draw a floor plan of that house on the blackboard, and instructed her to mark the boy's bedroom where Van Hook took her for sex. He questioned her at length about the bed there, and she could describe it only as a regular bed; she said repeatedly she did not remember the exact size, but it absolutely was not a baby crib. That was an important point for Gitchoff, and he went over it several times. She was unsure of the children's ages when she baby-sat for them, but she knew they were not in diapers. Another important point.

When Gitchoff tried to get a more specific date for the Saturday that Sarah baby-sat, the result was an almost comical set of exchanges as Sarah, Gitchoff, and Weber argued over the dates of the Saturdays between Thanksgiving and Christmas in 1977. The conversation was so confusing that Gitchoff ended up mumbling, "Now, Saturday before December the fourth would be Thanksgiving Saturday, wouldn't it? Saturday falls on a Thursday—I mean, Thanksgiving falls on a Thursday." Weber chuckled as this dramatic court testimony degenerated into a poor imitation of Abbott and Costello's "Who's on First" routine. The result was a loose agreement that Sarah was talking about a Saturday on November 13, 20, or 27, and perhaps on December 4 or 11.

Gitchoff switched gears. He suggested that Sarah rarely had cried over the incident that she kept hidden for six years before filing a suit seeking money.

"Why is it that you cried today, and you don't remember crying before?"

"Because I put myself back into that spot, and I felt the same way I did then." A common reaction while testifying at trial, Weber knew.

"Okay. You put yourself back into that spot when you filed a lawsuit for money, didn't you?"

"Yes."

With a slight edge in his voice, Gitchoff snapped, "You won't cry if you get money, will you?"

Sarah looked him right in the eye and said clearly, "I might."

Weber was angered again. He understood that technique for impeaching a witness, but it was a cheap shot at this one.

Shortly after that, Judge Ferguson recessed court for the day. Weber's strategy of putting on a difficult witness late in the day to catch the weary defense off guard had failed. Gitchoff would get a chance to come at Sarah again the next morning, when he was fresh and had spent the night analyzing her testimony.

Weber and his team spoke briefly with Sarah after court adjourned. Weber reassured her that she was doing a great job. He thought her experience on the stand, and in chambers, had toughened her up. She knew more about what to expect, and she seemed more resolute than ever to stand up for what was right.

Then, Weber went home and lost himself in the next installment of *Winds of War.*

Gitchoff resumed his cross-examination the next morning with the same tactics—long questioning about a smorgasbord of details, especially dates. Weber didn't think the defense was scoring many points with the jury; in fact, some of the exchanges seemed to reinforce Sarah's credibility. The more she repeated the facts in consistent and confident terms, the more believable she seemed. During a long discussion about the liquor Van Hook gave her, Sarah repeated several times that she never had drunk alcohol before, and still didn't. She remembered feeling light-headed and giggly after she and Debbie Weaver drank the little bottles of whiskey sours Van Hook gave her, but Sarah couldn't remember much more about it.

Weber was more impressed with Sarah as her time on the stand progressed. She avoided a common mistake by witnesses; many feel obliged to guess at an answer just to say something. When Sarah couldn't remember the color, make, or model of the car in which she rode with Van Hook to his mother's house, she said so; no amount of interrogation by Gitchoff could get her to guess. She insisted that she had paid no attention to the neighbors' houses when she arrived at Stella Van Hook's, or to whether any of the siding on Stella's house had been removed. Weber wondered where Gitchoff was going with that question.

And Sarah wouldn't guess how many packages of prophylactics she saw under the mattress when Van Hook lifted it—"pretty many" was as specific as she would get.

Had she seen packages like that before? "Not like that," she said.

"What kind had you seen before?"

Weber objected; the questions were getting very close to the issue of sexual history again. He was surprised when Ferguson overruled him. But Weber didn't need to worry; Sarah's answer was perfect again, and it stung Gitchoff one more time.

"Well, I remember a couple of girls showed me some that came in little boxes."

"Do girls show each other these things?"

"Yes."

The old pro smiled. There wasn't much he could do with this answer, either, but accept it gracefully. "Do they? Sometimes you are a little smarter than we give you credit for, huh?"

As much as Weber enjoyed that exchange, he was repulsed by the description of what happened when the mailman's arrival startled Van Hook after he began performing intercourse with her. Sarah even remembered that she was lying "the wrong way—crossways" on the bed, and Van Hook peeked through the window beside the bed when they heard footsteps.

"He said it was the mailman," she remembered.

"Okay, but he never stopped the intercourse?"

"That's right," she said in a voice suggesting that was exactly what she would expect from the man she had come to know on such intimate terms.

"Kept going?" Gitchoff asked.

"Yeah," she said with disdain.

Another exchange that added even more to the perverted portrait of Richard Van Hook.

Weber was pleased when Gitchoff ended his cross-examination shortly after that. The prosecutor decided to take full advantage of the two-minute rule he had learned so long ago from another old pro, prosecutor Bob Trone. For two minutes after a lawyer completes his questioning of a witness, he is absorbed in remembering what was said, evaluating the performances of the witness and himself, and determining the effect of it all on the case. The other lawyer has almost carte blanche to ask anything he wants because his opponent's mind is elsewhere.

The first order of business was a long question by Weber, almost testifying himself, to give Sarah the opportunity to explain that she couldn't remember details of the outside of Stella Van Hook's house; she simply wasn't paying attention to that. She remembered so much of the inside, however, because she was there longer and the events were more important. That would cancel any concerns raised among the jurors because Gitchoff had dwelled so long on what Sarah couldn't remember.

Weber also ran quickly through the list of M.O. items again, fearing that she might have missed some of them before, and giving Sarah a chance to remind the jury about the endearing little comments from Van Hook they would hear later from the other witnesses.

The prosecutor also wanted to address another issue. He referred to the years that passed before Sarah told anyone in authority what had happened, and linked that period to Sarah's impression about whether Van Hook was sexually involved with any other girls. She explained that in the car after the first incident, she had asked him, "Do you do this to everybody?" He had assured her, "No, you are the only one."

She told the jury softly, "And when I heard about all the other little girls, I just felt so—I felt responsible."

What a great answer, Weber thought. She realized she could have stopped Van Hook years ago, and decided that she had to tell the truth to stop him now. How could the jury hear anything in that but the unvarnished truth?

Weber then asked Sarah if the man who did all of this, the teacher who had intercourse with her, was in the courtroom. Yes. Point him out. She gestured toward the defense table and said clearly, "He's seated at the table, and he is wearing a blue suit and a blue tie with white stuff on it."

Weber hoped her testimony would end on that note, but Gitchoff wasn't about to let that happen. He asked Sarah how she decided to file a suit against Van Hook, and dwelled at some length on her answer that she was told

she could by Pam Klein and other counselors at the Rape
and Sexual Abuse Care Center. He also tried to make
something of the fact that Sarah had talked to Weber and
others the night before. Weber returned to clear up any
doubts about that for the jury.

"What did I tell you the bottom line was in your testimony?"

"Tell the truth," Sarah said.

The rest of the prosecution's case would focus on corroborating Sarah's testimony. He began with Belinda Barnett, who was Belinda Carr now because she had married
Jay Carr's brother. Weber ran through a quick series of
questions for Belinda to confirm that Sarah had told her
about the incidents with Van Hook shortly after they
happened—the legal point called "prior consistent statements." Such statements were exceptions to the rule bar-
ring "hearsay" evidence because they showed that a
witness had not recently fabricated the story.

But Gitchoff was not about to let in that kind of evidence without a fight. His prompt objection landed the attorneys back in Ferguson's chambers for another lengthy
discourse on the rules of evidence. Weber insisted
Belinda's testimony was proper because Gitchoff had implied Sarah fabricated her story to get money through a
civil suit against Van Hook and the school district. Weber
still was angry over the "You won't cry if you get
money" line—a low blow, the prosecutor thought, and
one that had opened the door for evidence supporting Sarah's story. But Gitchoff insisted the testimony from
Belinda was inadmissible hearsay, and that his questions
showed Sarah's greed, not fabrication of the story.

"As a matter of fact, all I was trying to show was her
greed, not her lying," Gitchoff protested.

Weber couldn't believe it. He threw his head back and
rolled his eyes upward in frustration. Gitchoff caught the
reaction and didn't enjoy it. "Well," he cracked, "it's the
truth. That's why she's suing for money—her greed."

The exchanges between Weber and Gitchoff in chambers grew increasingly testy. Gitchoff complained that a

case that started as one-on-one—Sarah versus Van Hook—had become forty-on-one with Weber's horde of M.O. witnesses. "That's right," Weber snapped with no small amount of satisfaction. It wasn't exactly an accident.

Gitchoff retorted, "There's no way you're going to prove the charges against my man with Sarah Cramer. What you have to try and prove is everybody else."

Weber wasn't about to miss a straight line, or stand for that characterization of the evidence. With some exaggeration in his voice, Weber shot back, "With all due respect, Mr. Gitchoff, I could have tried this case with only Sarah and convicted 'your man.' The evidence is overwhelming."

Judge Ferguson stepped in, ruling that the defense's suggestion that Sarah's motive for telling her story was money or greed was a classic attack on her credibility. Weber was entitled to prove she had made prior consistent statements. The parties returned to the courtroom for Belinda to recount how Sarah told her about the first sexual encounter with Van Hook.

"She said he had taken her to his house, and more or less trapped her," Belinda remembered. Weber almost nodded; what an appropriate description.

"What did he do then?"

"They had sex."

"How was Sarah's demeanor when she was telling you this?"

"She cried as she told me."

Belinda confirmed that Sarah told her about the towel in the nightstand, and about the second incident almost a year later at the home of Van Hook's mother. Weber asked if Sarah said anything about liquor, and Ferguson sustained Gitchoff's objection that the question was leading. Weber asked what else Sarah said, and Gitchoff gave him a shot by mumbling to Belinda, "Now tell him about the liquor." Weber grinned; he could appreciate a dead-center zinger like that.

Gitchoff's cross-examination bore in on the liquor in great detail again, only to hear one more time that Sarah didn't drink alcohol. When he questioned Belinda about Sarah's account of the second incident, he asked what she thought about Sarah in light of that. "I felt very sorry for her because I didn't think that would happen to her by one of our teachers."

As Weber moved down the list of people Sarah had told, Mark Richter took the stand to explain that he had become curious after seeing Sarah and Jay Carr, his best friend, crying at a Halloween party in 1978; they wouldn't tell him what was wrong. But Sarah divulged her secret in January 1979, telling Mark all about both incidents with Van Hook. That explained why Jay Carr had been so upset when he was around Van Hook, Mark said. Sarah said she hadn't told any officials at school or the police because she didn't think anyone would believe her. Mark had told a teacher, Charles Wandling, but Gitchoff's sustained objection kept Mark from saying any more about that.

On cross-examination, Gitchoff had Mark talk at length about the night Sarah and Jay were crying. Then Gitchoff called for a conference in the judge's chambers, where he said he wanted to go into Mark's knowledge of Sarah's pregnancy to suggest that was the reason the couple cried, not because of anything Van Hook had done. Weber winced; he realized that he may have opened the door by asking Mark about the Halloween party. Weber bluffed, insisting to the judge that Gitchoff's question would violate the order against getting into Sarah's sexual history or conduct. Ferguson agreed and sustained Weber's objection. Gitchoff was plaintive as he turned to the judge. "Well, he opened it up, didn't he?"

"I don't think he did," Ferguson said.

"Judge, can't I get just one," Gitchoff protested. "How come I always open it up for him."

But Ferguson wouldn't budge. He grinned. "I think I at least have to be consistently wrong."

Sarah Cramer's mother, Margaret, was an older woman whose deep concern about this situation was evident as she took the witness stand. She explained that Sarah was adopted at six weeks old—really the daughter of one of Margaret's nieces. Margaret had allowed Sarah to baby-sit for Van Hook only because he was a teacher. Margaret and her husband decided that if he was a teacher, they could trust him. When Sarah came home that afternoon, she went right to her room without saying a word, and stayed there all evening.

Weber hoped this decent woman had showed the jury that this case was about real people and real pain. Sarah was adopted, perhaps making her an easier victim for Van Hook; he chose prey who had some weakness in their background.

Gitchoff got stung again as Margaret Cramer rolled off a series of simple but profound observations. He repeated her line that she thought she could trust a teacher, and she nodded. "I never dreamed of such a thing."

"Neither did I. Neither did I," Gitchoff added solemnly.

"No, sir. Huh-uh," she said sincerely. "It hurt me, because I think the man needs prayer. He needs help."

Led by Gitchoff's questions, Margaret said she had learned only recently that Sarah smoked and had drunk the liquor from Van Hook; those discoveries wounded Margaret because Sarah attended church and was raised in a good, Christian home. She was hurt, too, when she realized that Sarah had confided in her friends, but not her mother, about Van Hook. Gitchoff seemed to give up some ground when he offered sympathetically, "Well, that happens sometimes when you are that age." Weber thought the defender had just made Sarah's whole story easier to believe by agreeing that's the way kids are.

Did she ever suspect there was something between Van Hook and her daughter? Gitchoff wondered.

"I felt something within me very strange. I can't put it into words. I don't know just what it was. I felt like there was something wrong with him. It could have been his problem that he has, you know."

"You know he has a problem?" was Gitchoff's curious response.

"That's . . . Sure, he has a problem," Margaret said indisputably. The tone of her voice was unmistakable: What else would you call it when a teacher sexually abused little girls who trusted him precisely because he was a teacher?

Weber moved quickly to the next witness, Debbie Weaver. In just a few questions he established that Debbie had shared the whiskey sours while riding the school bus with Sarah, and that Sarah had said she got them from Van Hook.

Gitchoff had little to attack there, and he opened his cross-examination with one of his off-the-wall references. He had noticed something protruding from her hip pocket, just like something he had seen one of the other girls carrying during the pretrial hearings the other day. What was it? A comb with a big handle, she replied. "That's the thing to do today?" The old veteran smiled.

After that he spent several minutes proving that Debbie's memory of when this all happened was almost nonexistent. On redirect examination, Weber asked simply whether she was sure the event happened and Sarah made those comments. "Yeah," she said. That was all that counted, Weber knew.

The next witness made him nervous. The teacher Charles Wandling was important, and Weber wasn't sure how this would go. Wandling not only had to confirm Mark Richter's story, but he had to show the jury why reporting the offenses to another teacher would have been useless.

Wandling backed up Mark's story right down the line, adding a few credible details. The boy had been in Wandling's shop class and seemed uncharacteristically upset one day. When Wandling inquired about it, Mark asked if he knew Van Hook, and then said he and a friend wanted to beat him up. Wandling was surprised, of course, and urged Mark not to be silly. Mark then explained that Van Hook had forced Sarah Cramer to have sex.

"I said, 'That's a pretty serious accusation.' But the main thing I was trying to get him to do was not to go running down to Caseyville and starting a fight on campus," Wandling explained. He counseled Mark not to do anything that would get him into a lot of trouble.

Wandling said he thought and thought about the situation, but decided not to report Mark's accusation to school authorities or the police. Teachers hear a lot of stories from students, he explained. This one about a teacher he knew well had flabbergasted him, but he decided not to pass it on.

Weber got what he needed, and was more convinced than ever that Wandling's decision was unacceptable; a serious allegation like that should have been reported to someone.

Gitchoff obviously knew a hot potato when he saw one. He asked Wandling only if Mark Richter was the same imposing size then as he was now, and Wandling said yes. Weber figured that was a suggestion that Mark was capable of pounding the smaller Van Hook if he really had felt there was reason.

Weber called a series of witnesses from the school district to establish some necessary facts. Collinsville High School got out at two o'clock, giving Van Hook time to drive Sarah to his mother's house two minutes away and be engaged in sex when the mailman arrived sometime around 2:45. Secretaries also produced school records showing that Sarah and Katherine Howes had been in Van Hook's classes.

Then Weber called his first hostile witness, Stella Van Hook. From the fire in her squinted eyes, Weber knew this would be tough. When he asked if Sarah Cramer had ever been to her house, he got the nonanswer, "Not that I know of." She was going to play it very tight; she had caught on to the damage inflicted by her testimony about the condoms. He asked her to describe the appearance of her bedroom in 1977. "Just like any other bedroom," was the curt reply. What furniture did she have in the room? Sarcastically she responded, "What does everybody have in the bedroom? A table, a bed, a dresser, and a chest of drawers."

"Did your husband pass away almost two years ago?"
"He certainly did," was the odd reply.

"Did he keep some prophylactics under the mattress of that bed?"

"He did not."

Despite this woman's obvious hatred for Weber, he was surprised by that answer; he didn't expect her to deny it flatly. But since she had, Agent Kuba had just been tagged as the next witness. As Weber persisted, Stella insisted that all she said to Kuba after the fruitless search under the mattress was that, if he had found some prophylactics, they could have been her husband's.

"Is it safe to say that you are not exactly a willing witness for the state in this case?"

With more defiance she shot back, "I am not telling any lies." Weber was sure the shrill tone of her testimony would convince the jury that she was a mother protecting her son; that was understandable.

But the jury heard the story differently from Kuba. As he started to lift the corner of the mattress, Stella had said, "Now, wait a minute. If you do find some prophylactics underneath that mattress, they belong to my husband." Kuba asked if her husband normally kept them there, and she said yes.

Weber asked if Richard Van Hook had access to his mother's house after the investigation began, and before Kuba looked under the mattress. "I guess he would." Weber remembered Van Hook's quick visit to the Bear's Cave after he was tipped off. A repeat performance, perhaps, with Van Hook cleaning out his father's stash of condoms this time?

Kuba described Stella's house, confirming all the points remembered by Sarah. All of this was vastly important to Weber's case. The jury had to believe that Sarah had been to that house when Stella wasn't there.

If Don Weber thought Stella Van Hook's eyes showed malice toward him, he discovered a whole new plane of hatred when he looked into the face of his next witness, Sandra Van Hook. Her eyes sparked with loathing and her lips were pressed tightly together as she glared at him from the stand. He could sense this nurse's version of the "doctor knows best" attitude—no matter what evidence

Weber had, Sandra Van Hook, R.N., knew the real truth and she would be unshakable.

"Did you ever discuss your menstrual period with Sarah Cramer?"

"Not that I can recall," was the cool nonanswer.

"Did you ever talk about sex with Sarah?"

"Not that I can recall."

With some resignation Sandra confirmed the towel in the nightstand and its purpose, major points for Weber to score from this witness.

"Had you ever discussed the use of that towel with Sarah Cramer?"

"Not that I can recall."

Weber shifted gears abruptly. How many baby-sitters had the Van Hooks hired? There were too many to remember, but she named five. Who was best? With her comments aimed critically at Sarah, Sandra said none of those smoked in her home, brought people to the house without permission, or talked on the telephone. The others may not have cared for the children any better than Sarah, but she did some things Sandra did not like.

Weber produced a high-school yearbook and asked Sandra if the inscription on the page was her husband's handwriting; it was. Weber told her to read it aloud. She looked at it, glanced back at Weber coldly, and then read, "Here's wishing the best of everything to the best baby-sitter I ever had. You weren't a bad student either. I hope I get to see a lot of you in the future. Always, Dick VH."

"And," Weber asked, "which words did he underline in the phrase, 'the best baby-sitter I ever had?' "

"He underlined 'best' and he underlined 'ever had,' " Sandra Van Hook said calmly.

"No further questions."

Now the jurors knew about the emphasized, double-entendre message from Van Hook to Sarah, and they had heard it from a source who couldn't have missed the obvious meaning.

Gitchoff had no questions for his client's wife.

* * *

"Neither rain nor sleet . . ." As Weber called the mailman who had walked the route at Stella Van Hook's home for years, the prosecutor wondered if the postal creed might not apply to Richard Van Hook as well; it seemed nothing had deterred him from his self-appointed rounds. Postal worker Charles Haywood testified that he delivered the mail at Stella's house about 2:30, give or take 30 minutes depending on volume. He walked onto the porch to drop it in the mailbox.

But John Gitchoff promptly stood that simple testimony on its head by asking Haywood if he remembered ever seeing a strange car parked in front of Stella's home. No. Would he have told her or a neighbor if he had seen one? "Oh, yes, always," Haywood said. When Weber objected to the speculative nature of the question, Gitchoff asked it again in more detail. This time Haywood mentioned that new siding was being installed on Stella's house in September and October of 1977. Other than vehicles from that, had he seen any strange cars parked there? "No."

Weber struggled to keep from getting angry. For some reason, this struck him as a typical bit of nonsense from a Collinsville resident amid this Van Hook mess. On redirect, he asked impatiently, "Mr. Haywood, are you saying that, in September or October of '77, there wasn't a car parked in front of that house?"

"I said there wasn't a strange one that I know of, outside of the siding people that were working, whenever they were there. Most of them had pickup trucks."

"You wouldn't really remember if there was another car there, would you?" Weber asked incredulously.

"Well, I think I would," the mailman responded defiantly.

From that frustrating exchange, Weber moved to a reading of the transcript from Van Hook's appearance before the grand jury. Under an agreement with Gitchoff, Assistant State's Attorney Randy Massey read the questions and answers on which the perjury charges were based.

With that, Don Weber completed the evidence about

Sarah Cramer. He thought her testimony had been extremely believable, and unscarred by the defense. Weber hoped the jurors agreed with his analysis that this intelligent, articulate young woman, who went to church and didn't drink, was motivated by a sense of justice, guilt, and responsibility, not monetary greed. But could 12 adults really believe the essence of her story? Could they understand how a young girl could just lie there, frozen, while her body was defiled and her trust shattered? Could they understand why a girl would keep such a dark secret from almost everyone she loved and trusted? And could they believe—beyond a reasonable doubt—that the man in the blue suit had done all of that?

CHAPTER 14

Another slim young woman walked to the witness stand Wednesday afternoon and swore to tell the truth about Richard Van Hook.

"Would you state your name, please," Don Weber asked.

"Stephanie Lorraine Knight."

"And, Stephanie, how old are you?"

"Twenty."

This would be different from the testimony by Sarah Cramer, the prosecutor knew. Different situation; different victim. But it was the same Richard Van Hook, and almost the same routine. That was why Stephanie Knight was so important to this case.

She described the visits to Van Hook and some other teachers at Caseyville School after she finished her classes at the high school in September of 1979. Van Hook was letting her use the overhead projector in the library to make a life-sized drawing of a goddess for a class in mythology. One day Van Hook gave her a short kiss on the lips as she was leaving. That was unusual, but she didn't do anything about it. If her friends were with her after that, nothing happened. But when she was alone, Van Hook made more moves on her after taking her into his little office. The kisses became more intimate, more passionate—French kisses.

"How did you feel?"

"Well, I was kind of taken off guard, you know. I didn't expect it. He's a teacher, and I was still in high school."

Soon he began to take off her blouse and fondle her breasts; then he removed her bra and kissed her breasts.

Before long he removed all of her clothes. Sometimes they laid down on the floor in the little office. He asked her once if she had touched a man, and then he put her hand on his penis.

"What did you do?"

"Well, I kind of jerked away. And he made a statement that, 'George won't bite you.' "

"What was he referring to as 'George'?"

"His penis."

The two reporters in the audience found no humor this time.

Stephanie recounted the series of lines Van Hook used: he wished she was older; she made him feel younger; he wondered where girls like her were when he was in school; he had dreams about her; he said she was the only girl he was involved with; he asked her to go to his house with him. He talked about his wife; they were having marital problems. He asked if she was taking birth-control pills, and said he could arrange that with a doctor friend. He offered her wine and gave her gifts—an initialed necklace and a pewter statue; she identified them as Weber handed them to her.

"How did you feel about him?"

"Well, I was 16 or 17, and I had a crush on him."

There it was; that was why this victim was different. Unlike the other girls, Stephanie had an adolescent infatuation with Van Hook. Weber hoped her admitted emotional involvement wouldn't disqualify her as a victim in the jurors' minds.

She said Van Hook told her they couldn't date because he still was married and would get into trouble seeing a student. She didn't have intercourse with Van Hook because she wasn't ready for that; it wasn't what she wanted.

"Did he want that?"

"He said he would like to make love to me."

She finally ended the relationship after several weeks because it got too serious. "I didn't want anything to happen. Like, it probably would have led to me going to bed with him, and that isn't what I wanted at all."

Stephanie told her best friend, Betsy Woods, but gave her few details. She told her mother after the first kiss. Her mother ordered her to stay away from Van Hook, and threatened to go to school and put a stop to it. Stephanie disobeyed her mother by going back to see Van Hook; some kids that age rebel like that.

Had Van Hook said anything about Stephanie's virginity? "He said I was the sweetest virgin he ever met at 17."

"Do you see that person in the courtroom today?" Weber asked.

"Yes. He is right there." She pointed nervously.

Weber turned to the judge. "Would the record reflect she's identified the defendant, Richard George Van Hook?"

It was the first time Weber had used Richard G. Van Hook's middle name—drawing it out for effect—and it was devastating. He had used his middle name to provide a separate identify for his own penis, a practice so absurd and juvenile that it was pathetic.

Weber completed his questioning on that crushing note, but the final exchange had left Stephanie so upset that Gitchoff asked for someone to bring her a drink and offered to let her take a break; she declined. Weber wondered again how Gitchoff planned to tread the fine line between impeaching a prosecution witness and looking like an oaf battering a vulnerable young woman. Weber even thought that Gitchoff might be making a mistake by being too nice to Stephanie; after all, the defense wanted the jury to believe that these girls were telling horrible lies about poor Mr. Van Hook. If that were true, would Gitchoff really be so nice to the members of this coven of malicious little schemers?

Gitchoff backtracked over Stephanie's story, concentrating on times and dates. He stressed that she started visiting Van Hook, and kept returning, on her own; he did not invite her, she agreed.

"Okay. So, you kind of had a crush on him?"

"Yes."

"And you wanted to go?"

"Kind of."

"And this was even after he was kissing you and fondling your breasts?"

"Well, I thought he had the same feelings for me as I had for him."

There it was again, Weber thought. She loved him, and his special attentions made her hope, perhaps believe, that he loved her, too.

Gitchoff edged close to portraying Stephanie as a home wrecker. "You knew he was married?"

"Yes."

"You knew he had children?"

"Yes."

"But that didn't stop you?"

"No, because he said he was having problems."

"Okay. And then, of course, if you had never gone down there in the first instance, there wouldn't have been any problems, would there, between you and him."

"I don't consider it a problem," she said quietly.

There was the key. This confused young woman may love her teacher, Weber realized, even after everything that happened.

"But you wanted this to happen to you?"

"No, I didn't want it to happen. I just, you know, I had this teenage crush on him, and I liked talking to him. I didn't want or expect this to happen."

"But you kept going back?"

"Yes."

"He didn't drag you in there, did he, honey?"

"No," she said as her eyes lowered.

That didn't make any difference, Weber thought. When it's a teacher and a 14-year-old girl, the law said it didn't make any difference.

Gitchoff delved into the investigation that led the police to Stephanie, and one of her answers struck Weber as the turning point in Van Hook's downfall. Stephanie said she had decided to call the police and tell them about Van Hook, but Dennis Kuba contacted her before she could volunteer to help. Was she doing that because of what had happened between her and Van Hook? Gitchoff asked.

"No, because I had read in the newspaper about incidents with other girls," Stephanie said firmly.

Weber heard the echo from Sarah's statement that she had felt so responsible. Living with secret memories of being abused was one thing; keeping quiet while knowing that the abuser was finding more victims was something else. On redirect, Weber asked if Stephanie loved or hated Van Hook when she agreed to talk to Kuba.

"Well, I didn't love him."

"Did you hate him?"

"I can't say I hated him."

"How did you feel about him?"

"Well, I . . . At this . . . I felt kind of . . . I don't know," she said, finally accepting her confusion.

Weber closed with a series of questions designed to battle the rumors floating through Collinsville. Had the police or anyone else told her what the other girls were saying about Van Hook? Did anyone tell her which room was being identified as the location of these activities? Was she close friends with any of the other girls? "No," Stephanie answered to all the questions.

Thursday, February 10, the final day for prosecutorial evidence against Richard Van Hook. Weber felt rested after blocking out the courtroom activity for two hours Wednesday evening watching *Winds of War,* and then getting a good night's sleep. He felt ready for the task ahead of him that day. He prayed the witnesses on the long list would come through, and would withstand the wearying cross-examinations by John Gitchoff.

The first that morning was Betsy Woods, who had accompanied Stephanie to Caseyville School several times to see Van Hook and at least one other teacher, Mrs. Alcorn. Once, when she went to the library with Stephanie, Van Hook had asked if Stephanie always needed a chaperon. Betsy took that to mean he didn't want her there. She thought Stephanie was in love with Van Hook; Stephanie told her later that Van Hook had kissed her.

Teacher Barbara Alcorn took the stand next, starting a

long series of teachers who would give Weber only the evidence they had to and nothing else. Alcorn remembered the visits by Betsy Woods, but thought they were during school hours. A perfect example, Weber thought; the evidence was clear that the visits were after school. Alcorn remembered seeing a girl she knew only as "Steph" with Betsy on a couple of occasions; Weber ended with that.

On cross-examination, Alcorn—whose room was directly across the hall from Van Hook's—could not remember having a student named Stephanie Knight, and seemed perplexed when Gitchoff said Stephanie had testified that Alcorn was her favorite teacher. "Well, I don't remember having her in class at all," Alcorn replied.

"Did you ever notice any unusual behavior by Mr. Van Hook with his students?"

"Not at all," was the steadfast reply Weber was sure he would hear many more times before the defense was done.

The next witness would be better, Weber knew. Stephanie's mother, Diane Knight, said she learned about the kiss from Van Hook accidentally when she overheard a conversation between Stephanie and her younger sister. Mrs. Knight threatened to go to school and talk to Van Hook, but Stephanie asked her not to do that, and not to tell her father. Stephanie insisted that nothing more than a kiss was involved, and Mrs. Knight decided to take no more action than forbidding her daughter to visit Van Hook again. She assumed that was the end of it.

Gitchoff started off with a friendly observation: "Your daughter favors you," he told the slim woman with the light brown hair. But then he took the issue to her in an accusatory tone, asking if she wasn't upset by what her daughter told her. Yes, but she doubted any action would be taken over one kiss. Why hadn't she told her husband?

"Because he would have done something."

"Wouldn't you think Van Hook had it coming?"

"Well, I figured my husband would have been the one that would have ended up in jail for assault or something."

"But it's all right to kiss the daughter?"

"No, I just didn't really know what to do or who to go to."

The kids were right all along, Weber thought: nobody would do anything. And he wondered if the jury was struck by the contradiction in Gitchoff's questioning. Hadn't Gitchoff just suggested that a teacher who kissed a girl deserved to be beaten by her father?

Weber turned his attention to another issue, calling crime-scene technician Louis Reddo to back up Kuba's account of the condom conversation with Stella Van Hook. Reddo also testified about his examination of the Bear's Cave—a room that was six-foot-eight by eight feet, and had clear floor space of four-foot-eight by six-foot-one. Reddo identified Kuba's favorite photograph—of him lying so embarrassingly on the floor.

A check of that room just a week ago, Reddo added, had discovered what appeared to be a book, but actually was an empty shell. Weber knew the importance of that would become clearer with his next witness, Katherine Howes.

Katherine had waited nervously for her turn, and as it approached, she had thrown up in the rest room again. She had looked to Pam Klein for assurance that being frightened was normal, and it would be okay. "You can do this, Kate," Pam had said softly. Mr. Weber had promised her earlier that day that this would be the last time. Even so, she wasn't sure she could do it, facing all of those people packed into that courtroom, and telling her story again while Van Hook watched her. When the bailiff called her name, Katherine felt her heart pound; her knees turned to jelly. Pam held her arm and escorted her to the courtroom door, and it seemed a long walk down that aisle to the witness chair. Pam felt helpless again as the door closed behind the thin figure.

She was pale and fragile-looking as she sat down, barely visible behind the oak buffer that separated her from the rest of the room. She was thin, but Weber thought she looked slightly more mature than she had before. The first step was to have her identify a picture taken of her sixth-grade volleyball team. Weber would show that to the jurors later so they would know how young she had been more than two years ago.

She explained that her family lived in Kentucky now, and her father was a minister. He had lost his other job while she was in the sixth grade. Weber hoped his next question would help the jury understand how Van Hook picked his victims.

"Was your family rich, poor, or medium?"

"A little bit on the poor side," she said wistfully.

"Okay. Were you having some problems because of money and your dad being out of work?"

"Yes." There was some of the vulnerability Van Hook had seen.

After she started the sixth grade in Van Hook's class in 1980, he started getting friendlier with her. Her grades the year before were lousy, she said, D's and F's; but they began to improve as Van Hook got friendlier. Just after Christmas vacation, in January 1981, he kissed her on the lips, and soon was slipping his tongue into her mouth. From there Katherine led the jurors through a relatively detailed description of the increasingly intimate encounters with Van Hook behind the locked door in the little room he used for an office off the library. Weber was sorry he could not spare her feelings by skirting around the acts and words that upset; he had to be frank and straightforward in court. He hoped he could make it up to her later. But he had to let the jurors hear from her mouth what had happened.

Weber wondered how many of these sordid tidbits would be published by the newspapers; he wished they would print it all. So many people in Collinsville were shaping their views from the reporters' accounts, and those stories often were so vague that they fed the rumors that Van Hook was being persecuted for nothing more than a friendly kiss on the forehead or a fatherly pat on the fanny. But Weber knew the papers had to be cautious with such matters; he just wished they would print the full facts.

As Katherine reluctantly revealed the depth of the activity, Weber asked where Van Hook kept the prophylactics in the room.

"On a shelf, in a box that looked like a book." She identified a picture Louis Reddo had taken in Van Hook's little room as the kind of book she had seen there. Weber realized it probably was a book-shaped sleeve to hold a collection of *National Geographic* magazines.

What did she do while he performed this variety of sexual activities with her, including intercourse? "I was frozen; I didn't know what to do." There was the word again.

The childish innocence came through at such peculiar times; Weber wondered if the jury was struck by that as he was. When he asked what would happen during the times that Van Hook rubbed his penis between her legs, she said with disdain, "Make a mess."

How often did he take her into this room for intercourse?

"Two or three times a week," she said softly. Weber wondered if it really was that often, and he thought immediately of a scene from one of his favorite movies, *Annie Hall.* On a split screen showing Woody Allen on one side and Diane Keaton on the other as they talked to their psychiatrists, they are asked how often they had sex. Woody Allen bemoans that it was hardly ever, while Diane Keaton complains that it was all the time. A matter of perspective, Weber thought. He was sure it seemed like all the time to Katherine.

"Did Van Hook tell you whether or not it would be okay for you to talk about what he was doing to you?"

"He said if I did, he could get in trouble, and it could ruin my dad's reputation as a minister."

Weber looked at the jurors. Did they realize how Van Hook had emotionally extorted silence from this girl? Could they see another in a course of despicable acts?

"How did you feel about him doing this to you?"

"I didn't like it," Katherine said softly but firmly. "I was scared. I was only 11 or 12. I didn't know what to do."

Weber looked at Van Hook; his face was almost blank.

He seemed to be deep in thought, and Weber wondered cynically if Van Hook was reliving some fond memories.

Katherine reeled off the list of M.O. points—all the little things he told her. He even said he wanted to take her to a bar. A new one for the jury was, "He said if he looked at me in class, he would lose his train of thought and start thinking about me."

The witness recalled the list of gifts bestowed by Van Hook, including the wood carving that proclaimed so innocently, "Love is contagious; We get it from one another." She held up the trophy for the jury to see.

And there was a little brass elephant—its trunk broken off—that he gave her on a class trip to the Magic House. Gitchoff perked up. "I didn't get that, dear." She repeated it for him.

For her twelfth birthday, he gave her a five-dollar bill in a folder on which he had drawn Winnie the Pooh. Weber almost winced again; if Katherine ever had children, she certainly wouldn't be able to read them all those wonderful stories. Winnie the Pooh would hold an entirely different set of memories for that mom.

"Did he do anything else on your birthday?"

"The same thing."

"What do you mean, the same thing?"

"He took my clothes off and his clothes off, and we had intercourse," Katherine said almost blankly. There was no disgust in her voice; it was a simple statement of fact.

As another reward for her compliance and silence, Van Hook supplied the answers to her homework. If she did poorly on a test, he gave her another chance—a blank test, the answer sheet, and instructions to fill out the new one and mark only one wrong.

She hated going to school while all of this was happening.

"What would you do to try to stay away from school?"

"Fake being sick; throw a fit."

"How would you do that?"

"I told my mom one day that I had a headache, and I cried and cried; and she still made me go to school."

Weber was glad Sheila Howes wasn't in the courtroom
at that moment; what a heartbreaking memory for a
mother who didn't realize she was ordering her only
daughter to deliver herself into the hands of a child molester.

Katherine described all the unsuccessful attempts she
made to avoid Van Hook's lunchtime rendezvous. She
even hid in the rest room until he sent another girl in to
get her.

As Weber completed his questioning, he decided to try
a dangerous tactic for a trial lawyer—he asked a question
without knowing the answer.

"Did he ever put your hand on his penis?"

"Yes," she said quietly.

"Did he ever mention any names that he had for his penis?"

As Katherine looked back at him, Weber was sure he
knew the answer now.

"George," she almost whispered.

Judge Ferguson called a ten-minute recess, and Weber
escorted Katherine into the waiting comfort of Pam Klein
and Dennis Kuba in the hall. She had done well, but still
faced the most difficult part. When Katherine went into
the rest room, Weber turned to the investigators and
stunned them with, "Kate said he called his penis
George." Two mouths dropped open in unison. They
should have known, but no one ever asked her that. How
much more corroboration could the jury want? How
could two girls who didn't know each other, were different ages, and had different friends, make up the same ridiculous notion that a grown man called his penis by his
own middle name?

Katherine was anxious as she climbed back onto the
stand, but the first exchange with Gitchoff made Weber
proud of her.

"Are you nervous?"

"Yes."

"Are you scared?"

"No," she said with a touch of defiance.

Gitchoff went back over the dates, the sequence of the

events, and the times of day when the incidents happened, and asked her again about the particular sexual activities. She kept nodding, giving little more than one-word answers if she could get away with it. He asked the time when she usually went into the room with Van Hook, and Weber thought the answer offered a deeply disturbing image: "Maybe ten minutes to twelve, or whenever he found me."

Weber was impressed again when Katherine refused to allow Gitchoff to misstate the facts.

"And on those occasions, as I understand, you would take off all your clothes?"

Quickly and emphatically, Katherine corrected, "*He* would take off my clothes." Her rebuke was so stern that Gitchoff said, "I'm sorry."

Echoing the testimony of Stephanie, Katherine described the desk in the room, as well as the green sleeping bag, gray gym mat, and orange corduroy pillow Van Hook used to cover the tile floor when they laid down. Gitchoff asked if Van Hook had taken the mat back to the gymnasium after "your affair with him." Weber almost exploded out of his seat, and Gitchoff withdrew it before the judge could rule. "Sexual activity," Gitchoff rephrased it.

Katherine explained how Van Hook kept the sleeping bag stuffed in a trash bag under the shelves, and the pillow hidden in a box of Christmas decorations; the gym mat slid into a space between two shelf units. Weber shook his head again. Everything was tucked neatly away in the Bear's Cave, and nothing was what it seemed. The binder for *National Geographics* was really a container for the condoms. The box of Christmas decorations held the pillow. The mat the kids used for tumbling in the gym was used for trysting in this room. How could this man find so many ways to pervert so many of the trappings of childhood?

Now it was time for Gitchoff to get down to the nitty-gritty. His first move toward impeaching Katherine's credibility came as he asked if she remembered testifying before the grand jury in St. Clair County that she first had intercourse with Van Hook before Christmas of 1980. No, she said. Gitchoff read the exchange from the transcript; she had said that, indeed, even though she had told everyone else it was after Christmas.

"I don't remember," she said in confusion. She began to tremble. "I am trying to forget this. This has been two years ago."

"I understand that, dear."

"I don't want to remember it," she said as she began to cry.

"I understand that. And, believe me, I don't enjoy this," Gitchoff said sincerely. "Do you want to take a little break?"

"No, I want to get this over with," she said, almost angrily.

"I do too, young lady. Let me tell you, this is no pleasure for me. Okay? But you have to appreciate—"

That was too much for Weber. "Your Honor, I am going to have to object to him lecturing the witness."

Gitchoff turned toward the prosecutor. "I am not lecturing. I don't know what else I can do. I asked her if she wants to take a break."

Katherine broke in, "Yes. Can I get out of here?"

As Katherine was ushered out of the room by Pam Klein, Weber shot a disgusted glance toward the defense table. Van Hook wasn't even looking his way, however, and Weber's eyes were drawn to the doodles on the yellow legal pad in front of the teacher. As the girls testified, Van Hook had amused himself by sketching a long, narrow dagger that trickled drops of blood into the open neck of a curvaceous Coke bottle. The Freudian, phallic images were so obvious in a drawing by this man that Weber was astounded. And the depiction was more than sexual; it was vicious. Van Hook was more disturbed than Weber had imagined.

Outside the courtroom, Katherine was crying as Pam escorted her toward the conference room where the girls were awaiting their turns on the stand. Pam whispered reassurance, promising Katherine she had just a little longer to endure; Katherine nodded, "I know."

Weber felt sorry for Katherine, again, but for her to break down probably was beneficial for everyone, except Van Hook. It would relieve the pressure building up for her; it would remind the jurors that these witnesses still were children; and it would emphasize how difficult it was for them to recall the events that scarred them so badly. And it made it even more delicate for Gitchoff; making her cry again would not ingratiate the defense with the jury.

Gitchoff picked up his cross-examination by taking Katherine through a long series of questions about lunch hours; she explained that Van Hook would keep her in the room for about 20 minutes on those days. He even sent other kids onto the playground to look for her, or found her himself while she played on the monkey bars.

Some seductress, Weber mused; she'd rather play on the monkey bars.

Katherine said Van Hook would tell her he needed help grading papers or putting books away. Then they went into the library, where he locked the doors, took her into his little office, and locked that door, too. She eluded him a couple of times, however, by going to the other end of the playground and playing baseball with the boys.

The defense attorney wanted to know why Katherine never told her parents, especially her father, the minister who counseled other people with problems. She didn't know. She didn't think her mother would have believed what was happening; she trusted Van Hook because he was a teacher. Katherine didn't know whether her father would have believed her or not.

Gitchoff repeated her earlier comment that she was only 11 and didn't know what to do. "Eleven is young; I grant you that," he agreed. He looked at the picture of her volleyball team and asked Katherine to point out herself.

"You do look young there, don't you?"

"Uh-huh."

Gitchoff looked up and smiled sympathetically. "You look young now. Pretty, but young." It was the soft smile of a father—a man who really loved children, too—and a man who had mixed feelings about all of this.

"Thank you," Katherine said.

He returned to the comments she said Van Hook had made, asking particularly about the teacher's suggestion that he wanted to take her to a bar. "And you could have something to drink at the bar?"

"He didn't say that. He just said he wished he could take me to a bar."

"Oh. Well, what would you do at a bar?"

"I don't know. I've never been to a bar."

"Well, why would he want to take you?"

"I don't know," she said with another answer so innocent that Weber wondered how Gitchoff could keep leading with his chin. Weber loved it; the more Gitchoff searched for a scarlet woman, the more he found a nice little kid.

What about Van Hook's comments about his wife, and her complaint that she didn't turn him on the way she used to? Had Katherine seen Sandy Van Hook outside the courtroom? Yes.

"Do you think she's an attractive lady?"

"I don't know. I don't judge women."

Another great line, Weber thought.

"Has a nice figure?"

"I don't know. I wasn't paying any attention."

"But he told you she didn't turn him on?"

"No," Katherine corrected again. "He told me, she told him that."

"Oh, okay. I'm sorry. What did that mean to you?"

"I don't know."

Gitchoff turned back to the timing of the first incident. Had Katherine also told the medical personnel who examined her at Cardinal Glennon Hospital for Children in St. Louis that it happened before Christmas? No, she insisted. He asked about the St. Clair County grand jury again. No, she said one more time. He read much of her testimony aloud, thrilling Weber as it all sounded absolutely consistent with everything else she had testified to here. Besides, the prosecutor hardly thought one slip about the date was valid impeachment for this witness, an emotionally distraught 14-year-old girl. Why would she lie about the date, anyway? It made no sense, except as an error by a nervous kid.

Gitchoff ended his cross-examination by focusing on Katherine's grades. Did she get good grades from Van Hook just because of their relationship? Yes. She earned C's, and he gave her A's and B's. She earned her A's in gym and art, she said, and Van Hook gave her extra help in math; he gave her second tests to grade herself in math. What about Mrs. DeConcini, the math teacher? She just passed out the tests in class.

That was all for the defense, and Gitchoff returned to his seat.

Weber hoped that was strike three for Van Hook. Three young women had told their stories, and Weber didn't think the defense had gotten to any of them at all. Katherine had one problem with a date, and Weber was sure he could argue that away with the jury later. He looked at Van Hook, who wore essentially the same face he had throughout the trial—concern and pained wonderment about why these girls would say such things about him. Was he more worried now? the prosecutor wondered about the defendant.

After lunch Thursday, Greg Becker renewed the defense's request to keep Lori Parker from testifying and asked the judge to order the testimony of Stephanie Knight and Katherine Howes stricken from the record. Weber knew that was fruitless; if the judge did that, he also would be obliged to declare a mistrial because there was no way jurors could be expected to erase their own memory tapes of what those girls had said. But Becker argued that case law in Illinois said that such collateral evidence was allowed only if it was necessary to help the prosecution make its case. Listing most of the evidence produced by Weber, Becker was in the uncomfortable position of arguing that the case against his client was so strong that it didn't need the extra witnesses.

Weber couldn't resist the chance to tweak the defense again. Responding to Becker's argument, Weber said all of the other witnesses would have become part of the case in any event because Gitchoff asked the girls why they waited so long to tell the police what happened. Those questions would have allowed Weber to call witnesses to explain that the girls were found as part of the investigation into what happened at Caseyville School.

Ferguson rejected the defense motions, citing the same grounds as he had before. Weber's witnesses bolstered the credibility of Sarah Cramer, and that was the essence of the case. Lori Parker could testify and the other girls' testimony stayed on the record.

The trial resumed with Weber putting Sheila Howes on the stand so the jury could see this family and hear firsthand how this abuse had devastated a little girl. Sheila recounted Katherine's radical personality change during the 1980–1981 school year; the formerly loving girl stayed away from the rest of her family, hibernating in her room, and sometimes even missing supper. She did everything imaginable to stay home from school, even shoving her hand down her throat to make herself vomit. Weber ended his questioning by having the picture of Katherine's volleyball team circulated among the jurors. He hoped they would be looking at that while Gitchoff began his questioning. But Gitchoff had been around too long to fall for that; he told the judge he would wait until the jurors were finished.

The defender tried to suggest that Katherine was a much better than average student whose grades may have fallen off a little because she had transferred to Collinsville from another school district that year. Gitchoff implied she certainly didn't need help from a teacher in exchange for sex. Sheila said Katherine had done well in earlier years, but her marks had fallen drastically in the fifth and sixth grades. They improved again during the period Katherine said Van Hook was having sex with her.

Gitchoff asked if Sheila Howes hadn't talked to Van Hook about Katherine's poor grades once, even suggesting that the deterioration could be linked to the time Katherine discovered boys. Sheila said she may have said that, but her assumption had been based on the age at which she remembered discovering boys.

Weber came back on redirect examination with one question, asked in his best tone of sarcasm.

"At the time you talked to Mr. Van Hook, you didn't realize that a man had discovered your 12-year-old daughter, did you?"

"No," Sheila said sadly. "I thought she had discovered boys."

Don Weber was about to produce a chain of witnesses unlike any he had ever called, or even seen, in a trial. Ten girls were about to parade into the courtroom with testimony that should prove beyond a reasonable doubt that Richard Van Hook was a man capable of the acts with which he was charged. Except for Lori Parker—one of the court-approved M.O. witnesses—none of the girls would be permitted to say whether Van Hook had abused them. They were being called for the limited purpose of corroborating other girls' testimony.

Outside the courtroom, Pam Klein and Dennis Kuba were trying to keep the nervous children corralled and occupied until their turns arrived. The purpose of this ordeal seemed to be lost in the pressure and preparations for getting through it. They were intimidated by the crowd and nervous about being cross-examined by Gitchoff; but they were ready to face Van Hook. Sarah Cramer, the oldest, was actually the shy one in the group. But the presence of her and Stephanie Knight seemed to reassure the younger ones.

Pam had brought something special she hoped would give the girls a spiritual crutch during their times on the stand—a polished black teardrop rock made as a good-luck piece for the girls by a rape victim counseled by the crisis center. Pam gave the "magic stone" to the first girl called to the stand with instructions to hang onto it to ward off evil, and then to pass it to the next girl as she headed toward the stand. Pam didn't know until later that one of the girls had brought in her own talisman—a stuffed Garfield cat—and several of the girls clung to it as they testified, too.

Pam kept the girls in a small conference room on the other end of the third floor. In addition to the girls, the group included an occasional parent, several of the staff members from the crisis center, and some other victims being counseled there; they came to offer a special kind of moral support to the kids.

They all were jammed into the room, and the close quarters seemed to heighten the girls' anxieties. They took turns dissolving into tears and being comforted by their friends or Pam. She had the list Weber gave her each day with the order of witnesses, and she kept the girls advised of the lineup, and who was on deck. She tried to give them appropriate pep talks as their turns approached. She knew their time in this room was something that would stay with them for the rest of their lives, perhaps even in nightmares. But right now Pam wanted it to be a place of comfort where people walking the same path could hold fast to each other.

She also had to be there when each girl returned, exhausted and looking for arms into which she could collapse and cry. The girls were not so upset as they were drained and relieved it was over. None of them complained about their treatment by Gitchoff; Pam had explained the defense attorney's job, warning that he had to try to trip them up. She tried to make a game of it, challenging them to listen closely, tell the truth, and be as smart as Gitchoff.

Pam Klein was struggling with her own emotions, too. She knew she had to be strong for the kids, but it was difficult. It helped when, each day of the trial, one of the rape victims from the center would walk up and pin to Pam's lapel a rose that matched the color of her suit that day. That kind of extra care from a friend reminded Pam how important all of this was, and it gave her the strength she needed so badly.

One small table in the conference room held an assortment of candy bars and sodas, good-luck charms, and stuffed animals. Klein and Kuba also took the girls to the snack bar in the basement for refreshment runs, and to get them out of the stuffy room for a while. It helped release some of the pressure.

Kuba couldn't take the claustrophobic room and spent most of his time prowling the hall, subjecting himself to continuous glares from Van Hook's relatives and supporters. Stella Van Hook walked the hall almost incessantly, going round and round the banistered atrium that offered a view of the two floors below. Each time a girl was called as a witness, Stella and another one or two of the other partisans stationed themselves by the courtroom doors, forcing the girls to walk right past them to get in.

Pam sometimes thought of the situation in the conference room as waiting to make an appearance on a Hollywood set to make a movie. As the bailiff announced each girl's turn, Pam would think, "We're on." Even the look of the courthouse—so Middle America—seemed like the perfect set for a movie.

Pam Klein often escorted the girls close to the courtroom doors before sending them on alone. On the long walk, the girls kept Kuba in sight as he stood on the other side of the hall. He would flash them a grin and a thumbs-up. And then the two adults watched helplessly as the little figure—her heels clicking on the marble floor—slipped through the huge door and was swallowed up by the crowd inside. How could anyone believe these girls were lying, putting themselves through this hell for some ulterior motive? Kuba stood in amazement as he realized how much these kids trusted him and Klein; the thought was humbling and Kuba hoped he had been up to it.

Weber had no idea all of this was going on across the building, or how hard this was for the girls. As he began to call them to the stand, in fact, he was impressed by how strong they seemed. Their courage confirmed his confidence in Pam, Dennis, and Virgina Rulison; they had prepared the kids well, and it was comforting to be able to let them take over that part of this trial. He had his hands full inside the courtroom.

As Weber turned to his long list of children, Elizabeth McBride was the first to sit on the hot seat. The cute, short blonde recalled the gym mat, pillow, and desk in Van Hook's office, and remembered Van Hook taking Katherine Howes into that room on many, many occasions. Elizabeth once tried to open the door when they were in there, but it was locked. He never took boys in there like that, she said.

On cross-examination, Elizabeth explained that she and several other girls worked with Katherine in the library for Van Hook. These episodes in the office were at lunch and during recesses, just as Katherine had said.

Weber enjoyed watching Gitchoff try to keep from opening the door to more revealing questions; after all, one wrong step by the defense might allow Weber to ask Elizabeth about the time Van Hook unzipped her jumpsuit and slid his hand onto her buttocks. Gitchoff nearly opened the door by asking if students could go in and talk to Van Hook while he was working in that little office. She said yes. On re-direct, Weber asked if anything had happened to her when she went into the room. Gitchoff's objection was sustained; apparently the judge did not think Gitchoff opened the door that time. Weber hoped the jury was astute enough to catch the subtle suggestion.

Bethany Crothers echoed Elizabeth's testimony, as did Connie Hill. Gitchoff's cross of Bethany went nowhere; his only comment to Connie was, "You're cute." When Weber began questioning tiny Sharon Bailey, he quite unintentionally asked if she had seen Van Hook and Elizabeth McBride together; Sharon said yes before Weber caught his slip and corrected himself. He had meant Van Hook and Katherine, and Sharon's answer was yes again. Weber also used Sharon to introduce something new about Van Hook's personality.

"Did Van Hook have a temper while he was teaching?"

"Well, I know of one time when he was mad, he kicked the podium instead of taking it out on the class."

"Were you scared of him?"

"Well, sometimes, whenever he was mad, yes. But other times, no."

He even told the girls they could come and talk to him if they had problems, "like the monthly," Sharon almost whispered. Weber missed her answer and asked, "About what?" She said quietly again, "About the monthly." It still didn't sink in on Weber. "About the what?"

She said even softer, "The monthly that you have—that girls have every month."

Gitchoff volunteered, "Your period?"

Sharon nodded in relief. "The period."

Gitchoff had no cross-examination for her, either. "Thanks, honey."

Tammy Pauley remembered perfectly all the items in the office, and all the times she had seen Van Hook take Katherine into the room. He had sent Tammy to fetch Katherine for him a few times. And she added that Van Hook had a bad temper, cussed a lot in class, and kicked the podium and his desk.

Then Lori Parker—a tiny, delicate 12-year-old—took the stand to begin the account of what Weber had decided was proof that Dr. Jekyll had surrendered to Mr. Hyde—that Richard Van Hook was ruled completely by George.

She described how Van Hook had come to another teacher's room on January 7, 1982, with an almost transparent excuse to call her and Sally Morton out of the class and take them to his office. He took Sally into the room with him first and told Lori to get the rest of the class and bring them back to the library. When Lori returned, Sally came out of the room; she was crying, and she told Lori to go in. Behind the closed door, Van Hook told Lori that she made him feel like he was back in high school, and he remembered how a girl he liked then had left him. He asked Lori how she wanted him to treat her, declared that he didn't care if she got him fired or arrested; then he French-kissed her. She ran crying from the room and joined the still-weeping Sally in the rest room.

Weber thought again how this episode had convinced him that Richard Van Hook had been a man out of control on that January day just a year ago. The master manipulator; the schemer who knew when it was safe to sneak a girl into his own home and when his mother's home would be available; the evil analyst who could find the weakness in a girl's life; the devious stalker who picked his quarry so expertly—that man was losing it after years of careful conduct. The more he indulged his darker side, the more he was willing to risk. Was he moving steadily down the age scale, from victims 12 or 13 years old to those just 10, maybe even 9? Didn't he fear discovery as two little girls fled his office in tears? Was George the dominant personality then; did Richard exist only to bring George his sacrifices?

As Lori described more of their conversations, the young age of his most recent victims was even more obvious; many of his smooth lines were sailing far over their heads. Lori explained, "Before that all happened, he used to say to me that he wished I was 20 years younger, or 10 years younger . . ." Her brow furrowed as she realized that couldn't be right. What had he said? Oh, yeah. "No, that I was ten years older and he was ten years younger." Yeah, that made sense, she guessed. She wasn't even sure why Van Hook was wishing away the years that way.

Lori had avoided Van Hook for several days after the incident in his office, and he finally had someone call her out of the rest room so he could ask if they still were friends. "I said, 'I don't know,' " she explained with a singsong voice and a slight turn of her head up and away. Weber was pleased; so childish, and so appropriate.

"And then he asked me if I had a boyfriend, and I said yes. And he asked me if he kissed better than him, and I said, 'I don't know.' " Same voice, same gesture; Weber almost chuckled out loud. "And then he said, 'You haven't found out yet?' And I said, 'No.' And then I went back in the bathroom."

Was Lori having problems outside school then? Yes, her father was drinking a lot; another perfect, vulnerable victim.

Van Hook asked her to stay after school to help him with the files, but she said she had to go home. He held out Katherine Howes as an example; she used to call her father to tell him she was staying after school. Van Hook even offered Lori a dollar to stay. Was the man who did

that in court today? Yes, she said as she pointed at Richard Van Hook.

Weber turned and sat down. John Gitchoff smiled and
said only, "Thank you."

Sally Morton was 11—a stocky, athletic-looking girl
with short golden hair and blue eyes. She confirmed the
event Lori had described, although Weber was not allowed to ask her what happened between her and Van
Hook in the room. She and Lori cried in the rest room,
and told their friends what had happened.

Under the court rule that allowed an exception to hearsay evidence so a witness could repeat an "excited utter-
ance," Sally could quote Lori. "She said he embraced her
and kissed her in a very improper way," Sally remembered with an air of indignation.

"Did you girls decide to do anything about this?"

"Yes, we decided we wouldn't tell no one, except for
our friends, until he tried it again, because we were afraid
he was going to hurt us. And if he tried it again, we were
going to tell. We didn't think it was very serious at the
time."

Another 11-year-old, Bobbie Hunter, started to sob as
soon as she sat down. Through tears she told of seeing
her friends, Lori and Sally, crying in the rest room. The
girls said Van Hook had called them out of class and
taken them into his little office. Bobbie was talking fast
as she remembered the girls telling her that Van Hook had
made these odd comments to them.

"He took Lori and he French-kissed Lori, and then it
was Sally's turn. He took her and embraced her, and held
her real tight, and told her all this stuff."

Gitchoff asked if Bobbie was in the class with the other
girls and saw Van Hook call them out. "Uh-huh." Did
Lori come back a few minutes later and get the rest of the
class?

"No."

"All right."

Bobbie turned abruptly to Judge Ferguson and, with a
plea in her moist eyes and a quaver in her voice, she
asked plaintively, "Can I leave?"

It was obvious Gitchoff had more questions, but he was not about to keep her any longer after that. He smiled and said, "Sure." Ferguson seemed thoroughly surprised as a faint smile crossed his bearded face.

The 11-year-old girl who had started it all, Michelle Sedlacek, stood solemnly as she took the oath before testifying.

". . . and nothing but the truth, so help you God?"

And the little voice said, "Amen."

"Michelle, did you say 'I do,' or did you say 'Amen'?" Weber asked with a smile. "I said 'I do,' " she insisted. Weber laughed. "Okay. All right."

She recalled Lori saying Van Hook had French-kissed her, but she couldn't remember any of the other things Van Hook had said. Weber tried to help her by mentioning her statement to the Caseyville police, where her stepfather was Officer Ron Tamburello. But it didn't work, and Michelle was excused.

Weber's last witness was little Ellen Spanos, who explained that she was just three days shy of her twelfth birthday. All the girls had been terribly upset about what had happened to Lori and Sally, and they had agreed they wouldn't tell. Ellen added brightly, "But Michelle Sedlacek told somebody, and we were all happy that she did."

Gitchoff smiled. "Spanos. Is that a Greek name?"

"I guess. Yes, it is."

"Do you speak Greek?"

"No, I don't."

"That's all."

That was all, and that was the end of Don Weber's case against Richard Van Hook. The finale had been a series of girls who kept getting younger and tinier as they marched to the stand; Weber hadn't planned it that way, but the effect was stunning.

Judge Ferguson sent the jurors home for a three-day weekend and told them to return on Monday, February 14. He also warned them not to begin weighing the evidence before the defense presented its case. "Don't start making any judgments on half-a-loaf," he said.

The prosecutor liked the way the case had sounded in court. Sometimes what looks like a good case crumbles in the courtroom; for some reason, the evidence never gels and the progression of witnesses never seems to progress. But this case had tried well. Weber knew better than to guess what the jury was hearing. But he thought the girls had presented consistent accounts of abuse in terms that made it real and, in some cases, horrifying. The M.O. points came across well, and those improbable details seemed to make the girls' stories all the more believable. After all, how could a group of 12 adults think some kids had made up such a list of warped idiosyncracies, especially "George"? Surely the girls had put to rest those absurd rumors that they had concocted this elaborate conspiracy to "get" Van Hook. The kids who took that stand obviously lacked the motive, the malevolence, or the maturity to put together that kind of diabolical scheme. And Gitchoff certainly hadn't brought out any suggestion of that on cross-examination; in fact, Weber thought his opponent hadn't scored any points at all.

How would the defense handle all of this? Unlike his experience in most cases, Weber had been unable to glean much about the defense's strategy from Gitchoff's cross-examinations. Obviously, the dates were extremely important, but Weber wasn't sure where Gitchoff would go with that. There was likely to be some evidence about the kind of bed in Van Hook's son's room; Sarah Cramer had insisted it wasn't a baby crib, and Gitchoff had asked repeatedly if she was sure.

Would Richard Van Hook take the stand to defend himself? What could the man say after hearing so many of his students tell such damning tales on him? Weber had heard a lot of defendants try to escape such snares. The smart ones knew they had to give up the facts that had been proved—like some of the little kisses—while adding a spin to make them seem less intentionally criminal—an innocent, fatherly act sadly misinterpreted by adolescent girls with active hormones. There had been plenty of time for Van Hook to perfect a good story to fit most of the facts, and to explain why these girls would want to see him destroyed. Weber thought the man had to get up there and offer the jury something in his defense.

So, facing a three-day weekend at the end of his case, Weber was feeling pretty good. Little did he know how abruptly his mood would change Monday morning.

CHAPTER 15

John Gitchoff shuffled casually over to the jury box and began to speak, less like a defense attorney delivering an opening statement in an emotionally charged trial than an old friend about to relate an entertaining story. His voice was calm and reassuring, restrained enough to promise no bombastic pronouncements or artfully drawn phrases. His tie was characteristically loosened at the collar. One hand rested comfortably in a pants pocket, and the other gestured gently as he made his points. Vintage Gitchoff; you had to love the guy.

But before long Don Weber's brow began to wrinkle as he listened to the old pro. Gitchoff and the Van Hooks had been very busy, and a substantial defense seemed to be shaping up. Some things the prosecutor hadn't anticipated were coming to light, and he was beginning to get concerned.

The veteran defender promised that teachers from Caseyville School would testify that Richard Van Hook's lunch hours were crammed with activities that would allow little time for such absurd dalliances in a school closet; and custodians would say they never found evidence of Van Hook's alleged activities in that room. In fact, the entire student body spent part of the lunch hour lined up in the hallway right outside the library where this teacher supposedly was defiling little girls. Many witnesses would swear they never caught Van Hook in that room with any students.

Gitchoff went down the list of activities that filled Van Hook's spare time and lunch hours—running off copies of tests and other materials on the mimeographing machine outside the door of the principal's office; coaching the teams for the kids' athletic contests called Junior Olympics; meeting with other teachers to discuss a special class they were taking together; instructing another teacher on the use of wood-carving tools; even leaving the school grounds to pick up films or other materials for class.

What about the math tests Van Hook supposedly slipped to Katherine Howes so she could forge one for an A? Well, they were kept under lock and key in another teacher's cabinet, and that teacher distributed, graded, and returned the tests.

Gitchoff slammed Weber between the eyes with a particularly unexpected move; it wasn't devastating, just very effective. Remember the little brass elephant Katherine claimed she got from Van Hook during a field trip? Well, the gift shops at the Magic House and the St. Louis Museum of Transportation say they never sold any such item.

The defense also hammered at Sarah Cramer's story about sex with Van Hook at his mother's house right after school. First, Van Hook had "bus duty" after school on those days; he couldn't leave the playground until all of the children had boarded the buses and they had pulled away. On other days he met with teachers after school for a variety of activities and bull sessions. Other factors weighed in against Sarah, too; new siding was being installed at Stella Van Hook's house, and workmen were there every day. One of them, in fact, was Jay Carr's brother, Matt, who was visited there by a lot of girls who could have wandered into the open house. Could a visit to her boyfriend's brother explain Sarah's familiarity with the house?

Then came the most staggering series of alibis Weber ever had heard. In an amazing effort, the defense had been able to reconstruct what Richard Van Hook had been doing on almost every Saturday in 1976 that Sarah Cramer had listed as possible dates of the incident at his house. On November 20, the evidence would show that the Van Hooks's television was in the repair shop; Sarah obviously hadn't watched *American Bandstand* on it that day. The next Saturday, the Van Hooks were at home, waiting for a call from Sandra's sister to announce whether or not she was pregnant; the doctor's office would verify that and the sister would testify that she called Sandra at home between 11 and 11:30 that morning. On December 4, a canceled check would prove that the Van Hooks had driven to Belleville to buy two rocking chairs for their children; that afternoon, they went to a diving practice at a swim club. The weekend of December 11, Van Hook was attending a diving meet in Iowa. On December 18, the entire Van Hook family had been at the home of Sandra's mother, who had been injured in an automobile accident. The next two Saturdays were Christmas and New Year's days, so they were ruled out.

The defense was chipping away, bit by bit, at what Weber had thought was a rock-solid case. It wasn't time to panic, but he was troubled.

It was not about to get any better, either. Sarah had said the Van Hook kids weren't wearing diapers when she baby-sat for them, and that the little boy had a bed, not a crib, in his room. Well, Gitchoff drawled, home movies at Christmas 1976 would show Van Hook's son clearly in diapers; and several witnesses and another canceled check would prove that the Van Hooks purchased a bed to replace the boy's crib—in June 1977—at least seven months after Sarah's visit.

By the time John Gitchoff ended his long statement, Don Weber was unnerved. He reminded himself about the routine ups and downs during a trial; it was okay to be a little worried after the defense began, just as it was normal to feel good after presenting your own evidence. He also tried to convince himself that he wasn't more concerned than necessary, but his belly told him something else. He was quite anxious now about what had seemed just three days ago to be an overwhelming case.

After his opening statement, Gitchoff launched into his list of witnesses with vigor. His secretary took the stand and read Katherine Howes's testimony before the grand jury in St. Clair County to establish that she had said the first sexual incident was before Christmas 1980. That point didn't concern Weber too much; he could argue that such a slip from a nervous child meant nothing. Anyway, the testimony reinforced many of the details Weber thought added to Katherine's credibility. She had been an 11-year-old virgin for whom intercourse was painful, and she was innocently unaware of the meaning of words like "orgasm and climax."

Three janitors at Caseyville School testified they never found anything suspicious in the storage room in the library, nor saw Van Hook there with students. But Weber got one to say he had seen Van Hook in that room; the other one, who didn't start work until after the lunch hours, remembered seeing a desk in the room. A school secretary said Van Hook often used the "ditto machine" outside the office door during the lunch hour. One of the teachers said Van Hook used the machine so often that she and his other colleagues had to remind him to share.

Another teacher recalled she had been taking a graduate course with Van Hook and some other teachers. Weber chuckled when she said the class was on "storytelling" for children's literature; there was a certain irony to that. The class was held in the library at the Caseyville School one afternoon a week from 3:30 to 6:30. She also remembered Van Hook at the ditto machine in the hallway at lunchtime.

Weber asked if she was aware that Van Hook had an office in the library, and was surprised when she responded haughtily, "I don't think any teacher has an office."

"Did Mr. Van Hook have a special room there in the library that you knew of?"

"No, not that I know of."

"Did he ever take you into any room there?"

"No."

Weber decided to prime the jury as he handed the woman a photograph of the office/storage room. "Did you ever notice any signs on that door?"

"No."

Weber already was tiring of the testimony that dripped

of sugar-coated sweetness while slanting everything in Van Hook's favor.

The march of the colleagues to the stand continued, and Weber recognized the next witness as one who had spoken strongly in Van Hook's defense in the newspapers. She had taken the storytelling class with Van Hook and spent some lunch hours with him; she also was an avid user of the library and spent a lot of her free time with him there. She knew he occasionally left the school at lunch to pick up films and other material at the Collinsville Public Library.

Weber tried to distill her testimony to its essence with his first question. "Sometimes you saw him at lunch and sometimes you didn't see him at lunch. Is that correct?"

"Yes, sir."

Weber asked about Van Hook's office in the library and got the response he expected. "I'm not aware of a specific office. The library is an open room—a large, open room," she said.

Weber handed her the picture of the storage room. "Was there a desk in there?"

"Not to my knowledge. No, sir."

"Were there pillows in there?"

"No, sir."

"Was there a beanbag chair in there?"

"No, sir. There was a beanbag chair in the library itself."

"Was there a gym mat in there?"

"No. sir."

Weber handed her a photo of the inside of the room, and pointed to what clearly was a student desk to one side. "Does that look like a desk to you, right there by that doorknob?"

"No, sir. I'm sorry. Were you pointing to this box?"

Weber was losing his patience and he jabbed his finger almost angrily at the desk again; his finger thumped hard against the wood under the photo. "No, right here. See? There's a shadow there."

"No, sir."

Weber gritted his teeth. "That doesn't look like a desk to you?"

"No, sir."

In the hundreds of cross-examinations Weber had conducted, no witness ever had denied the evidence in a photo before. It was all he could to do to restrain himself.

"And are you as sure about the pillow, and the beanbag chair, and the gym mat as you are about the desk?" he asked sarcastically.

"Yes, sir."

Gitchoff tried to give her an out. What did she think of as a desk? "I think of it in terms of a teacher's desk, sir."

Weber asked, "Well, was there another kind of desk in there?"

"No, sir, not to my knowledge."

The next teacher called to the stand was Dennis Craft, a boyhood acquaintance of Weber's from Collinsville, and someone Weber knew would tell the absolute truth no matter what. Craft, who was the athletic director at Caseyville School during the period covered by Katherine Howes, told Gitchoff that Van Hook had helped Craft coach the Junior Olympics teams in April and May of 1981. They practiced at noon on the playground two days a week. Craft also said the gym mats at the school were heavy, awkward beasts, 8 feet by 12 feet; the clear implication was that Van Hook wasn't whipping out one of these for lunchtime liaisons in the little room.

Weber smiled as he approached the witness. His favorite memory of Dennis Craft was when he had asked a girl if she wanted to go a dance and she said, "Yes, but not with you." Weber decided to let the jury see a friendlier prosecutor, and he grinned as he asked, "Have you seen Jeannette lately?" Unfortunately, his little joke bombed as Craft, completely puzzled, said, "Pardon me?"

Weber shook his head. "Never mind."

After Craft said he never had seen Van Hook's little office in the library, Weber decided to let the jury in on the little secret.

"He never showed you the inside of what he called the 'Bear's Cave,' did he?"

"The what?"

"You never saw any signs on the door referring to the room as the 'Bear's Cave'?"

"No, sir."

Weber hoped the jury had caught the implication. This was something else that Van Hook hid from his colleagues, and shared only with his chosen victims. The other teachers were ignorant about many important things concerning Mr. Van Hook, despite their absolutely, self-righteously, positive testimony.

The large woman with the very dark hair told the jury, "My name is Maria DeConcini." Weber had been waiting for this one.

Gitchoff led DeConcini on a long, boring presentation of her duties and the team-teaching program she shared with Van Hook; they combined their classes so he could teach physical education and she could teach math. DeConcini kept the tests locked in her cabinet in her room, and her teacher's aide, Carol Freeman, took them to Van Hook's class as needed; only the number of tests necessary were distributed. The aide then collected and graded the tests, and posted the grades. Van Hook had no access to the tests.

DeConcini said she often spent lunch hours with Van Hook in early 1981 so he could teach her to use wood-carving tools, or so they could discuss the students in their shared classes.

At several points during the testimony, Weber decided to keep Gitchoff's feet to the fire and show disdain for the witness by objecting to leading questions. The objections usually were sustained, and carried the added benefits of irritating Gitchoff and breaking his train of thought.

DeConcini explained that she had Katherine Howes as a math student—an A student, she explained—and had been Sarah Cramer's homebound teacher while Sarah was "disabled." Gitchoff asked if Sarah ever had confided in Mrs. DeConcini. The teacher said yes, that Sarah had wanted to go to work instead of returning to school when she was ready; the principal refused to give Sarah a work permit, however, so she returned to classes.

Weber girded himself for what he assumed would be a battle royale as he approached the witness stand. He decided to prod Mrs. D right from the start.

"Is it fair to say that you are pretty good friends with Mr. Van Hook?"

"No, sir. I am not 'pretty good friends' with him," she said with an air of superior indignation. "I have a good working relationship with Mr. Van Hook. We are not friends, especially, at all."

"Well, is it fair to say you are very, very supportive of Mr. Van Hook in this case?"

"Oh, yes," she said with satisfaction.

Without identifying his source, Weber trotted out a recollection of Sheila Howes from a class trip. "Is it fair to say that you are pretty chummy with him when you go on field trips, like to the Transportation Museum?"

She was insulted. "I am not 'chummy,' " she pronounced.

"Well, do you put your arms around him and confide in him on those trips."

"I do not."

"How are you with Katherine Howes?"

"Katherine Howes and I got pretty close, and especially so during the spelling bee when she came and clutched my hand and cried."

"Would you expect Katherine Howes to confide in you? Were you that close with her?"

"Perhaps. We did not have a lot of talking time, though, because I only saw her in class."

"Since Katherine Howes has come forward and made these statements, how have you felt about her?"

"I feel very sorry for Katherine. My heart breaks for the girl." DeConcini's eyes narrowed and she bore in at Weber with them. "She's been—she's being used."

"Have you seen Katherine since she made these allegations?"

"Once."

"Have you seen her outside the school room?"

"When she was parading in front of school," DeConcini said with scorn.

Weber turned up the heat. "Did you ever see her at her house?"

"Never," she spat back.

Weber was surprised that she would deny her surveillance visits. He leaned forward. "Did you ever go to her house, and sit by the driveway, and stare at her when she was outside?"

"I don't even know where she lives," she said with an indignant wave of her hand.

Weber was incredulous as he leaned in closer. "Have you been there twice?"

DeConcini's head jerked up in anger; she was about to rocket out of her chair. She blurted, "What? Sir, you are mad! I have no idea where Katherine Howes lives."

Weber hesitated, letting her outburst sink in on the jury. His assistant, Randy Massey, grinned as he noted on his legal pad, "Don Weber is mad."

Weber changed course and asked how much DeConcini knew about Van Hook's little office. He didn't have one that she was aware of, she said. Weber showed her the photo of the room, and she described it as a crowded storage space for movie projectors and similar equipment. Weber asked about the floor space, and she said she never even saw the floor through the clutter, and never noticed a desk in there. Weber asked whether she had seen a "Bear's Cave" sign, looking at the jury as he mentioned that again; she didn't remember that, either.

Weber decided to provoke her more by referring to a report he had just received that DeConcini had popped off to a sister of Susan Williams just the week before, saying Susan shouldn't be involved in the activities against Van Hook. But DeConcini denied saying that, and the judge sustained an objection by Gitchoff when Weber tried to probe further.

Weber headed for the finish line. "You were present at the grand jury in Madison County, is that correct?"

"Yes."

"Did you say anything to any of these girls after the grand jury had returned?"

"What girls?" she asked innocently.

Weber was amazed by that. "The girls who testified."

"I never saw them, ever," she said emphatically.

"You didn't stand in the hallway and say things to them in a loud voice?"

DeConcini was getting furious and her fist shot into the air. She spat out, "Never. I said something to you, though, in the hallway, and you lied back."

"Tell the jury what you said to me," Weber said calmly.

Gitchoff had heard enough and knew he needed to stop his witness's hemorrhaging on the stand. He objected that Weber was trying to harass the "lady." Weber said the question went to the witness's bias or prejudice. DeConcini pointed at Weber and interjected, "I think they should know what he said to me, though."

Gitchoff wasn't surrendering the floor, even to his own witness. "Ma'am, if you want to sit at the table, that's all right with me," he huffed.

"I'm sorry," she said.

Judge Ferguson sustained the objection, and Weber sat down to punctuate the end of what he hoped was an enlightening exchange for the jury. He leaned forward on the table.

"Just one last question," he said softly. "You were one of the teachers that these girls were expected to report these things to?"

"Huh? No," she said huffily.

"Do you think that Katherine or Sarah might have been a little bit reluctant to report anything to you because of your attitude?"

"What attitude?"

Weber almost laughed at that. "The one you have just displayed here."

"You made me display it by lying," she shot back.

"No further questions."

Gitchoff wanted no part of that and dismissed the witness. DeConcini stomped up the aisle, pausing near Weber to glare at him and sputter, "Liar," as she passed his table.

Weber looked at the jurors, who seemed startled. He hoped the ferocious demonstration had shown them the hostility these girls had met when they came forward with the truth; Maria DeConcini personified why kids are frightened to tell adults, and she had explained it better than any psychologist. Weber thought that surely had to put to rest any belief that the girls should have gone to a teacher to report what another teacher was doing to them. Hadn't Van Hook warned them about that, after all?

Weber turned to Randy Massey and asked, "Was I too tough on her?" Massey grinned and said, "No way. She had it coming."

Pam Klein had watched the confrontation and explosions through the door from the hallway. By DeConcini's face and actions, Klein knew Weber had got what he wanted. The woman had shown all the sensitivity of a runaway bulldozer. How could the jurors fail to see why kids kept their silence?

John Gitchoff called a long series of witnesses to fill out the rest of Monday afternoon. The teacher's aide for DeConcini, Carol Freeman, confirmed that the tests were held in a locked cabinet, and DeConcini kept the key. Freeman said she also had received help with wood carving from Van Hook. She was on the field trips with him, and remembered Sheila Howes going along; everyone got along fine, she said. But she was sure Van Hook did not buy a brass elephant.

As Weber approached for cross-examination, he smiled and said, "Mrs. Freeman, after the last witness, I am almost afraid to ask any questions. But is it safe to say you are not very antagonistic toward me, that you are just here to tell the truth? Right?

"Yes, sir."

Gitchoff smiled and quipped to Weber, "To know you is to love you."

Weber showed Freeman the wooden plaque Katherine

Howes had been given by Van Hook, the one bearing the motto, "Love is contagious; we get it from one another."

"I have never seen that one," Freeman said.

Gitchoff called three boys from Van Hook's class. One had worked as a library captain, too, and had gotten a wooden plaque from Van Hook. The plaque had the name of the school and the date on it; Van Hook had not asked him what he wanted on it. Van Hook had never taken him into the room in the back, and he didn't remember the teacher taking any girls back there, either. But he remembered a desk there. He also remembered that a girl had come in after school and used an overhead projector to make a poster.

The next two boys had seen the incident with Lori Parker and Sally Morton, and both said Van Hook had talked to the girls one at a time in his little office. They said they thought Van Hook had left the door open about eight inches while he talked to the girls. Both girls had been crying when they left.

Van Hook's trip to Iowa over the weekend of December 11 was confirmed by a doctor who had accompanied his daughter—a diver on Van Hook's team—and by two young men who were divers and rode in a rented van with Van Hook. One of them told Weber that Barbara Maxwell was on the team then and made the trip; Weber wondered if Van Hook managed to pin her into a corner and kiss her then, too. The diver mentioned that he believed Barbara eventually quit the team.

Ronald Russell, a contractor, testified that he had installed siding on Stella Van Hook's house in late September, October, and the first part of November 1977; he had a check dated September 2 for the down payment. He said he and a worker, Matt Carr, had been there every day until 5:30 or 6 o'clock. Oh sure, Weber thought, just like every construction crew. Russell said the house was open to the workers to run electrical cords, or use the bathroom, and a carload of girls stopped by to talk to Matt almost every afternoon.

To counter the obvious suggestion about how Sarah Cramer had learned about Stella's house, Weber delved deeper into the schedule for the siding job. Russell said he and Carr were on the job every day for a week or a week-and-a-half in September; after that, it was less frequent, while they waited for the windows to be delivered. That was more like it, Weber thought. Russell also testified that the girls who visited Matt had never been allowed in the house or even on the porch; the workers were especially careful when Stella was gone to get groceries or run other errands.

Weber decided to demonstrate just how useful all of this information really was. "Do you know where Stella Van Hook's husband kept his prophylactics in that house?"

"No, I do not," the contractor said in surprise.

"You wouldn't have any way of knowing that, would you?"

"No" was the response that conveyed the unspoken question "Who the hell would know that?"

Two more teachers were brought in. The first said teachers were required to stay an hour after classes ended at 2:10, and they usually gathered in her room for bull sessions. She could not recall any time that Van Hook had left before three o'clock in September or October 1977. On cross, she told Weber the first time she had been asked to remember if Van Hook ever left early was just two days ago, on Saturday—more than five years after the time period in question. Was she saying Van Hook couldn't have left early? No, just that she didn't recall that happening.

"It's hard to remember six years ago, isn't it?" Weber suggested.

"No, sir. I can remember a lot of things six years ago," she responded.

Here we go again, Weber thought. The teachers were hanging together like a bunch of bananas, refusing to concede even the most obvious point if it tended to count against Van Hook in any way. Weber tried to test her memory by asking who was in her classroom on the second Monday in September, but she hung tight and offered the name of a teacher who was there "most days." Not good enough, Weber said. But he knew he was butting his head against a brick wall, and he changed course. Was Van Hook in her room every day in September and October until three o'clock? No, she never said that. "He was there every day that I can remember that I happened to be there," she offered.

Weber held his temper as best he could. "Okay, so generally he was there every day?"

"Yes, sir."

"Okay. But there could have been days when he wasn't there?"

"Yes, sir."

Weber remembered the next teacher from his days as a student. He never had a class with Dennis Diaz, but he remembered him as a competent and popular teacher. He had been Van Hook's department chairman for social studies at the high school, where Van Hook was teaching when Sarah Cramer said the second sexual incident happened. As Gitchoff got close to the point, he made the slip of tongue he had feared all along.

"In the fall of '77, do you know that Dick Van Dyke"—the crowd began to laugh as Gitchoff chuckled and corrected himself—"Van Hook, Richard Van Hook—I knew I was going to make that mistake once. That Richard Van Hook had bus duty?"

As the laughter subsided, Diaz explained that Van Hook was required to keep order in front of the school as the students blasted onto the buses after school. That took no more than ten minutes, and then Van Hook returned to the building until he could leave at three o'clock. Before three, Diaz and Van Hook often met to discuss Van Hook's new and unfamiliar duties teaching social studies. Generally, Diaz agreed, with some prodding by Gitchoff, Van Hook was present every afternoon until three o'clock.

That was another silly suggestion by Gitchoff that Weber had to clear up immediately. "But there could have been one day when he wasn't there, right?"

"Certainly," Diaz willingly agreed. With a humorous mention that the spectators in the courtroom included administrators from the school district, he explained that there was a simple procedure—reporting to the principal in person or by note—for a teacher who wanted to leave before three o'clock. The policy was very liberal, Diaz said; no third degree for teachers wanting to leave a few minutes early.

Weber smiled. "Do you remember me?"

Diaz returned the grin. "Yes, I do."

Weber dropped it there, but Gitchoff cracked, "I was going to ask you if he was brilliant." Diaz smiled again: "He probably was."

Weber smiled weakly. Good times at old Collinsville High seemed a dim memory now, despite the kind words.

Gitchoff turned his guns next on two important points from Sarah Cramer's account of the incident at Van Hook's house. A nurse and friend of Sandra Van Hook's testified that she helped Sandra find a twin bed for her son in June 1977—six months after Sarah remembered such a bed in the boy's room. The nurse said she visited the Van Hooks in December 1976, and saw a crib.

A damaging blow to Sarah's story, Weber knew. He tried to test the nurse's memory of the furniture in the house, but didn't make any headway. He asked if she knew whether there was a towel in Dick and Sandy's nightstand, and she said no. It didn't help much, and Weber felt uneasy as the nurse left the stand.

The next witness was the Van Hooks' former baby-sitter, who also was a nurse now. She had been a junior in high school when she watched the Van Hooks' kids in December 1976. She remembered that the little boy still wore diapers—she changed them. And she remembered that he slept in a crib—she put him to sleep there.

Another kidney punch. With some rather terse questioning, Weber got her to agree that it was difficult to remember some details six years later. But she was certain there was a crib in that room then and, as she began to cry, she complained that Weber was trying to confuse her. Weber tried to avoid bullying young women on the stand, but he had to test her memory. He didn't get very far. She even explained that she remembered baby-sitting for the

Van Hooks on the Tuesday after Christmas in 1976; she knew because she listened to the radio to hear Collinsville High School's Kahok basketball team play in the holiday tournament at Southern Illinois University at Carbondale. The team won, she remembered. That drew a quip from Gitchoff that people from Madison, like him, always rooted against Collinsville.

Weber remembered all the fun and excitement of those basketball games, and he knew that a good Kahok fan could, indeed, recall the dates. Gitchoff had called 22 witnesses Monday, and the last two had inflicted significant wounds to the prosecution's case. Weber had an uncomfortable night; *Winds of War* had ended, and he had a different war to fight.

CHAPTER 16

Richard Van Hook still had the same expression on his face Tuesday morning as he watched the first four witnesses testify. Weber couldn't read much in the face, and he wondered if Gitchoff had been genuine when he told reporters the evening before that Van Hook would testify. Van Hook still seemed to be playing a role.

Gitchoff picked up where he had left off on Monday. The assistant director of the Magic House gift shop said the shop had never stocked a brass, bronze, or copper elephant like the one Gitchoff showed her—the one Katherine Howes said she got from Van Hook on a field trip to that attraction and the St. Louis Museum of Transportation. Weber had talked to Katherine about that again, and she had explained that Van Hook said he bought it at the St. Louis Zoo while he was there with his family; he just had given it to her after the trip to the Magic House. Weber really didn't think this point was a big deal, and he tried to let the jury know that. He simply asked the gift-shop operator if she had any idea whether such charms were sold at the zoo; she didn't.

Richard Van Hook's sister, Susan Meadows, testified she had lived next door to their parents in Collinsville while the siding job was being completed between September and November 1977. Sometimes the workers still were there when she got home from work at 4:30, and sometimes they weren't. Susan also described an all-American, family-tree odyssey for the crib that belonged to her nephew. Her brother had given it to Sandra's sister for her children, and she had given it to Susan for hers. Gitchoff went so far as to have the crib rolled into the courtroom so Susan could identify it; Weber thought that was an extraordinary effort and an effective use of a solid piece of evidence for the defense. Quite a journey for a piece of furniture.

But he saw a chance to slip in a zinger. Could the workmen have been at her mother's house without Susan knowing it? Yes.

"And your brother could have been at your mom's house and you wouldn't know that either, would you?"

Meadows knew the program, however, and resisted the obvious answer in favor of skirting the issue. "He was in school," she insisted.

Weber wasn't going to back off that easily. "Until 4:30?" he asked impatiently.

"No."

"Well, if the workmen could have been there without you knowing about it before 4:30, isn't it true that your brother could have been?"

"Yes, sir."

One more question. "Did you know, prior to this trial, where your father kept his prophylactics?"

"No, sir, I didn't."

The implication in Weber's recurrent theme was obvious; if no one knew but Sarah, how did she find out?

The next two witnesses—Sandra Van Hook's sister and brother-in-law, Jo Lynn and Jacob Deck—really nailed down several points in the alibis. They testified they got the crib in June 1977, and helped Richard and Sandra pick up a new bed for their son at the same time. Jacob remembered the date because he used the new truck he bought just days before; he even had the documents from the vehicle purchase. The Decks also testified about calling the Van Hooks on the Saturday morning after Thanksgiving 1976 to announce that the doctor had just confirmed that they were expecting their first child. The check for the payment to the doctor was introduced into evidence. Jimmy Wallis had been busy.

Weber was slowly coming to the conclusion that Sarah Cramer somehow had mixed up the date of the incident at Van Hook's house. He was convinced the sex had occurred, but the date must be wrong. It certainly wasn't

December 11, and maybe it wasn't even in 1976. He believed Sarah and the other girls unequivocally, and he hoped the jury would overlook such a flaw in memory and accept the essence of their testimony, too.

On cross-examination, Jo Lynn Deck remembered that the sofa in Dick and Sandy's family room was a Hide-A-Bed—a point for Sarah. And Jo Lynn admitted she would have no way of knowing what might be in the drawer in her sister's nightstand—another point for Sarah.

The almost circus atmosphere in the hallways during the trial continued, with camera crews from the television stations scrambling to tape Van Hook and his wife every time they walked out of, or into, the courtroom. Van Hook obviously was tiring of being the center of such attention. When one cameraman got too close as he backpedaled to keep Van Hook in view, the teacher made the mistake so common to people unused to that kind of media scrutiny; Van Hook angrily reached out and gave the camera lens a shove. What better and more incriminating tape could a TV station ask for than a hostile defendant interfering with the rights of the press to get the news? Everyone who succumbed to that desire looked so guilty.

Reporters from the St. Louis newspapers were more diplomatic. They went to Gitchoff, politely explained that their photographers were on the way, and proposed a cooperative venture. They could engage in a hallway dogfight, getting shots of a reluctant and guilty-looking Van Hook trying to dodge the news cameras, or Gitchoff could advise his client to pose pleasantly for a picture that would put his best side in the papers. Gitchoff didn't hesitate to arrange Van Hook's cooperation; the results were photos of a man who, if not exactly thrilled to be there, at least looked like something other than a guilty monster.

Other views of Van Hook and the trial were forthcoming from artists hired by TV stations and newspapers to capture the scene in the courtroom where cameras were banned. The artists had to scramble for front-row seats, squeezing in with their large pads and boxes of pencils.

* * *

John Gitchoff turned to the short, trim man in the medium-blue suit, and called Richard Van Hook to the witness stand at 11:20. This was Van Hook's chance to test his theory that no one would take the word of little girls over a teacher, and Weber had been looking forward to it. What would this man say now? He couldn't stonewall it and deny everything; there were too many witnesses and too much corroboration. Would he finesse the facts to fit his version of reality? Would he offer some reason that all these girls were out to get him? He was too bright to confuse easily, or to blow up and confess. But he had a lot of weak points to protect and contradictions to explain, and Weber thought cross-examination would be crucial.

Van Hook was mildly uncomfortable—hunched shoulders and a somewhat strained, poker face—as he recited his biography: family, teaching credentials, 15 years as a diving and swimming coach at six clubs. His voice was soft but firm. Weber thought Van Hook was determined to play out his bluff.

Gitchoff wasted little time getting to the heart of matters. He referred his client to the period when Katherine Howes was his student. "In December of 1980, before the Christmas vacation, did you have intercourse with Katherine Howes?"

Weber waited for some righteous indignation and wounded virtue. Instead, Van Hook delivered a firm but flat, "I did not." Too controlled, Weber thought.

"Was there any type of fondling, kissing, or sexual activity in any manner with Katherine Howes?"

"There was none," Van Hook said earnestly and quietly.

Did he have intercourse with her after that time? "I did not."

"Did you fondle her, or kiss her, or rub her breasts, or undress her at any time during that period of time?"

"I did not."

"Or at any other time?"

"No, sir."

Mutt and Jeff stuff for the attorney and his client, Weber thought, and not very convincing. Gitchoff knew the jury had to hear the defendant's denials from his own mouth, but Weber thought it rang hollow. Van Hook still hadn't figured out how to act innocent; he lacked the sometimes uncontrolled anger and frustration of a man unjustly accused of such a heinous crime.

Led adroitly by Gitchoff, Van Hook offered a long description of the library at Caseyville School, and confirmed that he used the storage closet there as a "part-time office—if you want to call it that." Amid the shelves and carts for projectors, there were a student desk and chair. Weber liked that, especially after the teachers—one in particular—had so carefully denied there was any furniture.

Van Hook identified the photograph of the empty box that looked like a book, and explained that it held *National Geographic* magazines.

"Did you ever, at any time, hide any prophylactics in a box or book like that?"

"No, sir," was the calm denial.

Was there a sleeping bag in that room? "Never." Weber knew that was too incriminating to admit, no matter how many girls had sworn it was there.

Pillows? Not in the storage room; there were some in the library. What about a gym mat? "Not that I know of."

Gitchoff moved to the M.O. points, and Van Hook denied them, one by one. He had never told Katherine she made him feel like he was back in high school; he never wished she was ten years older. Had he told her he had a dream about her?

"Of course not," he said with some pique and sarcasm. He was clever enough to alter his denials just enough.

"Or that you dreamed you would like to take her to a motel?"

"No, sir," he responded with his head shaking.

"Did you ever give Katherine a bronze elephant as a gift?"

"I never did."

Weber was unsure why Van Hook denied that; it really

wasn't that incriminating, and it seemed to be creating a lot of trouble for him. Weber decided he would have to put Katherine back on the stand to clarify that point, despite his promise that she wouldn't have to testify again.

Van Hook said the only jewelry he had given Katherine was a pin that cost $2.50 and said "World's Number One Student," in recognition of her achievement as the first in his class to get straight A's in all subjects from him and the other teachers. He bought it the same time he bought a pin for his wife that said, "World's Best Nurse." Nice touch, Weber conceded.

Gitchoff handed Van Hook the envelope containing an earring Katherine said she got from him; he had never seen it before. Weber was sure Van Hook would deny the earrings—they were too grown-up and suggestive for a teacher to give to kids.

He said he gave her a carved wooded plaque saying "Love is contagious, we get it from one another," for assisting him in the library. He explained that he gave similar plaques to all the student librarians who worked a full year, but they picked out the design from a book he had. The story about the design selection was new to Weber—an explanation that had been carefully thought through, even though it was an outright lie.

Van Hook said he carved another board with the slogan, "Katherine is Number One," for a class demonstration, and gave it to her at the end of the year. And he identified a third board that he said Katherine had chosen the slogan for—"Peace to All Who Enter Here." Another surprise to Weber, but he thought that sounded more like Katherine's choice than "Love is contagious."

Back to the storage room. Did the kids come in there to talk to him while he was grading papers? Yes.

"Now, did you ever invite any of your students into the room—that storage room that you used at times as an office—for any type of sexual activity?"

"Never," Van Hook said firmly.

"Did any of your students or any of those schoolchildren ever come to that room voluntarily for sexual activity with you?"

"No, sir" was the emphatic response.

Weber thought that probably was the most honest answer yet. He was sure none of those girls had volunteered for that duty.

Van Hook described his 45-minute lunch periods—11:30 to 12:15. A few minutes to get his class lined up at the cafeteria, and then some time to eat in the teachers' lounge. About 11:45 or 11:50, he prepared for later classes, talked to other teachers, studied for his college class, ran the ditto machine, stapled test pages together, graded tests, worked in the school library, drove to the municipal library to pick up materials, taught other teachers to use wood-carving tools, and helped coach the teams for Junior Olympics. It sounded pretty hectic. But Weber hoped the jury would accept the idea that Van Hook could find time on one or two lunch hours out of so many days to do something so important to him.

Van Hook had been on the stand for about an hour and 15 minutes when Judge Ferguson broke for lunch. Weber decided that he had to finish his cross-examination of Van Hook that afternoon; he didn't want to lose any momentum, and he especially didn't want to give Gitchoff and Van Hook all night to decide what to discuss on re-direct examination the next morning. Weber pumped himself up for a challenging cross-examination by skipping lunch; he got very testy when he didn't eat, and he certainly didn't want to be lethargic from a big meal. So, he sat in his office alone and kept himself focused on the man he would face that afternoon in a crucial confrontation.

Lunch hour was another example of the unprecedented attendance at this trial; some of the spectators were refusing to leave the courtroom at the break for fear they would not get a seat when they returned. Eventually, the judge had to order the room cleared, and the people simply walked out, did an about-face, and formed a new line to await the reopening of the doors. The number of spectators was such a problem that some were lining up outside the courthouse in the 7 A.M. cold before the building opened each morning, and then dashing up the stairs to the courtroom, only to line up again and wait until the trial started at 9:30. Some of them brought their breakfast or lunch with them, and ate in line.

Bailiff Wes Edwards eventually resorted to handing out numbered tickets to the first few in line who were eligible for the limited number of seats left after space was taken up by the reporters and the official observers for the defense and prosecution. Even then, few of the "wannabe" spectators would leave. No one could remember a trial that attracted that kind of fanatical attendance, but a huge knot of people outside Judge Ferguson's courtroom soon became a common sight.

Some of them were Van Hook supporters; others just curious citizens. Several days into the trial, Weber noticed the crowds and realized what was going on outside the courtroom. He thought the people were anxious to hear the evidence so they could decide whether these distressing charges against an upstanding member of the teaching profession in their own area could be true. Pam Klein was less charitable; she thought the people probably were attracted by the spectacle—the Roman Coliseum meets Ringling Brothers.

Van Hook climbed back onto the hot seat at two o'clock to offer his version of the incident in the storage room with Sally Morton and Lori Parker in January 1982. He had called them out of their other class to talk about problems they were having with a boy in the special-education class. It was partly their fault, Van Hook had decided, and he wanted to tell them to get off the other kid's back. That was a creative story, Weber had to admit. The girls were out to get poor Mr. Van Hook because he tried to protect the boy from "special-ed."

Van Hook testified he had been standing between the bookshelves in the library when he started talking to Sally, but moved back into the doorway of the storage room for more privacy as he was "chewing her out." She became upset, but he didn't think she cried. The conversation lasted only "a minute, minute and a half," and the door never was closed. He denied touching or kissing her.

But Weber thought he heard a door slamming shut—on Van Hook's story. He had just given the prosecutor several weapons. First, he had discussed the content of his conversation with Sally Morton in that room, which meant Weber now could ask her what really happened there. Van Hook also had put himself in the cramped position of talking to a girl in the doorway for 60 to 90 seconds when his own witnesses—the two male students who testified—said the door was open only a few inches and the conversations lasted 15 to 20 minutes. Additionally, all of the girls had said it was closed, and Weber could ask Van Hook to explain that.

Van Hook told the same story about the session with Lori Parker, and held his hands up to show how far the door was open while he talked to her. Weber suggested that was about three feet, and Van Hook shot back, "Three feet would be this . . . This is about a foot." Getting a little testy after the big lie, Weber thought. Van Hook denied all the things Lori testified that he said to her—all of the M.O. points—as well as her accusations that he kissed her and, as Gitchoff put it, "grabbed her by the buttocks." Van Hook said Lori didn't cry, either, but she was upset because he hadn't been quite as gentle in his conversation with her. He said he already was "a bit on edge" after talking to Sally.

Weber thought that probably was true. Van Hook had been losing control that day, and he probably was more anxious after the first girl had run crying from his clutches in the Bear's Cave.

On to Stephanie Knight. She had visited him three or four times, and used the overhead projector in the library, but the rest of her story was false. He never touched her, gave her any gifts, or did anything to lead her to believe he returned the affection she felt for him. He treated her nicely but did nothing to encourage this crush she admitted.

What about Sarah Cramer? She baby-sat for his children one afternoon after school on September 27 or 28, 1977, while he and his wife went to Southern Illinois University at Edwardsville to register for a class they had

taken together. He had driven Sarah to his house in
Maryville from school. She baby-sat for him again on a
Saturday evening in early October; he picked her up at
her home about 7 P.M. and took her home about 11 or 12
that night. On both of those occasions, his son was not
wearing diapers and was sleeping in the captain's bed that
had been bought the previous June to replace the crib.

During that same period, Gitchoff asked, did Van Hook
ever take Sarah to his mother's home in Collinsville?
"Not that I know of" was the stock answer. Weber knew
Van Hook was equivocating on this one because he had a
very serious problem with his story. If he hadn't taken
Sarah there, how did she know about the prophylactics?

"Did you ever take Sarah Cramer to your mother's
house and have intercourse with her?"

"I did not."

"Did you ever take Sarah Cramer to your mother's
home and show her where your father allegedly kept his
prophylactics?"

"Of course not" was the slightly exasperated answer.

"Did you know where your father kept his prophylactics?"

"No."

Weber was surprised this time. Van Hook had just dug
an even deeper hole for himself. With this testimony he
was asking the jurors to believe that the only people who
knew where his father kept his prophylactics were his
mother and Sarah Cramer. That made a lot of sense.

Gitchoff handed Van Hook an object. "Can you tell me
what that is?"

"An earring; a monogrammed earring."

"Okay. What is the monogram that's on it?"

"I guess it's supposed to be an S."

Weber almost flinched. He had looked at that earring,
and he never realized it was a monogram, an S; it looked
like just a swirled design to him. Weber looked at Van
Hook's cuff links and shirt pocket, and noticed the ini-
tials. Of course; Van Hook knew all about monograms.
He had given Sarah and Stephanie monogrammed jewelry; that was his style.

Did he have intercourse with Sarah Cramer at his home, on a sofa bed or his son's bed, in November or December of 1976? "I did not."

Van Hook ran through all of his alibis for the Saturdays during that period, impressing Weber again with the effort taken to sort through checks and accumulate memories detailed enough to fill in all of those blanks.

To wrap up more than two and a half hours of direct testimony, Gitchoff had Van Hook identify the home movies he brought to show that, during Christmas 1976, his son still was in diapers. The movies would be shown to the jury later, Gitchoff said.

At a recess at 3:10, Weber steeled himself for what he knew would be a contentious cross-exam. He was not about to let Van Hook set the agenda or repeat his lies; he would not get the chance to slant things his way. He would have to deal with Weber and his questions. But Weber would have to be quick about making his points; as the hour grew later, he had little time to be sure Van Hook's stint on the stand ended that afternoon. The prosecutor could take no more than 60 to 90 minutes to challenge the very foundation of Richard Van Hook's defense.

The men squared off at 3:40, and Weber moved immediately to establish for the jury that Van Hook had prepared for his testimony by going over all police reports and transcripts of his various appearances before grand juries, as well as discussing everything with his attorney.

Weber slipped in his first cutting remark. "I imagine you have had a lot of discussions with your wife about these events, haven't you?"

"In the last year, quite a few."

I'll just bet you have, Weber thought.

To help the jury understand that Sarah Cramer easily could confuse a date, even by a year, Weber reminded Van Hook that he had told the Madison County grand jury that he moved to Collinsville from Maryville in 1977, when he really moved in 1978. An innocent mistake in memory, just like Sarah.

Then it was time to get serious. How much extra salary

did Van Hook receive for serving as librarian at Caseyville School?

"Nothing."

"It was a volunteer job, right?"

"Yes."

"And this volunteer job allowed you to set up what you called the 'Bear's Cave,' right?"

"I don't understand what you mean by 'set up the Bear's Cave,'" Van Hook said cautiously.

"Did you have a sign on your door in that back room that labeled that back room as the 'Bear's Cave'?"

"Oh, yes."

"And what else did the sign say?"

"It was a picture of a Walt Disney bear, and it said something about, you know, 'Bear's Cave. Enter at Your Own Risk.' And it had my name on it and it was stapled inside, or thumbtacked inside of the door."

Now it was time to get down to brass tacks. Weber drew Van Hook's attention to the incident with Lori and Sally. "And they were only back there for a minute or two?"

"Yes."

"Now, you heard your own witnesses testify they were there for 15 or 20 minutes." It was time to let Van Hook know what the rest of the cross examination would be all about, and who would be in charge. "Can you explain that to the jury?"

"He was wrong."

Okay, thought Weber, try this. What had Van Hook said in one or two minutes that upset both girls so much that they ran crying from the library and hid in a rest room?

Van Hook paused; this was taking his story further than he had prepared for, and Weber thought Van Hook could see the train coming down the track, straight at him.

"I don't remember," was the weak response.

"Do you remember testifying at the St. Clair County grand jury and being asked about that?"

"No, I don't remember that question."

Weber referred Gitchoff to page 21 of the transcript and then read Van Hook's answer when he was asked what he told Lori. "Okay, go on back to class. I'll talk to my kids. I'll try to get my kids working with you, and I'll try to straighten out—keep this boy from bothering you down here." He looked at Van Hook. "Is that what you said?"

Van Hook's voice was very soft as he said, "I guess so."

Weber put an edge in his voice. "And that got both of these girls upset, and they went running out of that room, and went to the rest room." He looked at the jury, and then back at the defendant. "Is that your testimony?"

"I guess that is," was the hushed response.

Weber kept the edge in his voice as he mimicked, "I guess it is."

He prodded Van Hook to explain where he had stood when he was talking to the girls. He said they started out in the library, moved to the storage room doorway, and eventually stepped into the room as he pulled the door partly closed. Hadn't he told the St. Clair County grand jury that he talked to the girls in the library? Yes, but he meant that was where the conversation started. Weber zinged him again; hadn't he also heard one of his male students testify yesterday that the girls were in the storage room? "Yes, I heard that."

Time to turn up the heat again. Didn't Van Hook tell the Madison County grand jury that he didn't take the girls into that room? "I don't know."

Weber read the exchange from the transcript: "You didn't take her in that back room?"

"No, I did not."

"You are sure of that?"

"I'm sure of that."

Weber leaned forward. "At that time you didn't know what the boys were going to say, and you weren't exactly sure what Sally had said, were you?"

Van Hook looked strained. "No, sir. At that time I was shook up."

He was on the ropes for the first time; Weber was starting to land jabs Van Hook hadn't seen coming. As Weber asked if Van Hook was changing his story because of what he had heard the boys say on the stand, Gitchoff tried to rescue his client with an objection and an accusation that Weber was putting words into Van Hook's mouth. Judge Ferguson sustained the objection.

But Weber kept his momentum. "So you were in error when you told the Madison County grand jury that you didn't take her in in that back room, right?"

"Yes, sir."

Weber shifted the questions to Sharon Bailey. Did Van Hook tell her she could talk to him about her monthly period? No. Did he hear her testify that he did. Yes. Time for another jab.

"Explain that to the jury. Why does she say it happened and you say it didn't?"

"Because it didn't happen, is why I say it didn't happen," Van Hook snapped.

"Well, Sharon Bailey doesn't have anything against you, does she?"

"The only thing Sharon Bailey would have against me is being turned in to the truant officer."

There it was again; taking a cheap shot at the girls while trying to make himself look so pure and proper, just like his implication that Lori and Sally were getting even with him because he chewed them out for pushing around some poor little kid from the special-ed class. Denigrate the kids; build up yourself. What a slimy defense.

Weber began a rapid-fire assault on the M.O. points, starting with the pillows and beanbag chairs in the Bear's Cave. Van Hook stuck to his pat answers; the pillows and chairs never were in his office, although a chair may have been there a day or two when it got a hole in it. His voice had started trailing off softly, and Weber thought the witness was struggling to stay controlled while his insides were beginning to churn. Judge Ferguson had to ask him to speak up.

The prosecutor kept pushing. Had Van Hook heard Elizabeth McBride, Bethany Crothers, and Tammy Pauley testify that the pillows were in his office? Yes. Weber turned to his favorite device for cross-examination; could the witness explain the discrepancy between his testimony and the accounts from the other witnesses?

"I am telling the truth, Mr. Weber. That's all I can do," Van Hook said quietly.

Weber looked at the jurors, hoping they realized Van Hook was admitting that he had no explanation for his obvious lies. Weber pushed further. Listing those girls one by one, Weber asked if there had been any specific problems between them and Van Hook. No.

"Well, then why would they say this? Do you have an explanation for why they would say it?"

Van Hook was resigned; "I have no explanation."

Weber turned to Katherine Howes's grades. In quick order he got Van Hook to agree that he gave Katherine an A in reading, a significant improvement from the D she received from a different teacher the year before; he also moved her up to an A from a B-minus in English, and to a B from a C-plus in social studies.

Abruptly, Weber switched to the wooden plaques; mixing up the topics that way prevented the witness from setting up answers too far ahead. Van Hook said Katherine had picked the "Love is contagious" design out of the book of patterns; he carved all the plaques with the slogans the students said they liked during the year. He had completed the plaque after school was out for the summer, so he called and told her she could pick it up. Weber pointed out that Katherine had sent her little brother, instead—a rather telling gesture, Weber thought.

"Katherine never picked this out. You picked it out for her, didn't you?" Weber accused.

"No. She picked out the pattern."

"This is one of those little secrets you and Katherine had between you, wasn't it?" the prosecutor growled.

Gitchoff's objection was sustained.

What about Sharon Bailey's plaque? She picked it out from the boards Van Hook already had carved with the slogans the girls said they liked. He agreed with Weber that Sharon had not picked her own pattern out of the book; he was starting to give up some ground to the prosecutor.

"So, it's not accurate to say that the girls picked out the pattern, is it?" Weber asked. Van Hook hesitated, and Weber insisted almost angrily, "Is it?"

"They picked out the board—the pattern that was there, that they wanted."

It was an awkward half-answer, and Weber wasn't accepting it. With more sarcasm in his voice, he said, "Yeah, yeah. You had these boards. They were already carved. They already had the slogans on them, and the girls picked out the boards, right? But they didn't pick the patterns out of that book, did they, and have you do them? That's not the way it happened, is it?"

Van Hook really was stumbling now. "Well, the one that I was asked about specifically, on Katherine Howes and stuff, yes."

Weber read again from Van Hook's testimony before the Madison County grand jury. He had said, "And these kids picked out their own designs from these pattern books as to which one they wanted."

"But now you're saying that's not exactly the way it happened. Right?"

Van Hook looked blankly at the prosecutor. Weber pushed again. "Right? It didn't happen that way, did it?"

Finally, Van Hook almost mumbled, "Partly."

Weber stayed after him as the men fenced back and forth; Van Hook insisted the girls had picked out the patterns. Weber pointed out that if Van Hook was right, that meant Katherine, Elizabeth McBride, and Sharon Bailey coincidentally picked out the same slogan from the hundreds in the books Van Hook used. The teacher explained weakly that "Love is contagious" was a favorite among students.

He tried to nail Van Hook about the earrings given to Elizabeth and Sharon, but Gitchoff was successful in objecting that Weber was exceeding the line of questions asked on direct examination. Weber disagreed with the judge's ruling, but was rebuffed every time he tried to circle and come in from a different angle.

Okay. Did Van Hook ever have Katherine in the storage room with the door closed? No. Could he explain the

inconsistency in his answer and Elizabeth's testimony
that she saw him and Katherine in the room with the door
closed and locked?

He retreated to his fallback answer. "I'm telling the
truth."

"But you can't explain the inconsistency?"

"No, I can't."

Weber's attempt to find out if he had taken Elizabeth
into the room was blocked by Gitchoff.

"Now, you've testified that you didn't know where
your father kept his prophylactics. Is that correct?"

"Yes."

"Would you venture a guess as to how Sarah Cramer
knows that?"

"I would have no idea."

"It's hard to explain, isn't it?"

Van Hook glared at Weber, but offered no response.

"Isn't it?" Weber asked louder.

"Yes, it is."

"You don't have any explanation for it, do you?"

He hesitated, and then offered, "Unless someone was
looking around."

Weber pounced on that. Hadn't Van Hook and his
mother testified that Sarah never had been to Stella's
house? Yes.

What about the towel at Van Hook's house? Had he
heard Sarah testify about it and Belinda Barrett recall
Sarah telling her about it? Yes. Did he ever talk to Sarah
about his wife's menstrual cycle? "No, I did not." Did he
talk to her about the towel? "I did not."

"Then explain to the jury how Sarah knows about the
towel."

"The only thing I can say about that, is that she had to
be snooping through the drawers when she was baby-
sitting."

"You are speculating that that's what could have happened?"

"That's the only way I can come up with it."

Weber moved in for the kill on a critical point. Hadn't
Van Hook forgotten about the towel when he testified be-

fore the grand jury, only to remember conveniently after he talked to his wife in the hallway? Weber had been looking forward to this. But suddenly the rug was yanked out from under him.

"You asked me if I had a chest of drawers in that room, and in the chest of drawers, if I had a towel in there."

Weber realized he had, indeed, slipped up back then; he had said "chest of drawers" when he meant "nightstand," and that had given Van Hook an escape route. Even the best laid plans, the prosecutor, thought. He bulled ahead. Hadn't Van Hook remembered the towel only after he talked to his wife?

"If you had asked me if we had a towel in the bedside table, I would have said yes. You never asked me that question."

Weber turned toward the home stretch with another unpredictable series of topics and questions. He started with Van Hook's experience as a swimming coach. "I count: one, two, three, four, five, six swim clubs, right?"

"Yes, sir."

"You seem to move from job to job pretty quick as a swim coach, is that correct?" Another implication about Mr. Van Hook that seemed clear to the prosecutor.

"Not half as fast as most coaches," Van Hook explained.

What about sleeping bags and gym mats—ever have any of those in your little office? No.

"Now, you heard Sarah Cramer, Stephanie Knight, Katherine Howes, and Lori Parker all say that you told each of them that you wished she was older, correct?" No response. "Is that right?" Weber insisted.

"I heard that."

"Can you explain that to the jury—how these four girls would come up with you saying the same line?"

"No, sir."

"Three of them testified—that would be Sarah Cramer, Stephanie Knight, and Katherine Howes—that you told them that they made you feel younger. Do you remember that?"

"I remember hearing that."

"Can you explain how they would get the same line out, or say that you said that same line?" No response. "Would you like to try?"

"No."

"Okay."

Gitchoff was getting tired of Weber's successful strafing runs against the defendant. "Now we are getting argumentative," he objected. "Let him ask him a question."

Ferguson agreed.

Weber stayed the course. "Sarah Cramer and Katherine Howes both testified that you told them that you had dreams about them in a motel. Can you explain to the jury how these two girls would say that?"

"No, I cannot."

"And then Stephanie Knight testified that you told her you had a dream about her. Can you explain that?"

"No."

"Sarah Cramer, Stephanie Knight, and Katherine Howes all testified that you either gave them liquor or offered to take them to a bar. Can you explain that?"

"Well, that—no, I can't explain that."

"Sarah and Katherine both testified that you told them that they made you feel like you were back in school. Can you explain how they would come up with that same line about you if you didn't say it?"

"I have no idea," Van Hook said in frustration.

Did he tell Betsy Woods that Stephanie Knight didn't need a chaperon?

"If I had said that, I would have just been teasing."

"Do you have any idea why Sarah would tell Debbie Weaver that you gave her some liquor when you didn't do it?"

"No idea in the world," Van Hook sighed.

Time to close in. "Now, with Katherine Howes, her grades went up under you, right?"

"Yes, sir."

"You gave her some gifts, right?"

"A couple of things."

"And, as far as you know, there weren't any grudges or anything else between you two, right?"

"No."

"Can you explain to the jury, then, why she's saying this if it's not true?"

Gitchoff finally blew. "Your Honor, I have tried not to interfere in this, but I would state to the court that it's not up to this man to explain anything. These charges are brought by the state. It's incumbent upon them to prove him guilty of these charges beyond a reasonable doubt. He's not required to explain anything."

Weber wasn't going lie down on that one. "Judge, I just want to know if he had an explanation," he said innocently. "I realize he isn't required to; I just want to know if he has one."

Ferguson surprised Weber by responding, "Well, I would assume if he had one, it could have come out in impeachment of those witnesses."

Gitchoff looked stunned as he turned toward the judge. "We would object, Your Honor."

"Yeah, the objection is sustained."

Weber wasn't sure which objection was sustained—one to his questions or one to Ferguson's comment. Weber still felt like grinning. The judge had slipped with that comment after being properly impartial all along.

Weber wrapped it up with a question he hoped would educate the jury on an important point.

"Did you tell Sarah that it wouldn't do any good to report this because you were a teacher and nobody would believe her?"

"No."

Weber leaned over and asked Randy Massey if there were points that hadn't been covered. Massey had one suggestion, and Weber turned back to Van Hook. "In December of 1976, did you have a roll-away bed in your house?"

"It's a Hide-A-Bed."

"And where was it?"

"In the family room."

A final point for Sarah.

As Gitchoff bounded back to try to repair some of the damage, Weber worked to focus his mind and avoid becoming a victim of the "two-minute rule." Even though he understood the rule so well, it was difficult to keep his mind on Gitchoff's questions instead of running an instant replay and analysis of the exchanges with Van Hook. Weber strained to listen.

Gitchoff asked if Sarah had been Van Hook's student when she baby-sat for him? No, she was in his class after that.

What about the "Bear's Cave" sign? "It was just a decoration." Van Hook shrugged innocently.

Gitchoff slipped in some of his endearing old-style, street-smart jargon. "Was it put there with the intent to keep everybody out while you went back in that room and dilly-dallied and had sexual relations with Katherine Howes?"

"No, sir."

Gitchoff was getting cranked up as he turned to the incident with Sally and Lori.

"Was your physical makeup at that time so hot that you had to go tell a teacher who knew who you were—who knew you were asking for two girls—that you were going to take them right out of his classroom, march them right into the library, right in that room, sit them down and tell them how much you loved them, try to French-kiss them, and get in their pants? Were things that pressing with you?"

"No, sir," Van Hook replied in a voice that suggested the whole thing was too silly to contemplate.

"Thank you," Gitchoff said as he returned to his seat.

Weber wouldn't allow that to resonate in the courtroom for long, especially with another two-minute rule going into effect.

"Mr. Van Hook, the evidence was that you had been getting away with it for years. So, you just figured you would take a chance that day, isn't that right?"

Van Hook's eyes narrowed. "No, sir."

How did Sarah rate as a baby-sitter—in the top five? No.

"Top ten?"

"I don't know how to rank baby-sitters as far as being baby-sitters."

"Best baby-sitter?" Weber offered sarcastically.

Van Hook knew where Weber was going and tried to head him off. He simply wrote that in her yearbook as a nice note to a girl who was returning to his class after being out of school in the "homebound" program. Another little jab at Sarah.

"And you underlined 'best,' right?"

"I don't remember underlining those things. I know they are underlined."

Van Hook just couldn't admit something so obvious, and so stupid, Weber knew. Weber pounded in more salt.

"And you underlined, 'ever had,' right?"

"I didn't say that."

"Did you?"

"No."

Weber slipped into his most sarcastic voice. "You wouldn't have had any reason to underline 'best I ever had,' would you?"

"No."

Gitchoff needed more damage control. "What's the purpose when you write in this thing? You know, why do people write in these things?"

"To remember somebody, hopefully fondly, at the end."

The end had come, indeed. As Van Hook left the witness stand after an hour of intense cross-examination, Weber felt as drained as he thought his target must be. As court was recessed for the day, Randy Massey shook Weber's hand and complimented him on a masterful cross that had left Van Hook looking completely unbelievable. Weber felt good; he was sure he had hammered Van Hook on every point and, even if he were acquitted, Weber had put him through hell for the longest hour of his life. Surely he realized he looked bad on the stand. Weber was angry at this poor excuse for a man, and had gone after him as harshly as anyone he ever faced in the courtroom.

Weber was sure the defense would rest in the morning, and he hoped the jury would score it with the prosecution ahead on points. For the first time in the trial, he joined Pam Klein and Dennis Kuba for some drinks. He planned a day of rebuttal witnesses on Wednesday, February 16, to slam some of the defense's claims. A fitting way to close out the trial, Weber thought.

CHAPTER 17

John Gitchoff turned to the bailiff first thing Wednesday morning and announced, "Sandra Van Hook." Weber was surprised. He had been sure Richard Van Hook was the last witness; the defendant is the traditional finale for a defense case. But Gitchoff had been craftier than that; he must have assumed Sandra would be a strong witness and a better way to close out the defense.

Mrs. Van Hook wore a stylish suit and looked every bit the professional nurse as she took the stand. She exuded confidence and Weber could see fire in her eyes when she looked at him. This would be interesting. She embarked on a biographical tour that moved quickly to the date in September 1977 when she and her husband registered for a college class at SIUE. Gitchoff handed her the check she wrote to the school on September 27, 1977, and the fee card she received from the registrar. Weber dismissed the evidence with a wave of his hand when Gitchoff offered it for his inspection.

Finally, the point. Sarah Cramer had been the Van Hooks's baby-sitter that evening. Sandra was sure it wasn't in November because of a traumatic experience that month. As her voice trembled, she recalled, "My daughter fell through a glass terrarium and almost lost the sight in her right eye, and . . ."

"All right. Well, just compose yourself," Gitchoff said kindly.

Sandra Van Hook went through all of the Saturday alibis in great detail and with credibility, and then it was time for the Van Hook home movies. A screen and projector were set up, and scenes of a typical family flashed before the jurors. Kids and parents and grandparents around the Christmas tree. A little boy in the bathtub. The baby-sitter who had testified earlier for the defense. When the movie ended, Sandra confirmed the obvious. At Christmas in 1976, her two-year-old son was wearing diapers that bulged clearly under his pajamas. More contradiction of Sarah's memory.

Weber stepped before Sandra Van Hook and began to test her memory by reminding her that the baby-sitter in the movie had testified that the boy was about 14 months old in December 1976. "Now, I'm a bachelor. I don't have any kids. But it didn't look to me like that baby was 26 months old."

Sandra's eyes turned cold as she snapped, "You don't know very much about children, then."

A solid blow to Weber's ribs. Sandra Van Hook would, indeed, be tougher than her husband. This woman was fighting to preserve her family, and she hated the man who threatened it.

Weber delved deeply into her memory of the alibis and the record provided by her checkbook, even asking her to recall the hour at which her television was returned from the repair shop and she wrote the check for it. He made no headway at all. "I think you have an unbelievably good memory for all of these dates and times and hours," he remarked.

Her face tightened as she retorted, "Well, when you have to go back six years in your life and start piecing together what was happening to you back then, believe me, I made it my business to find out what was going on."

Weber reminded her that her husband had trouble remembering what year they moved to Collinsville. The venom dripped as she snarled, "Well, you know, everybody is not perfect like you are, I'm sure."

Another slap. Weber was tiring of the abuse, but he wasn't going to be drawn into a nasty exchange that could make him look like a bully. Besides, he didn't think Sandra's attitude would play well with the jurors.

Weber kept plugging away. Sandra had said earlier that she "believed" Sarah Cramer was the baby-sitter when she and her husband registered for class. Now Sandra said she was sure it had been Sarah; was she sure or not?

"You know, Mr. Weber, I can only point out that I'm not perfect, either."

Weber kept after Sandra's memory by asking what time everyone left to pick up the rocking chairs in Belleville, and how they were dressed. After all, just how detailed was this memory of hers? "In clothes, Mr. Weber" was the abrupt retort. But this sarcastic line of questioning by the prosecutor was starting to draw some critical mumbling and insulted gasping from Van Hook partisans in the back. As Weber's questions became more insistent and detailed, the buzz in the back grew louder and more distracting. He finally stepped to the bench to ask the judge to issue the standard warning to spectators. Ferguson turned to the audience and said gruffly, "Ladies and gentlemen, if there are any more comments or remarks, you are going to be removed from the courtroom."

Weber kept pushing. What did they have for lunch when they went to the racquet club in Belleville for swim practice after they picked up the chairs? Mrs. Van Hook was beginning to tire of this. "Probably hamburgers and french fries. I don't remember. I don't remember what I had for supper last night. Do you?"

Weber agreed that remembering details from six years ago was difficult, and explained that he was inquiring about her excellent memory. But she snapped, "I have had help with my 'excellent memory.' However, your questions about what I ate and what I dressed my children in seem pretty ridiculous."

What about the Saturday the entire family spent at her mother's house after she had been injured in the crash? It seemed unusual to him that a woman in pain would want two little kids running around the house.

"We happen to be that kind of a family."

Would her husband have been mistaken if he told the grand jury that both times Sarah baby-sat were right after school, unlike Sandra's memories? "That's a possibility, I guess. He's not perfect, either," she said coldly.

She had been one of the toughest witnesses Weber ever

faced, and he was glad it was over. She had slapped him around pretty well and it had been unpleasant, even though he didn't think it helped the defense. She had done better than her husband, but Weber hoped it was in vain.

As Gitchoff rested his case after 29 witnesses, Weber looked back and decided the defense had done a good job with the alibis. The charge that Van Hook committed indecent liberties with a child at his home in November or December 1976 was in serious jeopardy; the jury might find room to acquit him on that count, even though Weber thought the prosecution had established clearly that the sexual intercourse occurred there on some date. But Weber hoped the jurors would agree that the evidence on the incident at Stella Van Hook's was uncontradicted.

Weber was ready with a lineup of rebuttal witnesses. Matt Carr was first, explaining that he hadn't even known Sarah Cramer when he spent less than two weeks installing new siding on Stella's house; he couldn't have let Sarah into the house to snoop around and find the prophylactics. He never let his girlfriend or anyone else into that house.

Belinda Barnett, who now was married to another of the Carr brothers, reaffirmed her memory that Sarah Cramer told her about the first incident with Van Hook in late November or early December 1976, while they were in the eighth grade. Weber had Sarah's mother recall that Van Hook picked up her daughter for a baby-sitting job on a Saturday morning in early December 1976, just as Sarah had said.

Then Katherine Howes returned to the stand. She seemed to be in much better emotional condition this time as she explained in no uncertain terms that she never had picked out the "Love is contagious" slogan. She hadn't even picked out the other that said, "Peace to All Who Enter Here." Weber showed her the bronze elephant, and she recalled that Van Hook gave it to her after the trip to the Magic House and the Transportation Museum, but said he got it at the zoo when he was there with his wife and kids.

Gitchoff asked why she hadn't explained that before. She said she didn't think it was important.

Sheila Howes confirmed her daughter's testimony, recounting that Katherine had showed her the elephant after they got home from the class trip and said Van Hook gave it to her. Weber asked Sheila to describe Van Hook and Maria DeConcini on that field trip. "Overly friendly. More friendly than I consider two teachers ought to be. While we were walking around, they would have their heads together in conference. But they were just acting very friendly."

Sheila also told the jury about DeConcini's two visits to the Howeses' home, where she sat in her car and glared at the children. There was no doubt it was DeConcini; Sheila even went to school the morning after the first visit to confirm it.

Weber asked about the wooden plaque; Sheila said Katherine seemed uninterested in going to school to pick it up after Van Hook called and said it was ready; her son went instead. Katherine's father had been upset when he saw what the plaque said.

Gitchoff wanted to know more about that. Did Mr. Howes do anything about it? Yes, he went to the school, but Van Hook already was gone. The Howeses decided not to pursue it, since Katherine wouldn't be in his class anymore. Did they call someone to complain?

"Why cause trouble?" Sheila asked.

Gitchoff's tone changed to indignation as he stepped closer and his voice rose. "I don't know. It's your child. I sure as hell would. Wouldn't you, you know, now that your daughter says that Mr. Van Hook had intercourse with her? Intercourse!"

Weber wasn't going to tolerate that kind of mock outrage from the defense, of all sources. He objected to Gitchoff badgering the witness, and Gitchoff apologized before the judge could rule. Gitchoff asked if Sheila understood that her daughter was charging now that Van Hook had intercourse with her.

"Yes, I do. And I believe everything my daughter says because children don't lie."

"I understand that, and a mother would. I understand."

"Not just a mother. A lot of people would believe it because children just don't lie to get in this kind of trouble."

Did the Howeses ever do anything after their daughter made such serious allegations? Sheila's voice quavered as she said, "After the allegations came out, we went to the school board. We were called liars by the officials of our school district. We were told that they had read transcripts, and that they knew these children were lying, and that he was innocent."

Weber winced; he certainly would have preferred for the jurors not to have heard that. Having the school board cast Van Hook in a favorable light against the girls certainly wouldn't help the girls' credibility, since the jurors couldn't know the whole story of what Weber and his team saw as the unconscionable failure of the school district to protect and care for the girls.

Gitchoff recalled Sheila's characterization of the actions of Van Hook and DeConcini. Had Sheila seen Mrs. Van Hook? Yes.

"Would you say she's more attractive than Mrs. DeConcini?"

"I don't judge other women," Sheila said. Weber smiled; Katherine had given Gitchoff the same answer to the same question.

Weber did some damage control of his own on re-direct exam; he needed to offer some perspective to counter Sheila's comments about the school board.

"Mrs. Howes, since that school board time, there has been a lot more evidence developed in this case, hasn't there?"

"Yes, sir."

Weber called Sheila's neighbor, Diana LaBlanque, who told the jury that she had seen DeConcini sitting in front of the Howeses' driveway on both occasions.

"What did she look like?"

"Well, to coin a phrase my son used, he was afraid of her because she looked very angry."

Gitchoff asked when Mrs. LaBlanque was asked to testify. She said that just the night before, she had reminded

Sheila about seeing the car and the woman with the dark hair sitting by the Howeses' driveway. And then La-Blanque dropped something unexpected on Gitchoff and Weber. She had been a spectator in the courtroom the day DeConcini testified, and could positively identify her. LaBlanque had heard DeConcini deny being at the Howeses' home or even knowing where they lived. That was why LeBlanque reminded Sheila about seeing the car when the incidents happened.

Perfect, Weber thought.

He turned back to what he believed was the strength of this case—the girls themselves; he would finish by calling four of them. Bethany Crothers recalled seeing the gray gym mat—much smaller than the kind the teachers remembered—in Van Hook's office. Sharon Bailey echoed Katherine by explaining that she did not pick out the design for the "Love is contagious" plaque she got from Van Hook; he gave plaques with the same slogan on them to Katherine and Elizabeth McBride, too. The only choice Sharon had was whether the plaque would be painted or stained. What about earrings? Sharon remembered the day that Van Hook gave earrings to her, Katherine, and Elizabeth.

Elizabeth was the next; she had no choice in the design of the "Love is contagious" plaque. When she got to choose the design for another one, she asked for "Home Sweet Home." He gave all three girls earrings, too, on a day when he called them out of class. He warned Elizabeth to take good care of hers, because they were expensive; they were hypoallergenic, he said.

The last witness was Sally Morton; now she got to tell the jury her version of what happened in the little room. Did he start talking to her in the library or the doorway? No.

"When did he start talking to you?"

"When we got in the room, after he double-checked the door was shut."

He asked her if she wanted to be treated like his child, a student, or an adult. What happened next? "He embraced me and he kissed me, and he wouldn't let go until I started tugging away. Then he finally let go."

She was crying, and he told her to send in Lori. What was Sally's emotional condition? "I was afraid he was going to do it again, and he might hurt me serious if he did." She said she stayed in the library and watched the door after Lori went in. After 20 minutes, Lori came out; she was crying, too.

"She was crying so bad I tried to calm her down. And then we went into the bathroom and she told me. Some other girls in the classroom came down and worried about us, so we told them."

"Okay. Were you so upset because he just chewed you out over some library work?"

"No," she said sharply. "He didn't chew us out about no library work."

She said the girls had decided not to do anything about what had happened, because they really didn't think it was very "drastic." But they were afraid he would do something else to them.

"We were thinking of taking something to protect us with, and a boy in our class overheard us, and he held up some jump-rope handles that were wooden." In an earnest little voice, Sally explained, "And we said, 'No, we could get in trouble for that.'" Later, Van Hook grabbed her arm and asked if the girls were giving him the "silent treatment"; she said no.

Gitchoff asked what she meant by "double-check" the door. "He looked at it first, and then he looked again to make sure it was shut."

The defender made no progress as he went through Sally's story again, so he asked if she had talked to anyone about her testimony. Had she talked to Weber? "Yes, but he didn't say anything. He just told me I had it all together. That's all he said."

"Okay. What about Virginia?"

"That's all she said, too. She said I had my story together."

Weber came back only to be sure the jury understood what Sally meant. Was this a story she made up? No.

Hadn't she told the police all of this a year ago? Yes. Was it all the truth? Yes.

And with that from his thirty-fifth witness, Don Weber had completed the prosecution's case. Surely, the jurors had to realize they had heard the truth from those girls, as Sally had just said. Did their uncontradicted testimony sound the most truthful, or did Van Hook's manipulated version, full of holes and inconsistencies, sound credible?

Weber made another big decision that afternoon; he dismissed one of the two counts of official misconduct and two of the four counts of indecent liberties with a child. He wanted the jury's deliberations to be as clear and clean as possible; the less he had to explain in closing arguments, the better. He threw out the misconduct charge alleging that Van Hook had acted to gain some personal advantage for himself; the remaining count charged that he committed an act he knew was forbidden. The dismissed indecent-liberties charges referred to lewd fondling; Weber kept the charges that Van Hook had performed intercourse with Sarah.

That evening, Weber spent about 45 minutes organizing his thoughts and coming up with some catchy phrases for his closing argument the next day; then he rested up for the big day. He never wrote out his closings; if he couldn't argue this case off the top of his head after living with it for a year, he should be in some other line of work. A closing that was spontaneous, with a few well-delivered lines mixed in, sounded better to the jury.

But his peaceful evening was shattered later by a surprising call from Kuba. First thing the next morning, Weber asked Judge Ferguson to reopen the prosecution's rebuttal case for a new witness—a woman who said Gitchoff had interviewed her a week earlier, but Kuba had just found the night before. She was a PTA volunteer at Caseyville School and would testify that she once found the doors to the library locked about two o'clock. When she returned a few minutes later, she saw Van Hook and Katherine Howes in the library, where the lights were out. When Van Hook saw the woman, he immediately turned on the lights and opened the doors. Katherine—looking "peculiar"—left hurriedly, and Van Hook explained that he had forgotten his keys and returned through a rear door to get them; he was helping the girl with her math homework, he added.

Weber argued that he should be allowed to reopen his case for this witness; her testimony would not be a surprise for the defense, but was support for the prosecution. Gitchoff objected; the testimony was too uncertain to be proper, and it would be highly prejudicial to the defense. The incident didn't even occur around noon, the time frame Katherine Howes set as the period when the sexual activity happened.

Judge Ferguson agreed, and barred the witness.

The parties returned to the courtroom, however, for a surrebuttal witness for the defense. The manager of the St. Louis Zoo gift shop testified that she never stocked brass elephants like the one Katherine said Van Hook gave her. Weber posed a hypothetical question to the witness: was it possible that a man could tell someone he bought such an elephant at the zoo when he really got it somewhere else? Gitchoff's objection was sustained.

The last question of the trial came from Weber: "They brought you over here to prove there aren't any elephants at the zoo, right?"

Gitchoff's objection was sustained, again.

But somehow that question seemed an appropriate ending to the evidence in this case. These little girls made it all up, and there aren't any elephants at the zoo.

CHAPTER 18

As Don Weber waited to start his closing argument, he glanced over his shoulder at the spectators and saw the cast of girls filling the front row. They wanted to be here for the final act, and Weber thought that was only fair; their lives were on the block every bit as much as Richard Van Hook's.

The prosecution and defense had agreed to divide up the limited space in the courtroom for closings, each getting half the seats to parcel out to their supporters; a crowd of more than 50 packed in. Pam Klein, Dennis Kuba, his wife, Joanie, and Virginia Rulison sat by the girls; Van Hook's family and friends filled the other side. The arrangements left many spectators, some of whom had attended every day, cooling their heels angrily in the hall and complaining about squeezing out the public.

Judge Ferguson offered a warning to the spectators. No comments or reactions would be tolerated when the verdict was returned; anyone acting up would be ejected immediately.

Finally, Weber stepped in front of the jurors for his closing argument. He began by telling them he had proved what he had promised about Van Hook's misconduct with Sarah Cramer, Katherine Howes, Stephanie Knight, and Lori Parker. Beyond that, the rules of evidence had permitted him to prove that Van Hook had forced himself on still another victim, Sally Morton. Mr. Gitchoff, on the other hand, had not proved what he had promised. He certainly hadn't proved that Sarah and her friends had easy access to Stella Van Hook's home. He had proved the first intercourse with Sarah wasn't on December 11, but he hadn't introduced a single doubt about the second incident at Stella's house.

Weber urged the jurors to listen when the judge instructed them not to single out one fact and disregard the others. Look at the big picture; don't get hung up on where the brass elephant was purchased. After all, the evidence was clear Van Hook was a liar. He had tried to contend that the girls had picked out the "Love is contagious" slogan, when every one of them had said they had no choice in the designs. When they got a choice, they chose "Home Sweet Home," not "Love is contagious."

Weber pointed at the "Love" plaques; "These are what a pervert wants to give to 11- and 12-year-old girls."

Pam Klein and Dennis Kuba almost fell out of their seats as they looked at each other in amazement; neither could believe that Weber actually had called Van Hook a pervert. They were afraid that would alienate the jury. But Weber knew the jurors had heard this sordid story; they were ready for straight talk.

He reminded them to use their common sense. Was it believable that four girls, most of whom did not know each other, would come up with such similar stories five years apart if they weren't telling the truth? Would Stephanie Knight and Katherine Howes come up with the same kinky application for Van Hook's middle name? And, what was their motivation to lie?

On the other hand, what about the prejudice of some of the defense witnesses? "The defendant's wife doesn't like me. I can't say, at this stage, that I blame her. I pity her, and I think I understand her feelings. Mrs. DeConcini, on the other hand, is somebody I do not understand. Why would a teacher—who helps disabled children—blindly and out of blind loyalty, go out to Katherine Howes's house and stare at her because Katherine Howes said these things? I think you should consider that, and judge Mrs. DeConcini's credibility on that fact. She called me a liar when I asked her about this, but yesterday I proved exactly what I was alleging. She said she never had been to Katherine Howes's house, and I proved that she had been."

What about Sarah Cramer; was she telling the truth? If not, how did she know where Van Hook's father kept his prophylactics? How did she know the floor plan at Stella's, and the time the mailman arrived? How did she know about the towel in the nightstand and the sofa bed at her teacher's house? Wasn't it more likely that the contradiction over the crib was a mistaken detail?

If Van Hook was right that Sarah baby-sat for him in September 1977, why did Sarah, Belinda Barnett, and Sarah's mother remember that Sarah knew about the towel in 1976? Weber put the monkey on the jurors' backs: they could not acquit Van Hook without a reasonable explanation for that question.

The prosecutor turned to Van Hook's "pattern of lying." Why lie about giving earrings to his students? Because he already had denied it to the St. Clair County grand jury. His pattern of lying had pushed him into a corner when he took the stand in Madison County; even after the testimony of the girls who received the earrings, he couldn't admit it. He was running a bluff; he kept his poker face even when he was confronted by facts he couldn't explain away or refute. What had happened when he was asked how Sarah knew about the prophylactics under his father's mattress if he didn't take her to that house? He equivocated; he squirmed. He wouldn't even offer a clean denial; he said he couldn't remember whether he had taken her over there or not.

"That, ladies and gentlemen, was a person who has had his bluff called, and who doesn't have an ace in the hole."

Weber pushed the ugly reality of an acquittal on the jury. He pointed at the girls, who looked even younger sitting there. "Let's send them back to the school, and they can walk around in twos and use the end of their jump ropes"—Weber looked angrily at Van Hook—"because 'I'm a teacher and you have to believe me.'"

Weber made eye contact with each of the jurors to be sure they were listening for this important point. "You have to consider Van Hook's testimony in light of the testimony of Sarah Cramer, Stephanie Knight, Katherine Howes, Lori Parker, Sally Morton, Elizabeth McBride,

Tammy Pauley, Bethany Crothers, Sharon Bailey, Betsy Woods, and Debbie Weaver. All of those people would have to be lying in order for you to acquit the defendant, because they all saw the pillows; they saw the beanbag chairs; they saw the gym mat; they knew about the bachelor pad that man had set up to trap and ensnare 11- and 12-year-old girls at Caseyville."

There was the essence of the case; either Van Hook was guilty, or every one of those girls was lying. There was no middle ground.

What about the blind loyalty from some of Van Hook's cast of supporting characters? Some of it seemed literally blind; one teacher refused to see a desk when it clearly was in the photograph before her. Another teacher insisted stubbornly that Van Hook was at school until three o'clock every day, even though another teacher said it was relatively simple to leave early. Weber didn't believe they were lying. "I believe they started with the idea that he couldn't have done it, and worked their memories backward."

Why hadn't the girls told anyone about these traumatic events before the police found them? Three reasons. First, each girl believed she was the only one involved with Van Hook. Second, the girls were embarrassed by sexual conduct they could not even understand, much less sit down and discuss with an adult; they didn't want anyone to know. Weber pointed at the children as he listed the third reason: a 33-year-old man had run one hell of a bluff on a bunch of little girls. He told them no one would believe them, and the girls had no reason to doubt that.

Weber's voice became a little harsher. "And, in fact, there were certain people who didn't believe them. You might have had a problem believing just Sarah and Stephanie, but I think by the time you got to Sarah and Stephanie and Katherine, any shadow of a doubt would begin to be removed. And once you got to Sarah and Stephanie and Katherine and Lori and Sally and Bethany Crothers and Sharon Bailey and everyone else, there wouldn't be a doubt in your mind about it."

What about the dates and the alibis? Weber found room

to believe Van Hook had sex with Sarah the first time on December 4 or December 18. The canceled check from buying the rocking chairs didn't completely rule it out on the fourth. And it was hard to believe that Sandra's mother really wanted her son-in-law and grandchildren at her home on the eighteenth when she was so badly banged up. If he had been there, wasn't it possible Van Hook had left his mother-in-law's for a couple of hours that day?

Weber addressed the bed in Robbie's room with one of the lines he had come up with the night before. "The evidence has shown that the defendant has been robbing the cradle for years. I don't think it's any surprise, at this point, to find out that he's trying to hide behind the crib." Even if the jurors believed the crib was in the boy's room in December 1976, that didn't rule out Van Hook having sex with Sarah in that house. Couldn't the home movies and the family's memories of the crib really be from 1975, when Van Hook's son would have been the 14-month-old toddler the baby-sitter remembered?

Did Van Hook exploit his position as a teacher to commit these crimes? Of course he did. Sarah even was afraid he would flunk her if she resisted or told anyone. Didn't Maria DeConcini's behavior in court indicate the reception the girls would have received if they had gone to other teachers for help? Wasn't there a chance the other teachers would have ganged up on the kids, just as they feared?

"You saw how she acted toward me," Weber remembered with recrimination in his voice. "She called me a liar; she said I was crazy. Now, if she would do that to me, what would she do to a student who had said those things about her real good friend, Richard Van Hook? It's obvious what she would have done." His voice boomed, "She would have come crashing down on them."

Van Hook's position as a teacher was the essence of the "Bear's Cave." Who knew about the cave? All the kids. Who didn't know? All the teachers and the janitors—the adults. And what did Van Hook tell the girls? No one would believe them, because he was a teacher.

Weber began his crescendo. "We are talking about the guilt or innocence of the defendant. We do have some innocent people here"—he looked at the children in the front and pointed at them—"and they are those little girls sitting right there. Look at them. Remember how they testified. They are the innocent ones. They have no guile in them. They don't know how to lie. They just want 'Home Sweet Home,' and they want peace when they go through a door. They don't want to go through a door, particularly with the teacher, when they have to enter at their own risk."

As Weber focused on the girls, Pam thought they seemed to sit up straighter in their seats, hold themselves a little prouder. This man was vouching for them, testifying for them. They were worthy of belief and they were innocent victims. The girls needed to hear that.

"It is impossible for them to have made these stories up and have them come together the way they did. It is unbelievable and preposterous that they could have made this up. You saw them testify. Sally Morton got on the stand, and when I asked her, 'How did you feel?' she gave you an honest reaction. She said, 'I felt it was very inappropriate for a teacher to be doing that.' "

Weber walked closer to Richard Van Hook's table.

"Well, what do you think? Is it okay for a teacher to do that?" He pointed angrily at Van Hook again, now from just a few feet away. "Are you going to call his bluff? Are you going to let him bluff his way through this? Or are you going to sacrifice these little girls on the altar of his erection? Because that's exactly what this case is all about."

Weber ended with a challenge for the jurors. They must demand that John Gitchoff provide reasonable explanations for the crushing list of lies by Van Hook and contradicting evidence Weber had recited. Unless the defense could offer reasonable explanations, Richard Van Hook must be found guilty. It was a bold way to close, and an attempt to put Gitchoff in a trick bag. It was an old maneuver, but sometimes it worked. Weber sat down, and waited to see if his challenge would be accepted.

Gitchoff assumed his slump-shoulder stance, his position of comfort and familiarity before the jury, and promptly refused to be sucked into Weber's trap. Gitchoff was much too experienced to let his opponent set the agenda.

"Mr. Weber stands here in front of you and dares Mr. Gitchoff to come up and explain away this and explain away that," the defender sniffed. So what? The important part of this case was the evidence, not what Weber wanted. With a new vitriolic tone, Gitchoff turned on the prosecutor.

"He refers to my client as a pervert. Do you want to know where the perversion is in this lawsuit, ladies and gentlemen? It's the investigation and prosecution of this case by Weber. Every bit of evidence—every bit of evidence—that we brought in here, ladies and gentlemen, and put up to you in this courtroom, has been documented not by mere words, but by checks and by documents. We found it. Why didn't they? Why? Because they didn't want to go look for it."

Who checked out Katherine's story about the elephant? Not the prosecution; the defense ran out during the trial and found independent witnesses whose unchallenged testimony about that piece of evidence disproved the ever-changing claims by Katherine.

The state's attorney's duty is to investigate and prosecute, and to be fair, the defender said. "Let's see how fair he was." The investigation began with the grand jury in St. Clair County, where some of the girls and Van Hook testified. "Thirty days later, where are we? We are in Madison County, where Weber got a hold of it." He found the Cramer case and reached back six years to charge a crime that happened over a period of several months.

Gitchoff shrugged; the defense still had done its job despite the difficulty of going back so far in time. Gitchoff's team and the Van Hooks did what Weber should have done to find the truth. Then what did Weber bring to the jury? A day of testimony about Sarah Cramer, and several days of testimony about "Caseyville, Caseyville, Caseyville." Gitchoff called those witnesses "the same little select group of girls" who testified in St. Clair County. Four of them only knew what the other girls said in the rest room; they never saw anything and nothing happened to them.

What about Richard Van Hook the man? Lovely wife, two lovely children. A teacher with a master's degree in library services. Gitchoff's voice ratcheted up a notch to suggest disbelief. "He volunteered for the library at Caseyville because that would give him the opportunity to set up his bachelor pad and his den, and let him get in there and just ravish these little girls?" Too ridiculous to consider, the tone of his voice assured.

The Van Hooks were a family who spent time together, did things together. When one of them was sick, they all were there. Not all families do this, but they did. "They are a very stable family with a good, stable relationship."

Gitchoff sighed. "Sometime in January or early February of 1982, Dick Van Hook left his home and went to work. Sometime right after that, he entered into the most hellish nightmare of his life. He has been accused and condemned in the press—mouthed to death by a publicity-seeking prosecutor." He had been unable to strike back while "Weber has had free run with the news media to do whatever he wants to do."

Weber remembered the fawning news stories about Van Hook's absolution in St. Clair County, and the prosecutor couldn't let that distortion go without objection. "That's not true," he interjected.

But Gitchoff wasn't backing down and snapped, "Oh, get off of that."

Ferguson ordered the jury to disregard Gitchoff's comments. But the defender was not slowing down his attack against Weber, adding that he even had tried to have Van Hook fired.

"Weber runs for office; he's a prosecutor. What better kind of lawsuit, man, can a prosecutor have than to be prosecuting charges on little children?"

Weber even had attacked the teachers who testified in Van Hook's defense. "If they support him as Mrs. DeConcini—who is very supportive of him, that was ex-

hibited very well in here—because she's 'very, very supportive' of him, she's a liar. Or, as Mrs. Howes says,
'overly friendly.' "

Gitchoff took a great deal of time going through the
schedule for Van Hook's lunch periods. "Where have you
got the time for this man to go in there and have intercourse with her two and three times a week over four and
a half months?"

He echoed Weber's oft-repeated question of why Van
Hook had lied about the earrings. The old pro's voice
eased into that avuncular, casual timber. "You know, you
have got your butt hanging out on a serious charge, and
he's trying to remember whether or not he gave them earrings; he denied it. I think, myself, that he gave them the
earrings. But I asked him, and he says, 'I don't remember
giving them earrings.' So, he gave them the earrings and
he doesn't remember. Or, he's lying, as Weber wants you
to believe."

Weber thought that failed as a reasonable explanation
for the lie about the earrings, and was a dangerous tactic.
Would the jury infer that Van Hook was stonewalling on
the earrings and hadn't even convinced his own lawyer?

What about those plaques? Gitchoff held up one and
pointed to the design—two children sitting on a rail fence
under the slogan, "Love is contagious, we get it from one
another." He looked perplexed as he turned to the jury.
"Does that look suggestive? Does that look horny? Does
that look like the work of a pervert?"

Couldn't Van Hook be innocently mistaken about
which designs were picked out by which girls? "And remember, at the time they are asking him these questions,
they are also standing there and pointing a finger at him
and saying, 'You're a pervert.' I don't think he's lying
about it, because this man hasn't lied, I don't believe. But
that's for you to determine."

And the "Bear's Cave" sign. A Disney cartoon pinned
to the door. What is so sinister about that when you are
dealing with children? Gitchoff motioned at Weber. "He's
making a lot of hoot-hoot about it."

The storage room. A tiny space crammed with projectors and carts and shelves. A teacher said she hadn't seen a desk, but she was thinking about a teacher's desk. Weber even makes that evil. What about a gym mat? No one except the kids—none of the teachers, janitors, or coaches—ever saw a mat. Katherine remembered sleeping bags, pillows, and a gray mat, but she couldn't keep straight which one she was on when she lost her virginity; she couldn't even remember whether that important event happened before or after Christmas 1980.

Stephanie Knight. A former student asks for help with a school project and Van Hook obliges. Gitchoff slipped into the comfortable vernacular again. "Why? Because he wanted to get into her pants? No. Because he's a dedicated teacher; he's been helping people all his life." It was the young lady's love affair, not Van Hook's. He didn't lure Stephanie down there and drag her in. Gitchoff remembered his crush on his high-school English teacher, Miss Waters. Surely everyone could drift back to a similar sweetness in their past and remember the fantasy.

As Gitchoff shifted to another year, he made that slip of the tongue again. "In September and October of 1977, Dick Van Dyke is now employed at the high school"—he caught the error and said with a grin—"not Dick Van Dyke." He explained Van Hook's busy schedule there, and then drew Sarah Cramer into the picture.

"We go back now, during this same period of time, to Mrs. Van Hook's home on Constance Street where the famous phrase, 'Do you know where your father kept his prophylactics' came from." He looked at the jurors. "Do you know? Did you know? I never knew where my dad kept his. And my kid is not going to know where I keep mine."

Then Gitchoff rested one hand on the railing of the jury box and sighed deeply as he slid toward a precipice.

"How she knows about this, I don't have the slightest idea in the world." He sighed again. "God, I wish I knew. I wish I had an answer for you. I don't."

Weber sucked in his breath. Was that admission as devastating as he thought it was? It was one of the two pieces of the puzzle, the prophylactics and the towel, that

Gitchoff had to make fit, and he just admitted he couldn't do it.

"Because if I can create that doubt in your minds and it's reasonable, then you have to acquit the man. I am not giving you a song and dance here. I'm being right out front with you."

Weber looked at Van Hook. His expression still hadn't changed; Weber wondered if he realized what his attorney was saying.

Gitchoff recounted the testimony from the two men who installed siding on Stella's house. They couldn't say anyone went into that house, but at least the opportunity was there.

He attacked Sarah's explanation of her six years of silence; none of the victims had come forward, he marveled, until the police found them. "Isn't that strange? And why? They were afraid they were going to flunk. 'My father's a preacher and I didn't want to embarrass him.' 'I was frozen.' 'I was a zombie.' 'I was shocked.'" He shook his head. "That's what's unbelievable."

He knew that parents want to believe their children; that's only natural. But children do lie, the attorney said quietly.

None of the parents did anything about these abuses? "I don't know about others, and I don't know about preachers. But in my neck of the woods, I guarantee you that the old man would either have a baseball bat or a gun or something, and he would be down there stomping, and not waiting until now. It could be Christian or un-Christian, but I'm saying it's the human, emotional thing to do for any parent who finds it out."

Gitchoff made his way through all of the Saturday alibis, resting on the Van Hooks's visit to Sandra's ailing mother. "Weber says you don't believe that you can go visit a mother who wasn't feeling well with her children. Families do." He looked disapprovingly at Weber. "He may not, families do."

Weber was chafing under the continuing piety from the camp of a child molester.

On to the home movies of Christmas morning, 1976.

Gitchoff said the jurors should decide how old the dia-
pered little boy was. Common sense should explain the
contradiction of Sarah Cramer's story about the date she
baby-sat for the Van Hooks.

Was any part of Sarah's story believable? If Van
Hook's purpose for taking her to his house was to have
sex with her, does it make sense that he would open the
sofa bed, and then take her into the boy's room "and nail
her on the kid's bed"?

Even Weber flinched; pretty crude terminology.

Gitchoff was running out of time, so he started hitting
the last set of buttons. The defendant still is presumed innocent; the burden of proof always rests on the prosecution, not the defense.

"I submit to you, ladies and gentlemen, they haven't
done one damned thing about trying to bring out the truth
in this matter. We have; we have never quit trying."

He looked at the jurors for one last time and his voice
swelled with sincerity.

"You send Dick Van Hook back to his family, and you
walk out of here proud and tall."

Weber was stinging from the personal insults from
Gitchoff, and he decided to cut through the niceties and
let everyone know how things really stood.

"I think you all have got your minds made up that the
defendant is guilty," he said calmly as he looked at the jurors, one by one. "So, I'm not going to pound on the rail,
yell and scream, and reach a high point of drama, even
though Mr. Gitchoff might feel that, since all the press is
here, that this is all I am doing this for—for votes."

He paused, but kept his voice calm as he moved back
into the facts. "I think that what Mr. Gitchoff has said
here is basically this: the state's got Van Hook on the
Constance Street sexual intercourse. He has no explanation for these things. You saw him. He said, 'I wish I
had.' I bet he did. I bet he wished he was defending Dick
Van Dyke. It would be a lot easier to defend him than
Dick Van Hook. I think the issue boils down to whether
or not, beyond a reasonable doubt, you will convict him
on the incidents that occurred at his house in Maryville."

Since Gitchoff had tried to make an issue of Weber's decision to dismiss some of the charges, the prosecutor trotted out another unexpected line. "I dismissed the two lewd-fondling charges because—sort of like a perverted Santa Claus—he came down the chimney and went straight to his work. There wasn't any foreplay involved in this; this was sexual intercourse."

Okay. Surprising allusion number one was delivered. On to the second one. What about Van Hook's character and admirable family life? "You know, there was a guy in Boston who was a good family man and had lots of kids. He was Robert DeSalvo, the Boston Strangler." So much for the "family man" defense.

Weber brushed aside Gitchoff's personal attacks. "I don't really want to talk about the intimidation, the insults, the innuendo, and the personalities. Mr. Gitchoff has done a good job; I think I have been fair. If I haven't, please excuse me for that. But I didn't file this case because I would get a lot of votes, because I don't think I'm going to get a lot of votes over this. The passions are too high on both sides. As they say, 'Friends come and go, but enemies accumulate.' I filed this case because I couldn't sleep at night knowing he was back in the schools."

Did poor Mr. Van Hook just forget about the earrings? Hardly. Surely he wouldn't forget about similar gifts he presented to so many girls. Were gifts of wood carvings incriminating? Not really. But they became incriminating because the phony story, added to the lie about the earrings, proved the pattern of lying by the man wearing the monogrammed cuff links in court today.

Weber looked at Van Hook, who was easing his shirt cuffs back up his coat sleeves.

"Now, Mr. Gitchoff is evidently thinking this is a gigantic conspiracy by all of these little girls, and yet he's got his candle lit on the end when he says, 'But they didn't come forward with it.' Now, why would you go to the trouble of scoping out Stella's house, looking under her mattress, scoping out Van Hook's house, getting these five girls in some secret enclave someplace, getting this story about 'George,' about being in high school again, about being ten years older—get it all together, but then you don't say anything about it? Then you just sit back and wait. What were they waiting for if this was a big conspiracy?"

All the defense had shown were some insignificant inconsistencies that didn't shake the girls' stories when viewed as part of the big picture.

Weber took another shot at Gitchoff's earthy style. "We don't want, in a civilized society, for fathers to take baseball bats and knock the head off of that man's shoulders for what he did. That's why we have laws."

With that preface, it was time to hand the case to the jurors for real.

"Whether or not we have law and order in this county, and whether or not Lori and Sally have to go to school and hold hands, and walk down the hallways with their jump-rope handles because we have a pervert stalking them, is going to be up to you. You have a choice. I did the best I could; I can't do any better. I can't present any more evidence. It's up to you whether or not we are going to have justice for those innocent little girls, right there, by convicting this man, or whether or not we are going to have the second slaughter of the innocents if you let him go."

Weber took a step back from the jury box. "I will rest and abide in your judgment on this case."

His mind was racing and his heart was pummeling the inside of his rib cage as he sat down at 1:37; he was as nervous as he could remember ever being, but he made sure it didn't show. The judge read the instructions to the jury and Weber tried to retain his composure. Now the case was in the jurors' hands. Surely the jurors would convict on something; there certainly was enough evidence for a conviction on one charge. And a partial victory in the case would be enough for Weber.

He made his way through the handshakes and congratulations, and was back in his office by two o'clock. He collapsed onto the black vinyl sofa and stared up at the ceiling. The jury should be back with a verdict about six o'clock. The average length of deliberations was two and a half hours for a nonmurder case, four and a half hours for a murder. But this case was complicated; seven charges on five different sets of offenses had been discussed in testimony by 64 witnesses over seven days of trial. Four hours would be about right.

Exhaustion rolled over him as he replayed the trial. He didn't think he even closed his eyes, but he suddenly snapped back to consciousness. His watch read six o'clock; time for the verdict, surely, he thought. He hustled back over to the courthouse, amazed to see that nearly everyone who had been there four hours ago still was there. He was disappointed to hear, however, that the jurors had just left for dinner. Okay, no problem. The jurors had put in a hard day and figured they had earned a dinner on the county. They would come in with the verdict right after they ate. Weber tried to get some information from the bailiffs, who almost always had the real skinny on how things were going in the deliberating room. But all he could learn was that there had been no loud discussions, and all the jurors seemed to be getting along when they left for dinner.

An hour later the panel returned and filed back into the large courtroom at the opposite end of the hall. Thirty minutes passed; no verdict at 7:30. Four and a half hours of deliberations came and went, along with Weber's prediction. Everyone was hanging in there for the duration, however. The Van Hooks and their crew had taken up a position on the second floor, while the girls, their families, and others on Weber's team occupied the third floor.

He spent most of the time in his office, making occasional and nervous trips to the courthouse. Many others in the cast—Pam Klein, Dennis Kuba, DCI Agent Larry Trent, assorted other cops, lawyers, and reporters—were waiting it out at the Watering Hole where the blasting music, accumulating water rings on the tables, and animated conversations helped pass the time. Everyone pitched a buck into the pool to pick the time of the verdict.

The clock moved to 8:30; nothing. This was not good.

Weber had made his peace with whatever verdict was returned, because he had done the best he could, but now he was getting nervous for the kids. He hated to think how an acquittal would affect them—as well as Klein and Kuba.

By this time the two had returned to the courthouse to assure the girls that everything was okay; the kids were becoming worried about the delay. They were beginning to compensate for being tired by becoming more active and antsy.

Another hour passed and Weber began to sweat. This could be a defense verdict now, damn it. Suddenly it was 10:30. It was up for grabs by then, and speculation was rampant. A lone holdout perhaps, refusing to believe a teacher could do these things? Or worse yet, an even split? Was this headed for a hung jury and a mistrial? Weber wondered what he would do if that happened. He had no secondary plan; there was no other way to try this case. And office policy was that a retrial went to another prosecutor. Who could he dump this monster on?

Weber went back to the courthouse again and scanned the congregation still filling the benches in the hallway. Richard Van Hook looked like death warmed over. Judge Ferguson was in his chambers, taking the delay in stride. He said he would let the jurors go quite late before giving them the instruction about cooperation and compromise, or deciding whether to send them to a motel for the night.

The judge had received one note from the jurors about mid evening. They asked if they could convict Van Hook of official misconduct if they acquitted him on the indecent-liberties charge for the incident at his home. The judge had the bailiff tell the jurors they had the only instructions he could provide.

Almost at the stroke of midnight, the jurors sent word that they finally had a verdict, after ten hours. Weber felt his stomach flip and then tighten. The Watering Hole emptied in a flash. The crowd from several locations began pouring back onto the third floor in the eerie, late-night atmosphere set off by old marble and bright fluorescent lights. As the assembly grew, Judge Ferguson realized this event needed special attention. He decided to take the verdict in a larger courtroom; that would give the crowd now approaching 80 people more room and, perhaps, reduce the chance of an ugly confrontation. Just in case, the judge also called the Sheriff's Department and had several uniformed deputies sent to help with security.

The courtroom air was charged as the girls slid into several rows toward the rear of the courtroom; they held hands and bit their lips as they awaited a verdict that just as surely would pass judgment on them as on Richard Van Hook. His supporters crowded into the front rows, where his mother and sister held hands, too. Sandra Van Hook joined her husband at the defense table as the jurors, their faces showing the strain of long deliberations, filed into the box for the final drama at 12:14 A.M.

The verdict forms were handed to a solemn Judge Ferguson, who shuffled through them before beginning to read. Finally—as those gripping, endless seconds before the announcement dragged by—the judge read, "On Count one, official misconduct, we, the jury, find the defendant . . ."

Weber could hear his heart beating, reverberating in his ears.

". . . guilty."

There were a few soft gasps in the audience, but the reaction was amazingly restrained. Had the tension and the verdict struck everyone dumb? Weber resisted the urge to shout in relief and approval; that count alleged that Van Hook had had sexual intercourse with Sarah, and a conviction that would revoke his right to teach in Illinois again. Weber looked at Van Hook, whose expressionless face suggested he had not understood what he had heard. Had he still expected to win his bluff? Slowly, the reality took hold, and Van Hook turned to his wife with a forlorn grimace. As he shook his head slightly, Sandra gently placed her hand on his shoulder.

Ferguson moved to the next form, this one for indecent liberties with a child for sexual intercourse with Sarah at Van Hook's home. "Not guilty." Weber was not surprised; the defense alibis for all of those Saturdays had convinced the jurors. But what did this mean for the rest of the counts? Was Van Hook going to beat them, the way he had beaten everything else until this moment?

The girls were looking to Pam for an explanation; her heart sank. Did this mean the jurors had not believed the stories of sexual abuse? Was the system about to fail again?

The judge read the third form; on the charge of indecent liberties with a child for intercourse at Stella's—"Guilty." Weber tightened his fist. His analysis had been right; Van Hook's cute little remark about his father's prophylactics had been costly, indeed.

The girls' eyes darted to Pam again. "Did that mean they believed us?" they whispered. Pam smiled and nodded; inside she was screaming, "Yes! We got him!"

On the charge of perjury for denying that he had told Sarah about the towel—"Guilty." Weber nodded; the jurors had believed Van Hook had sex with Sarah at his house, but they weren't sure when it happened.

But then came another "not guilty," this one on the perjury charge for denying that he gave Sarah the bottles of liquor. A curious verdict, Weber thought. Pam and the girls were beyond caring about the perjury counts; they already had what they needed.

The last two verdicts came in guilty of perjury—for denying that he took Sarah to his mother's house and that she baby-sat while she was his student.

Five convictions, two acquittals. Weber was thrilled.

The smaller girls in the back of the courtroom finally began to loosen up, hugging each other, crying, and bouncing in their seats as their emotions took over.

Sarah Cramer sat calmly as she felt relief wash over her. She had wondered how the jury could do anything except convict Van Hook, but she had been a bundle of raw nerves as she awaited the verdict. She couldn't feel happy, but she certainly was relieved. At last everyone would know he was guilty and she had told the truth. Finally, all the rumors that he was innocent would end. She was bothered, however, by the acquittal on the incident at his house; she began to feel some anger. Damn it, she thought, it happened, and the jury was wrong to say it didn't. She had been so young then. How could the jury expect her to get every date correct?

Gitchoff broke the silence at the front of the courtroom to move immediately for a new trial. The former judge told the current judge that the communication from the jury had been mishandled. Ferguson should have disclosed it in open court to all attorneys and the defendant, and the court reporter should have made a record of the proceeding. Weber shook his head and said there was nothing improper about Ferguson's actions. The judge denied the motion.

Then Weber made a recommendation that would be more fateful than anyone could imagine. "Your Honor, the state would move to increase the defendant's bond to $10,000 on each count and have him placed in custody immediately."

That would raise the total to $50,000 from the $30,000 Van Hook already had posted, and would send him back to jail, at least until the rest of the bond could be paid. The request drew some grumbles from Van Hook's still-stunned supporters, and seemed to anger Gitchoff. But Weber didn't care; he told the judge that this was an emotional case, and a man under this much pressure and disappointment could consider fleeing. He even could be a danger to himself in the wake of such an emotionally devastating verdict.

But Gitchoff responded that Weber was just being vindictive and wanted to see Van Hook dragged off to jail. The defender said his client always had appeared in court and there was no reason to believe he would flee because of the conviction. His family would provide the emotional support he needed.

The judge nodded and ordered the bond continued at $30,000; Van Hook remained free. The judge instructed the Probation Department to prepare a background report for use in sentencing, which would be set some 30 days or so down the road.

The judge adjourned the court, and the emotional crowd headed for the hall. As the mob slowed at the door, one of Van Hook's relatives looked back at Sally Morton and snarled, "You little liar!" Sally's mother lunged for the woman, and Pam Klein quickly reached through the crowd to restrain her.

The crowd surged into the hallway, where the girls released a year's pent-up frustration with boisterous cheering, hugging each other and their parents. Klein saw the television cameras rolling, and realized this was not a scene everyone watching at home later would understand. She began herding the kids into a vacant courtroom across the hallway. As Weber followed the girls, one of Van Hook's supporters across the hall angrily offered the unbelievable criticism, "They're acting like little kids." Weber glanced back over his shoulder and spat out, "They *are* little kids."

He walked into the courtroom to a rousing round of applause and a deafening cheer. Some of the girls hugged him and he shook their parents' hands. Then he held up his hands and said, "Listen, I know you guys are all excited. But I think it would be appropriate to say a prayer right now." Quickly the group quieted. The kids and adults joined hands and bowed their heads as Weber offered thanks for the justice that had been delivered to them that night, for the truth that was restored, and for the chance for these girls to reclaim their lives and put this ordeal behind them. And then the jubilant celebration continued.

In the hallway, many of Van Hook's supporters cried and voiced their criticism of the nearby reporters for convicting Van Hook well before his case went to the jury.

The Van Hooks were badly shaken as they met with their attorneys for some time in the courtroom. Then the teacher and his wife stiffened their backs for the humiliating walk through the hallway and down the darkened stairs. As they left the courtroom, Sandra Van Hook glared at one of the girls' relatives and said icily, "God will forgive you for this." The television cameras moved in and reporters approached to ask for comment, but an ashen Richard Van Hook ignored them from the center of an angry group of family and supporters. The human ring formed a buffer zone around Richard and Sandra as they moved arm-in-arm toward the stairway, just as so many people defended Van Hook before the trial.

Someone in the other courtroom noticed that Van Hook was leaving, and the girls poured into the hall to call their farewell to him. Their high, singsong voices cut through the air.

"Good-bye, George. Good-bye, George."

Weber grimaced, but he understood. After all, they really were just kids.

A subdued but gracious Gitchoff met with the press to confirm that an appeal would be filed with confidence of overturning the convictions. One point would be the way Ferguson had handled the jury's note, although Gitchoff stressed that he was sure the error was unintentional on the judge's part. And there would be much more to appeal. In fact, the verdicts were inconsistent on legal grounds because Van Hook had been cleared of indecent liberties for the first incident, but convicted of official misconduct that referred to both incidents; he couldn't be innocent and guilty at the same time.

Weber emerged from the girls' pep rally to tell the reporters that these verdicts showed that the jury believed all of the charges. Despite the acquittal on one sex charge—which Weber attributed to uncertainty about the dates—the jury obviously believed Sarah's story about the towel. Weber was spin-doctoring here; he wanted to be sure everyone in Collinsville understood that the split verdict did not cast doubt on the girls' veracity or Van Hook's guilt. This was a definitive verdict vindicating the girls and confirming Van Hook as a sex offender and child molester. The community had to accept the truth about Van Hook.

Weber also wanted everyone to know that Van Hook would not walk away from this night with a slap on the wrist. He had refused reasonable plea offers, so he would get no consideration from the prosecution now. Weber told the reporters that he would take Van Hook to trial on the remaining two charges of indecent liberties and six counts of perjury; they were unrelated actions for which Van Hook had to be held accountable.

What about a sentence in this case? he was asked. Weber said he was not prepared to say what he would recommend, but the maximum sentence was 20 years—15 for indecent liberties and an additional 5 for perjury.

As the jurors headed home after being dismissed, they barely slowed down as they told reporters they had agreed not to discuss the case. But one juror and a reporter stepped into the shadows in a stairway for a few words in private. The juror, Calvin "Pokey" Bosworth, was one of the toughest men his nephew, reporter Charlie Bosworth from the *St. Louis Post-Dispatch*, had ever met. There were many similarities between Pokey and his late brother, Charles Bosworth, Sr., the reporter's greatly missed father and toughest man he had ever known.

But the hard crust and rough edges that were Bosworth trademarks had dissolved on this late night, and the gentle side buried beneath them was exposed. Pokey's eyes were red and wet, and showed the stress of what he had lived through for the last ten hours. "Man, this was rough. This was the hardest thing I've ever done." He swallowed hard and shook his head again. "I've never been through anything like this."

Charlie's colleague and close friend, Girard Steichen from the *Belleville News-Democrat,* approached and heard part of the juror's whispered remarks. "Can we quote an unnamed juror as saying that?" Steichen asked politely. Pokey's eyes flashed as he grinned and said through his teeth, "You do, and I'll break your neck."

Steichen smiled and said, "Yeah, he sounds like a Bosworth."

Months later, some of the jurors broke their silence to reveal they had convicted Van Hook early in the deliberations for having sex with Sarah at his mother's house. The rest of the debate had focused on the incident at his home.

* * *

Once Richard Van Hook had left the courthouse, the building emptied quickly. Weber and his group adjourned to the nearby home of an assistant prosecutor for a surprisingly brief victory celebration. On this night, exhaustion overcame revelry, and the participants soon headed home for some much needed rest.

Weber and Klein and Kuba were sure of one thing that night—the ordeal was almost over. Van Hook was guilty, adjudged by a jury of his peers after a full, fair hearing. Everyone would know that Van Hook had done the things the girls said. It would have to be accepted fact now.

Klein felt a new relief. A huge step forward had been taken. The girls had been vindicated, but this verdict was more than that. It was an important step in the fight against sexual abuse of all kinds, for all victims. If she had done nothing else, Pam felt she had accomplished something important for her own daughter, and her daughter's future as a woman in this society.

Kuba felt a huge burden lifted from his shoulders—the weight of months of questions and looks of doubts from friends, neighbors, fellow cops, even tennis partners. Finally, his assurances to these people that Van Hook was guilty had been corroborated. Finally, everyone would know that Van Hook was guilty.

For everyone, it seemed that only the sentencing remained before this case could be closed.

But no one dreamed then how the end would come.

CHAPTER 19

The state's attorney stared past his crossed feet on the corner of his desk and looked aimlessly out of his office window. A somewhat surprising conclusion had arrived with the morning. If Richard Van Hook received a reasonable sentence—anything other than probation, and the minimum sentence of four years in prison seemed acceptable—there would be no more prosecutions. One trial was enough; the point had been made and, almost as important, Van Hook would forfeit his teaching certificate as soon as a sentence was imposed. Even if he was convicted on all of the remaining charges, there was little chance he would get additional prison time. And Weber saw no weakness in the trial that would lead to a successful appeal and justify a backup conviction.

But the decision to be less aggressive on the remaining charges didn't alter Weber's other plans; no holds would be barred at the sentencing hearing. Van Hook had to go to prison, and Weber would spare no one's feelings on the last step in the journey for justice. Van Hook had cast down the gauntlet months ago, and he was about to find out just how brutal legal combat could be.

The rules of evidence were different at a sentencing; Weber would be free to call any witness and introduce any evidence that shed light on the severity of the defendant's conduct, and justified the sentence sought by the state. A review of the file showed that at least 20 girls had been molested by Richard Van Hook in some way, and every one of them would tell her story from the witness stand before Judge Edward Ferguson decided what sentence was appropriate.

Weber even sent Dennis Kuba back to the interview

trail to talk to former members of Van Hook's swimming teams and more former students to see if the conviction would encourage them to come forward. Kuba was sure there were another one or two Katherine Howeses or Stephanie Knights in the girls he already had interviewed, but they were too scared to admit what had happened.

Later Friday, Weber found himself explaining all of this to Charlie Bosworth when the reporter stopped by for a follow-up on the trial. The result was a story in the weekend editions disclosing the startling number of girls who had reported some improper sexual contact with this man. The indictment listed nine victims, and now Weber said more than twice that many could be documented. Who knew how many more were out there?

The story also explained that testimony from those 20 girls would support Weber's decision to ask Judge Ferguson to impose the maximum—20 years. After all, that would be a year for each girl the authorities knew Van Hook had abused. Weber hoped that much additional evidence would prod Judge Ferguson in the right direction; Weber wasn't sure whether the judge's kind heart would deter a stiff sentence.

Weber also was interviewed Friday by Ed Gurney from the *Collinsville Herald,* and it slowly dawned on the prosecutor that his hometown still was resisting the truth. Gurney asked about allegations flying around town that Weber had prosecuted Van Hook solely for political gain. "When are we going to put an end to these silly accusations?" Weber asked in frustration. "I had no vendetta against this man, although I was very angry about the things he did." Weber knew he would win no votes with this case.

Had Weber "overprosecuted" Van Hook, heaping on more charges and more evidence and more witnesses than needed? Weber shook his head; you can't "overprosecute" anyone. There are strict rules of evidence enforced by the judge. Only what is proper is admitted at trial; anything repetitive and excessive is barred.

Would there be people who still refused to accept Van Hook's guilt? Gurney wondered. Weber sighed again.

"It's utterly and completely unbelievable to me that people would doubt this man was doing these things." But he feared there would be plenty.

Other people caught up in these events also were talking to reporters on this Friday. Gitchoff was expanding on his plans for an appeal, citing points that included the statute of limitations and the admission of all of the M.O. evidence. The spin from this doctor was that the verdicts were a hollow victory for Weber in light of the acquittal on two counts and the pending appeal.

On Monday night, February 21, the Collinsville School Board met in closed session to discuss Richard Van Hook's status; he didn't attend the meeting. After less than an hour, Van Hook was fired in a unanimous decision by the seven members. The resolution passed by the board said Van Hook's offenses and convictions "constitute evidence of immorality and incompetency to teach."

Board president Dick Cain told reporters it was unnecessary to wait for the sentencing because a jury had heard all the evidence and determined that Van Hook was guilty. And the district had been informed by attorneys for the Illinois Education Association that Van Hook would not resign.

Career problems continued to mount for Van Hook. The day after he was fired, it became apparent he would lose his state teacher's certificate. The regional superintendent of schools for the county said he would arrange the automatic revocation through the State Board of Education as soon as Van Hook was sentenced.

Gitchoff even told reporters he had suggested that Van Hook should resign; even if he won on appeal, the attorney had cautioned, there always would be people who believed he really was guilty; it would be difficult to teach in Collinsville again. Gitchoff wondered if a change of careers would be advisable. With Van Hook's education, perhaps he could work for a company that published law books and needed researchers.

* * *

Two days after Van Hook was fired, the Collinsville school district was sued for the second time on charges of failing to protect a student who was molested by Van Hook and harassed by other teachers after reporting the abuse. Elizabeth McBride filed this suit, but did not include Van Hook as a defendant, unlike Sarah Cramer's suit filed three months earlier. Elizabeth sought punitive damages of $15 million on allegations that the district failed to investigate allegations against Van Hook or take other steps to protect the girls, and that "school officials embarked on a specific course of harassment intended to cause emotional distress" for Elizabeth after she talked to police. Those actions included vulgar remarks to her by teachers allied with Van Hook.

More litigation was filed in March when Katherine Howes sued Van Hook, the school district, and Gerald Ellis, the principal at Caseyville School. The suit said the district and Ellis failed to investigate allegations against Van Hook or protect Katherine.

Van Hook appeared to be sinking under the tide. In March, he wrote to the State Board of Education and waived his right to appeal his firing; he gave up without a fight.

Richard Van Hook sat for a long time in the office of probation officer Darrel Smith in Edwardsville. Richard was cooperative and controlled, and still maintained his innocence. He had developed a problem with a spastic colon and was on medication. But he said he never had needed psychiatric or psychological treatment. He was confident he could make a living and provide for his family once he got over this hurdle. He never would return to the public schools, and was considering a career in industrial education.

His wife no longer was working, so neither of them had any income. They were dependent on the generosity of family, friends, and fellow church members; many people still were raising funds to help out. They were in desperate financial condition.

Smith received several letters of support for Van Hook,

from his pastor, a school-district administrator, and an assistant professor from Southern Illinois University who lived in Collinsville. The first two were average examples of such letters; but the third was something different. The assistant professor not only vouched for Van Hook's fine character, but she expounded about the "highly emotional crushes junior high school girls develop for young men teachers." As a former librarian in a junior high school, she worried about some of the suggestive books these girls read. The books provided explicit details about puberty and sex, but lacked the guidance and moral perspective essential to young readers dealing with their first sexual experiences, the woman wrote.

She also was convinced that girls at that age fantasized about sex, and could allow exaggeration and gossip to become outright lies. As a teacher and a parent, she was of the opinion that adolescent girls had a "considerable difficulty in distinguishing between fantasy and reality."

Bull, Pam Klein fumed. When would this stop?

In the conclusion of the report he submitted to Judge Ferguson, Darrel Smith said Van Hook seemed to have the potential to complete a term of probation and become a productive member of society again. But Smith rejected that as a sentence. Van Hook had abused his public trust as a teacher, using that trust to sexually abuse adolescent girls; he had compounded that by perjuring himself repeatedly on the witness stand. Stern punishment was needed for his crimes, and to protect society from further abuses of its trust. Van Hook should go to prison for a term to be set by the judge, Smith said.

As time drew near for Van Hook's sentencing, now scheduled for April 13, Weber got a call from reporter Matt Meagher from KMOV-TV, the CBS affiliate in St. Louis. Meagher was working on a series about the Van Hook case, focusing on the school district's failure to respond after hearing about the allegations or to protect the girls. Meagher was interviewing some of the girls, their parents, and school district officials, and even was conducting some surveillance of Van Hook to get good vid-

eotape of him. Now Meagher wanted to talk to Weber and
Pam Klein. Weber was somewhat reluctant to fuel the
fires still raging in Collinsville, but his anger and frustration overcame his hesitance. Klein also agreed to help,
hoping that she finally could convince her hometown that
this man really was guilty. Weber and Klein realized they
still had to try to convict this man in the court of public
opinion. Maybe a hard-hitting television series now
would accomplish what a year of publicity and a trial had
not.

Don Weber had turned much of his attention in March
to other matters in his office, including a major murder
trial set for June. But the hubbub in Collinsville had not
abated after Van Hook was convicted; the verdict seemed
to inflame the situation. Letters to the editor continued to
rip Weber for his "persecution" of Van Hook. Anonymous letters were arriving in Weber's mail, including one
blaming Weber for putting the Van Hook family through
"the torments of HELL!!!" The writer said only divine intervention would heal the deep wounds Weber had
caused, adding that he never would have made such accusations against Van Hook if he knew him and his family.
Weber shook his head; it was precisely because he had
come to know Van Hook so well that he had to prosecute
him.

Sources that included Weber's mother and Pam Klein
said the rumor mill still was in motion; one popular report
had it "on good authority" that Weber and the police had
planted evidence in Van Hook's house to frame him.

For Van Hook's supporters, the verdict did not mean
the charges were proven; it meant the injustice of the accusations and public humiliation of this man had been
compounded intolerably. People who had known him for
years could not believe he was capable of doing what the
girls said. Those friends of Van Hook and his family said
that nothing less than a videotape of him in the act would
change their minds about Dick Van Hook.

On March 3, Weber opened a letter from a woman in
Laddonia, Missouri. It was short and to the point: "You

are making an extremely tragic mistake in the case of Richard Van Hook. I have known this Christian family all my life (72 years). There's never been a finer family. Life on this earth is too short compared to eternity. Let us live this to the best of our ability."

It was just enough to push Weber over the edge. He sat down and wrote a response, and then mailed it to area newspapers as an open letter to the public. The people needed to hear this again; obviously, many of them had not been listening before.

The letter turned out to be so chillingly prophetic that Weber would wonder later if another hand had guided his.

"I have received your letter of March 1 concerning your feeling that I am making 'an extremely tragic mistake' in the case of Richard Van Hook. Because there are a few people, like you, in the community who still believe that Van Hook is not guilty, I am taking the time to write you to fill you in on the *facts* of this case."

Weber recounted the basic allegations about Van Hook's reprehensible behavior and sexual abuse of little girls, noting that the charges came from a diverse group of girls who varied in age and background, many of whom did not even know each other. Even Van Hook's attorney had been unable to explain away evidence such as Sarah's knowledge of the towel. In the end, Weber said, 12 objective people Van Hook helped choose had ruled unanimously that he was guilty beyond a reasonable doubt, based on the same facts the public was trying to ignore.

And then Weber tried to focus the community on what really was important now.

"I know that charges such as these are hard for a friend of the family to believe. However, there comes a time when the question of guilt should be settled. In our country, that comes when twelve objective citizens find beyond a reasonable doubt that the charges have been proved. I can assure you that this prosecution was not embarked upon without the utmost consideration, deliberation, and prayer. The people who really care about Van Hook and, in particular, his family, I believe should, at this point, reconcile themselves to the fact that Richard Van Hook is guilty, and try to give him the type of support that a sick man needs. Further blind support of the defendant in this case only does a disservice to the community and, in the long run, to the defendant himself."

The mounting tension did not bode well for anyone in this case, and Weber felt something tragic in the air. He didn't know what it was, but it was there.

In early April, John Gitchoff asked Judge Ferguson to delay Van Hook's sentencing to give the defense more time to prepare; the judge agreed, and set the date for Wednesday, April 27. On Friday, April 22, Gitchoff and Jim Wallis filed a 23-page motion for a new trial that cited the communication between Ferguson and the jury, as well as a laundry list of other errors the defense said prevented Van Hook from getting a fair trial.

Weber shrugged off the motion. It was a rehash of the same tired arguments the defense made unsuccessfully before and during the trial. Weber knew Judge Ferguson would reject the motion quickly at the hearing the next Wednesday, and then would sentence Richard Van Hook. Weber still was unsure what the judge would do, but the prosecutor couldn't see any justification for letting Van Hook escape a prison term. He had to be punished; his day of reckoning was about to arrive.

CHAPTER 20

Monday, April 25, was the kind of spring day that held out the promise of new life, and helped bury a cold, bitter winter deep in the past. It was warm and sunny that morning, and new color was returning to every part of the landscape. Horseshoe Lake State Park near Collinsville was experiencing that reawakening, too, as a young man drove his blue and white car across the causeway to Walker's Island in the center of the lake. He stopped in a gravel parking lot at the end of the causeway and walked east about 200 yards past a picnic area, through scruffy underbrush, and along a section of plowed field. Then he turned down a gently sloping embankment to a deserted stretch of rough shoreline on the southeastern edge of the island. He sat under one of several trees scattered along that part of the shore.

The man was in no mood to appreciate the weather or the scenery or seasonal renewal. He had not come to the lake on this spring morning to contemplate new beginnings; he was there to find a termination.

He thought about what had happened to his life, and what awaited him, and then he drew a small pistol—an antique .22-caliber derringer—from his pocket. After he summoned his courage, he slowly put the barrel in his mouth and cocked the hammer. Finally he pulled the trigger.

The hammer struck the rim of the cartridge and the resulting sound was a harmless click. A misfire.

The young man had been frustrated again, as he had so often during the last 15 months and, especially, during the last two months. Once again, what he was sure would happen had not happened; his expectations had not been met. A situation so firmly in his control had slipped beyond his grasp.

But he was undeterred; he would not be denied this time. He put the barrel back into his mouth and pulled the trigger again.

This time he was successful; there was an explosion. The bullet blasted through the roof of his mouth and ripped into his brain, killing him instantly.

The shot echoed across the swampy lake; no one heard it.

State's Attorney Don Weber was on his way to Judge Edward Ferguson's chambers shortly after lunch on Monday, April 25, to discuss the hearing set for two days later when the judge would sentence Richard Van Hook. But Weber was met in the empty courtroom by the judge, whose startled face should have been a warning.

"They just found Van Hook at Horseshoe Lake," the judge said.

Weber had no idea what that meant. "What was he doing there?"

"They found his body. The Sheriff's Department just called."

"His body? You mean, he's dead?"

"He shot himself."

That's all there was to say. Weber turned and went back to his office. He wasn't surprised; he was shocked, but not surprised. Hadn't he said several times—at least twice publicly—that a man in that position could be dangerous to himself?

Weber felt an odd numbness. It wasn't grief; he couldn't grieve for this man. It certainly wasn't guilt; he had acquitted his conscience with reasoned warnings—issued from more sensitivity and insight than those closest to Van Hook had offered. Weber didn't even feel guilty when his reaction to the man's death was, "Well, at least we won't have to put all those girls through the experience of testifying at the sentencing."

His first call was to Pam Klein. He had to tell her three times before she would believe he wasn't kidding.

Finally, she erupted in anger. "Damn him! Damn that

son of a bitch," she yelled into the telephone. Weber didn't understand the anger.

"Don, he's raped the girls again. He's stolen their right to see him punished. He's taken the last bit of dignity from them, and he's taken the chickenshit way out. Damn him! He's taken it all away from them."

Don was silent for a moment as he tried to see the situation from Pam's viewpoint. "Well, anyway, you've got to call the girls and tell them, Klein. You can't let them hear it on the radio or see it on TV."

"Yeah, I know. I'll do that now," she said softly.

Klein hung up the phone, sat there for a second, and then began throwing things around her office in a rage. When she settled down, she flipped open her Rolodex and began looking for names and numbers: Howes, Cramer, Knight, all the rest. Oh, God, she thought, how do I tell these kids?

Dennis Kuba was going through some routine paperwork when he answered the phone. A deputy from the Sheriff's Department wanted to be sure Kuba knew the detectives were on the way to Horseshoe Lake, where Van Hook's body had just been found; he had shot himself. Kuba sat back and let it sink in. Unbelievable. After all of the crap of the last year—it had come down to this. He had to go to the scene. He didn't understand why; he just knew he had to go.

A deputy waved him past the roadblock near the parking lot. He walked across the bare soil and patches of mud in the plowed field, an irritant for a guy who was almost fanatical about his shoes and suits. A deputy directed him down the sloping bank. The body of Richard Van Hook was slumped back against a tree. In the detached way cops learn to look at corpses, Kuba's first thought was that he had never seen Van Hook in blue jeans before. The small pistol still was in Van Hook's left hand. Kuba looked again; some envelopes in plastic Baggies seemed to be sticking out of Van Hook's shirt pockets. Suicide notes, everyone guessed; perhaps a confession or a last defense. The police would check them out after the scene was combed for evidence.

Kuba looked up and scanned the view over the lake; he wondered what Van Hook had thought when he looked across the same poor-man's panorama not much earlier that day, and then stuck that gun in his mouth. For a lake in a state park, this was not a very picturesque setting. Kuba looked around again and thought about the moments before that shot exploded. Nothing had changed here since then, and everything had changed. Pretty metaphysical for a cop.

Kuba watched the coroner's team load the body ingloriously into a pickup truck from the park maintenance shed, and then drive it to firmer ground for transfer to a hearse. As Kuba walked to his car, trying to dodge the newspaper photographers on the way, he was sorry he had come. He turned his car toward the Sheriff's Department; he wanted to read Van Hook's notes before going to Klein's crisis center. He knew he had to be there for the girls, and for Pam.

Weber was still in his office, wondering what to do next, when a friend in Collinsville called with a warning that a relative of Van Hook's was armed with a gun and headed toward Weber's office. Weber thanked the caller, and then pulled the shoulder holster with the .357-magnum revolver from the bottom drawer of his desk. There was no security in the building, and Weber's open-door policy suddenly didn't seem like such a good idea.

He called the Sheriff's Department and talked to Captain Bob Hertz, the chief of detectives. Hertz told him what the police knew, and offered him a ride to the scene. Weber would regret the decision later, but it seemed right then. He didn't want to see the body, but he wanted to see where this story ended. When Hertz drove into the lot where Van Hook had left his car, Weber immediately wished he had stayed away. Stella Van Hook was standing with a group of family and friends, and she immediately spotted Weber. She glared at him as he drove by.

His arrival must have seemed ghoulish to her, and he was sorry for that.

He didn't hear the outburst that followed. One woman in the gathering of Van Hook's family saw Weber walking toward the lake and screamed at the police, "Don't let him go back there." When a deputy sheriff explained that Weber's position entitled him to enter the scene, she turned and yelled after him, "You look at him good."

But Van Hook's body already had been taken away, and Weber was thankful. The detectives told him what they knew about the events of the morning. Van Hook had driven his children to school, but hadn't returned home when his family expected. After a while they had become concerned and decided to look for him. Relatives including Sandra and Stella drove straight to the park because they knew it was Van Hook's favorite spot to be alone. They found his blue and white Dodge Colt and, fearing the worst, enlisted the help of park workers in a search. A few minutes later, at 12:45, they found the body.

Katherine Howes had just walked in the door from school; the look on her mother's face told her something was terribly wrong. The news of Mr. Van Hook's suicide was almost suffocating for Katherine. She ran out of the house, but there was nowhere to go to escape. She stood crying in the driveway. It was her fault, she just knew. She felt guilty now for what she had put Van Hook and his family through. Did that mean she still had some tender feelings for this man, after all she had endured? She didn't know. She just knew she hurt terribly, and she felt so guilty.

Sarah Cramer felt even more responsible. She was terribly angry at Van Hook, but she couldn't shake the feeling that it somehow was her fault. She cried uncontrollably.

By the time Kuba reached the crisis center, he was getting angrier and angrier. In four notes Van Hook had left, he had maintained his innocence and complained of a conspiracy to get him among the girls, Weber, Klein, the cops, and the media. He blamed everyone but himself. These people had left him dead inside; death was the only way to spare his family any more hurt and the financial burden of an appeal.

The girls who gathered at the crisis center that afternoon were devastated by the notes. They felt guilty about his death, but that soon turned to raw anger as each of them realized he had abused them again—even at the moment of his death. They felt badly for his children, but the girls soon spoke of a new hatred for Van Hook. He couldn't stop using them, even when he died.

Sarah was able to see through Van Hook's suicide as she heard more about the notes. He was doing it again—laying a guilt trip on the same girls he had abused, and trying to shift the blame for his misdeeds to them. The girls didn't want him dead; they just wanted him to sit in jail and think about what he had done to them. They wanted him to admit his responsibility, and to get help for his sickness. Instead, he took the easy way out.

Klein found herself reaching a new level of outrage; she could not remember ever feeling so much hatred for someone. This man had shattered these girls' childhoods and put them through hell. But he couldn't resist twisting the knife one more time—a classic example of the narcissistic personality. After all that he had done to them in life, in death he had taken away a vital part of their healing process—their just revenge.

Klein was grateful for the presence that afternoon of Kuba, Weber, and Lieutenant Randy Rushing, another DCI agent whose sensitivity had brought him there to help these girls any way he could. The adults kept explaining that this was not the girls' fault. Mr. Van Hook was responsible for what he had done to them and what he had done to himself; his own actions had brought him to this end. The girls remained victims; they had not become offenders by telling the truth.

The group spent quite some time that afternoon and early evening on the center's lawn, under the shade of the trees just beginning to show the new growth of spring.

The news of Van Hook's suicide was a crushing blow to his attorneys. John Gitchoff had talked to his client four days earlier, and the strength and resolve Van Hook had shown all along seemed unshaken; he still maintained his innocence. There were no indications that he was despondent or even considering suicide. He had complained, however, that he was worried about the costs of an appeal, and that a television crew from St. Louis had been following him.

Wallis and Gitchoff had remained optimistic about Van Hook's chances to win a new trial on appeal. Wallis said he still planned to see if there was some way to press the appeal to clear Van Hook's name, even though the defendant was dead.

Lawyer Bill Gagen, who still represented Van Hook on the suits filed against him by two of the girls, told reporters he remained as convinced of Van Hook's innocence as he always had been.

Weber, Klein, and Kuba met later Monday evening at the Watering Hole in Edwardsville with the sheriff's detective on the case, Sergeant Steve Nonn. He told them about the misfire, a staggering addition to the already overwhelming story. Everyone agreed that they would have taken that as a sign, and abandoned the suicide attempt. Van Hook must had been incredibly, tragically, determined to end it his way.

Nonn also brought copies of the four handwritten notes Van Hook left in his pockets or car. One of them, in an envelope marked simply, "Please Read," was dated March 3, evidence that Van Hook had been on the brink of suicide for eight weeks. In almost sloppy handwriting, Van Hook referred to a newspaper story about the approaching sentencing, and despaired that Weber would "get his chance to parade all of the kids who ever had a gripe about me to the front." His family and friends would have to hear all of those girls' "fantasy stories" about him, making him look even worse. He could find no way to combat all the lies, and pursuing an appeal would leave his family bankrupt. There was a conspiracy against him, he insisted in the letter, and people were changing their stories to make them fit together. Money and power had to be at the root of this effort to ruin him, but he wrote that he could not find the facts to prove it.

His existence was destroying his family, his friends, and his colleagues. His only way to "fight back," his only weapon to end the misery, was his death. He had been to the brink before, only to back away. This time, he would not stop, he wrote.

Weber shook his head. Van Hook's decision to kill himself and still blame everyone else for his sins was a sick way to "fight back."

Another note was addressed to whomever found his body. It went farther to explain his desperate act, saying, ". . . my insides are already dead." He had been unjustly accused by so many people whose lies portrayed him as a monster. And the court system prevented him from getting out the truth, while it gave Weber the right to trot out people to say whatever he wanted. The Constitution then gave the newspapers and television stations the right to report the lies. He wrote that he could only pray no other family had to suffer through this kind of hell, and that God would forgive those who had brought him to this end.

Van Hook was going to his grave unrepentant, and still wrapped in lies, Weber thought.

The third note was addressed to Van Hook's pastor, asking him to take care of Sandy and the kids. Although he was not leaving Sandy well off financially, he wrote that he knew she and the children were strong and would survive. But he worried that they would hate him for committing suicide, and he asked for understanding. "I've cracked and given up. No fight is left," he said. He closed by repeating his call for support for his wife and children, adding, "I love them much more than life itself." On the envelope, he asked for the hymn, "Abide With Me," to be played at his funeral.

In the last note, addressed to lawyer Bob Gagen and dated the day before the suicide, Van Hook wondered how these girls' lies had grown to such an insurmountable obstacle. "How many people have I made hate me and how did I do it?" he asked. He again proclaimed his innocence of "these damn charges." With a wife like his, he wrote, he would have had no reason to cheat, especially with little girls.

Pam Klein shook her head. The notes betrayed such despair and exhaustion. Van Hook had, indeed, run out of fight, but he lacked the courage to admit his guilt and seek help.

Weber was angered by the notes because they proved he had been right, after all. The people who so staunchly supported Van Hook had been so fanatical that they left him no room to deal realistically with his conviction or the plea-bargain Weber had offered earlier. Van Hook couldn't admit he had a problem and needed help. He had nowhere to turn, and he couldn't face what was going to happen on Wednesday.

Katherine Howes was on her honeymoon when she answered a knock on her door. When she opened the door, she was stunned to find Richard Van Hook standing there. He stepped in, and then shot her to death.

That was the dream that woke Katherine from a fitful sleep the night Van Hook killed himself. His death didn't free her from her fears; it just changed the way Richard Van Hook haunted her. But soon the guilt began to dissolve into relief. At least, she thought now, he couldn't hurt anyone else. And, before long, Katherine's feelings about Richard Van Hook changed again. Within a few months, Katherine told a visitor, "I wish I could have been the one to shoot him. Honest to God, I wish I could have shot him."

EPILOGUE

On the day Richard Van Hook was to have been sentenced—Wednesday, April 27—KMOV-TV in St. Louis began running Matt Meagher's frank, hard-hitting, three-part series about the scandal that had left Collinsville quaking. Despite the teacher's suicide and scores of angry calls to the station protesting the stories, Meagher spent 20 minutes over three evenings describing "how a school district turned its back on a problem that had many victims—a problem that could have been detected if the Collinsville school district had paid attention to the warning signs, and a problem that may scar the lives of many young girls for years to come."

Meagher concluded that students who had been sexually abused by teachers had good reason to fear that no one would believe them if they reported it. He cited a study by a legislative committee in Illinois which found that the small number of teachers who abused students usually went unpunished.

Don Weber and Pam Klein stood by everything they said in their interviews with Meagher. But Weber regretted that few people realized they had been taped long before Van Hook's death. As much as Weber detested Van Hook and his crimes, he would not have made those angry remarks on the night the man's family was greeting mourners in front of his casket at a local funeral home. Weber asked Meagher to delay the series, but he understood why it was broadcast then; Van Hook's suicide made it all the more timely.

That evening, an anonymous caller asked Pam Klein's son, "Is your mother going to march the children in front of the coffin tomorrow?" A day later, Pam got an unsigned note saying, "Ms. Klein, It is most unfortunate that Mr. Weber did not offer you the opportunity to view the body of Mr. Van Hook at the suicide scene. You could have joined him in all of his arrogance and self-righteousness. Is perhaps an ounce of satisfaction worth a pound of persecution?"

The series drew the ugliest, most violent reaction Matt Meagher had seen from anything he did in 12 years in St. Louis. Hate mail and angry, often obscene telephone calls came in for days, jamming the switchboard. Some people carried picket signs in front of the station with messages echoing the complaints in the mail that Meagher and KMOV were "Unfair to Collinsville."

More than a year later, Meagher was enjoying a St. Louis Cardinals baseball game at Busch Stadium when two men approached. One of them doused Meagher in beer, proclaiming "This is for Van Hook."

On Thursday morning, April 28, 1983, Richard Van Hook was buried in what was perhaps the largest funeral ever seen in the city of Collinsville.

In July 1983, Sandra Van Hook and her two children filed a "wrongful death" lawsuit charging that Richard Van Hook was forced to take his life because of a conspiracy. Named in the 26 counts were Weber; Klein and the Rape and Sexual Abuse Care Center; Matt Meagher, KMOV-TV, and CBS; the *St. Louis Globe-Democrat* and reporter Patrick E. Gauen. The suit charged that Weber and the others conspired to force Van Hook to plead guilty, forgo an appeal, or commit suicide. A ridiculous laundry list of supposed misconduct by those named in the suit included using eavesdropping devices on Van Hook, threatening to physically injure him and his family, and surreptitiously monitoring the Van Hook family's activities. Reports said CBS eventually settled the case with a small payment, but the rest of the suit faded away.

In late 1983, the U.S. Justice Department invited Weber, Klein, and Kuba to speak in Washington, D.C., at a seminar on sexual abuse of children. After Weber finished his presentation on the Van Hook case—standing at the massive podium before a packed crowd in the Great Hall of Justice—a member of the audience asked about political ramifications of such a prosecution. Weber grinned and said he would be up for reelection in a year. If he returned to lecture then as state's attorney, prosecutors would know they could embark on such cases without fear of political revenge. If he was defeated, it would be because of this case.

In November 1984, after four years of aggressive, uncompromising prosecutions that included two death penalties for murderers, Don Weber ran against a Democratic challenger with a philosophy more akin to the defense side of the bar. Weber had won his hometown of Collinsville by 750 votes in 1980, carrying him to a slim, 600-vote victory. But the Richard Van Hook case claimed another victim in 1984. Weber lost Collinsville by 750 votes, just enough to bury his hopes for a second term. He was defeated by 1,365 votes out of 103,000 cast.

Half of the community of Collinsville had killed the messenger who brought it such bad news about a nasty scandal at the town's very core; Weber was the fall guy. But his duty had demanded that he prosecute Van Hook. What could he have done differently? He had offered Van Hook the opportunity to plead guilty and avoid a prison sentence. He had warned everyone just seconds after the verdict that Van Hook could be a danger to himself. And he had written a sincere letter telling everyone who cared about the man to give him the emotional room to admit his guilt and get the help he so desperately needed. Weber had been fair and, in many ways, more compassionate than those who professed such dedicated support for Van Hook. Weber's conscience was clear. Richard Van Hook and his cluster of supporters had made their own decisions.

Weber married Virginia Rulison, and returned to private practice—a mix of patent law, personal injury suits, and the occasional, criminal defense case. He made a few forays back into prosecution as an interim state's attorney in another county, and an assistant state's attorney in Madison County. He remained close friends with Kuba and Klein.

In 1989, the Collinsville school district agreed to an out-of-court settlement in the suit by Katherine Howes. The district's insurance company paid her a sum the parties agreed to keep confidential; various reports put it at nearly $200,000. But the settlement did little to settle Katherine's life. She suffered from emotional problems her family was sure were her inheritance from the abuse by Van Hook. She had a child that she surrendered to adoption. She was plagued by a series of automobile accidents. Eventually, she married, used part of the money from the settlement to set up housekeeping, and had another baby.

Elizabeth McBride's suit went to trial in 1988 and a jury ordered the Collinsville school district to pay her $25,000 in damages for failing to protect her from Richard Van Hook. The president of the school board then, Susan Burroughs, called the verdict a partial victory for the district because it was so much less than the $500,000 Elizabeth's attorney asked the jury to award. The district paid the verdict without an appeal.

Elizabeth felt guilty about Mr. Van Hook's death for a long time before that was replaced by anger. Years later, she even could find a strange kind of solace in his suicide—at least he couldn't inflict such pain on any other girls.

Despite the passage of time, Elizabeth stayed angry about one aspect of the case. She still was furious that the school district provided counseling to the teachers to help them deal with the trauma of Van Hook's conviction and suicide, but the district never even offered a word of encouragement to the girls. No one ever asked if the girls needed counseling or could use some help from the district. The district's lawyers even told Matt Meagher that officials were unaware that any child was in need of

counseling. The girls abused by a teacher felt abused
again by the district.

Elizabeth still lives and works in Collinsville; she is
married and has a child. Few people know she was one of
those girls, and she seldom hears the case mentioned; she
hopes the community has learned to look at what happened in a different light—to see the girls' pain and understand that they were telling the truth. She works hard
at keeping her mind off the past; she thinks about Van
Hook as little as possible. But her voice chokes and her
eyes fill with tears when she does. What comes to mind
after all those years? "It all happened so fast, and it was
all so hush-hush. I'm scared that something like that
could happen to my daughter. I'm sure I'll talk to her
about it when she's old enough. I know it can happen."

Sarah Cramer dismissed her suit against Van Hook and
the school district shortly after his suicide; she did not want
to pursue the case against Van Hook's family. She would
wish years later, however, that she had pressed the suit
against the school district. She remained angry at the officials and teachers for their lack of concern, protection, and
support after the abuse that she felt ruined her life. She married Jay Carr in 1984, but they divorced three years later.
His family ridiculed her about the Van Hook case; the teacher's ghost remained one of the problems between Sarah and
Jay.

And the case remained a cloud over Sarah's life; it tore
her own family apart. A favorite aunt abandoned Sarah,
never speaking to her again. Sarah believed her aunt was
angered because she knew someone who had been involved with Van Hook the year before the investigation.

Sarah eventually was driven from Collinsville by the
stares and taunts of so many in the community who refused to accept Van Hook's guilt. She stopped seeing old
friends to avoid the issue; she never even attended a class
reunion. The town still made her feel as if she had done
something wrong. Even when she moved, the distance
didn't insulate her. She remarried and had another child.
But ten years later, she still couldn't be comfortable, even

on a brief visit to Collinsville. She would choke up as she explained that she couldn't accept the way Collinsville dealt with the case.

And the past came back to haunt Sarah in another tragic way. Her daughter said she was sexually abused by a woman several years after the trial. Dennis Kuba investigated, and charges were filed; but Don Weber no longer was the prosecutor, and Sarah was disappointed with the results. Weber's successor agreed to give the woman probation instead of jail if she would leave the state. Sarah had to explain to Amy that the "system" sometimes breaks down in cases of sexual abuse. But Sarah's experience gave her an advantage in helping Amy deal with what had happened. Amy got counseling, and had a mother who understood the tears.

Sarah still faces the pain from Van Hook's destructive legacy every day; it preys on her mind. She is convinced he ruined her life, and that his town—her town—found no guilt in him for that.

Pam Klein left the Rape and Sexual Abuse Care Center in 1985 when her husband's job took them to London for a while. In the months that she lived there, she helped Scotland Yard develop a training program for sexual-abuse investigations. She knew the English needed help when she saw a newspaper headline reading, "Vicar arrested for fondness for choirboy."

By 1992, she had returned to the St. Louis area and was called in as a consultant in an investigation into allegations that the popular principal at the middle school in a little town in the Missouri boot heel had molested a ten-year-old boy. By the time the investigation was completed, the 53-year-old man was indicted on 35 counts of abusing ten boys over a five-year period. The victims said all of the abuse happened on the school grounds—some during school hours and some after. The principal denied everything. He was fired, but was seeking reinstatement.

The publicity about the case brought grown men forward to allege that the principal had molested them as their teacher and Cub Scout leader as long as 23 years ago; authorities said victims could number in the hundreds. The adult victims said their abuser had chosen vulnerable boys giving them special treatment and rewards. The men described the damage they suffered— psychological problems, rebellion against authority, drug use. They said they never had disclosed the abuse because they were too scared, too embarrassed, too humiliated. They didn't think anyone would believe the word of a kid over the word of a trusted teacher and Scout leader. One victim grew up to become a Baptist minister, haunted by the memories.

The allegations against the solid citizen split the town down the middle, causing quarrels between old friends on opposite sides of a shocking, emotional issue. For some, the charges were evidence of a long-rumored evil, proving the need for more awareness of sexual abuse in Middle America, in the heart of the Bible Belt. For others, the charges were outrageous lies and distortions, ruining the career and life of a loving family man, a church member, and a Scout leader once recognized as Kiwanis Man of the Year. Some who watched the principal's career and life for 25 years refused to believe he could do such things.

So many crows, Pam Klein thought. When will they learn?